~ reviewed C W 69 (1975-1976)
475-76 Levy;
CP 73 (1978) 84 Cunningham

Latin Literature of the Fourth Century

Greek and Latin Studies
Classical Literature and its Influence

Editors

C. D. N. Costa and J. W. Binns

School of Hellenic and Roman Studies
University of Birmingham

Greek and Latin Studies
Classical Literature and its Influence

Latin
Literature of the
Fourth Century

Edited by
J. W. BINNS

Routledge & Kegan Paul: LONDON AND BOSTON

First published in 1974
by Routledge & Kegan Paul Ltd
Broadway House, 68–74 Carter Lane,
London EC4V 5EL and
9 Park Street
Boston, Mass. 02108, U.S.A.
Printed in Great Britain by
The Camelot Press Ltd, London and Southampton
© Routledge & Kegan Paul 1974

ISBN 0 7100 7796 3
Library of Congress Catalog Card No. 73-91031

Contents

Introduction

The fall of the Roman Empire has fascinated generations of men; and we, who have in our own day witnessed the passing away of western Empires, feel, it may be, a special affinity with Rome in the century and a half before her fall. There are those today who, with Spengler and Toynbee, would hold that western civilisation itself must decline on to the dust of previous cultures. There are indeed resemblances between the Roman world, preparing for its passing, and the twentieth-century west. The European hegemony has gone; new powers have arisen in the East; new peoples and cultures impinge upon our consciousness, even as Rome's power succumbed to the great movements of tribes and populations surging westward. We with the later Romans have witnessed the debasement of the coinage, the growth of a complex bureaucracy, the ceaseless demands of government for money to pay for its armies and officials, the lure of ideologies which sap the foundations of conventional thought. The half-empty churches bear silent witness to the withdrawal from them of the vital forces of religion, even as the pagan gods of Rome retreated before the onset of Christianity. In the terrible battle of Hadrianople in A.D. 378 Rome knew the slaughter of the Somme and Passchendaele. In the modish sterility of much modern art and literature, some would see the counterpart of that jaded weariness which is often thought to characterise Roman literature in the centuries after the Silver Age.

Yet human societies are not biological organisms with but a single life. They are capable of perpetual self-renewal. The differences between life today and life as it was lived in the fourth century are greater than any similarities. And Rome even as she drifted towards the dissolution of her power could yet produce great men and great writers such as St Augustine whose works and modes of thought are powerful even today. For many of the writers of Rome's last days were Christians, passionately so, or through convention. Christian compassion, which introduced a new heightening of inner emotion and feeling to the ancient world, was at odds with the Stoic ideal of Classical Antiquity. The Christian writers of the later Roman Empire are thus often set apart, the preserve rather of theologians than of students of Roman literature. And so the Latin writings of the fourth century, which survive in considerable bulk, have had less attention than they merit in modern times. Prudentius is no longer highly valued as he was in the seventeenth century as one of the great Christian Latin poets. The eighteenth century, refining and narrowing the concept of classicism, concentrated attention on the writings and the history of Augustan Rome.

Yet historians of the ancient world have turned of late more and more to the study of late Roman history; and I hope that the present volume will help to stimulate interest in the literature of this period too. Here are the writers – Augustine and Ausonius, Symmachus and Paulinus of Nola, Claudian and Prudentius – diverse in background and belief, who yet lived through the great changes whereby the ancient world yielded to the medieval. They experienced the tensions between Christianity and classical culture, they were alive, some of them in that fateful year, with all that it portended, of the sack of Rome in A.D. 410. They knew a world where vitality was ebbing from the old forms of political life, of religion, of literature, to mould new institutions, new manners and modes of life and thought. How to respond to this interaction between the old and the new? By pretending that nothing had changed, affirming, by restating its rituals in action and in writing, the validity of the past? Or by rejecting what had gone before, by adapting to or even embracing, with whatever degree of passive acceptance or of enthusiasm, the new political and emotional life of the times? These are the problems faced by the men whose writings are discussed in this volume, and the answer given has, in literature, consequences which affect an author's choice of poetic imagery, of literary form, his very Latinity.

We are facing, perhaps, problems not dissimilar which bear upon the life and literature of our own day. The fourth century has left us a record, in action and in writing, of how men faced these problems then, and the record is true.

Abbreviations

AE	L'Année Épigraphique
AS	Augustinian Studies
CC	Corpus Christianorum
CIL	Corpus Inscriptionum Latinarum
CLA	Codices Latini Antiquiores
CP	Classical Philology
CQ	Classical Quarterly
CSEL	Corpus Scriptorum Ecclesiasticorum Latinorum
CT	Codex Theodosianus
FHG	Fragmenta Historicorum Graecorum (Müller)
GIF	Giornale Italiano di Filologia
GL	Grammatici Latini (ed. Keil)
HE	Historia Ecclesiastica (Socrates)
HS	Harvard Studies in Classical Philology
HTR	Harvard Theological Review
ICUB	Inscriptiones Christianae Urbis Romae
ILS	Inscriptiones Latinae Selectae
JRS	Journal of Roman Studies
JTS	Journal of Theological Studies
MAH	Mélanges d'Archéologie et d'Histoire de l'École Française de Rome
MGHAA	Monumenta Germaniae Historica, Auctores Antiquissimi
OCT	Oxford Classical Texts
PL	Patrologia Latina
PLPLS	Proceedings of the Leeds Philosophical and Literary Society
PLRE	Prosopography of the Later Roman Empire
PP	La Parola del Passato
RA	Recherches Augustiniennes
RE	Real-Encyclopädie der classischen Altertumswissenschaft

ABBREVIATIONS

REA	*Révue des Études Anciennes*
RH	*Revue Historique*
RSI	*Rivista Storica Italiana*
SCH	*Studies in Church History*
SE	*Sacris Erudiri*
SGLG	*Studia Graeca et Latina Gothoburgensia*
TAPA	*Transactions of the American Philological Association*
VC	*Vigiliae Christianae*

I

Paganism, Christianity and the Latin Classics in the Fourth Century

R. A. Markus

That great historian, Norman Baynes, once remarked that 'we tend to foreshorten the religious struggle of the fourth century because we know its issue'.[1] The obverse of that struggle was the conflict within Christianity over pagan literature and learning. Of this, too, we know the eventual outcome, and we are apt to foreshorten that conflict too. We are conscious of the triumph, a triumph all but complete, of that current in Christian tradition which led to the wholesale assimilation of classical learning by Christianity. There would always remain churchmen ready to identify love of the classics with praising Jupiter or to recognise the devil as the first dialectician. But despite such survivals – reminders of an earlier intransigence – the fifth century witnessed the definitive adoption of secular learning by Christianity. In our foreshortened view of this conversion we sometimes fail to reckon with the hesitations and conflicts which attended it. Instinctively we think in terms of some image such as Arnold Toynbee's of the Christian Church as a 'chrysalis' carrying the elements of a new culture over from the old.[2] But this is the language of myth. In this paper I shall try to demythologise Toynbee's chrysalis. The crucial period for this enquiry is the century or so from about 350. Thanks to a number of important studies of Roman society, religion and culture during this period produced by the revival of interest in late Roman studies, such a survey has now become a possibility.

The survival of the Latin classics in Western Europe depended on many things: the existence of books which could be copied, of libraries where they could be found, of men who wanted to read and to copy them, study them and comment on them, and on the existence of places where the expensive luxury of scholarship was provided for. For securing some of these conditions, though not all, the period we are considering was crucial. At its beginning, we are on the threshold of a hardening of the official Christian establishment of the Empire towards paganism, and of the pagan reaction under the emperor Julian, with Julian's significant attempt to exclude Christians from teaching in the public schools of the Empire. At its end we see a christianised aristocracy, for instance the senatorial families who formed the backbone of the Gallo-Roman episcopate in the time of Sidonius Apollinaris in the 450s and for a long time yet to come, dedicated to upholding a literary culture indistinguishable from that of men such as Symmachus or Nicomachus Flavianus, the last pagans of Rome in the closing decades of the fourth century. Symmachus and Sidonius are landmarks: in the course of the two generations between them the culture which had been the preserve and pride of the pagan aristocracy of Rome in its last great conflict with Christianity passed into the hands of Christian bishops and aristocrats. The beginning and the end of the process of conversion are clear enough; its course less so.

It was certainly no steady, progressive softening by the Christian Church of its reserve about the pagan classics. In the Greek-speaking East there had never been the sharp sense of discontinuity between Christian and pagan, between sacred and secular, which in an earlier age had been so characteristic of the Latin, and especially of the African Christian tradition. But by now even in the Latin West Tertullian's *quid Athenae Hierosolymis?* (what has Athens to do with Jerusalem? – *Praescr.* 7) was a voice from a very distant past. Never, even in Tertullian's day, had Christians sought to provide their own alternative to the normal educational facilities available to their pagan contemporaries. Whatever misgivings they may have had about them in the past, by the middle of the fourth century few Christians had any reservations about sending their children to school, where they would receive the standard form of traditional education, with its strongly literary and grammatical bias.[3] The emperor Constantius II appears himself to have had pretensions to learning and to have taken an interest in education and the liberal arts.[4] In the 350s some distinguished rhetors such as Hecebolius and Prohaeresius, both Julian's teachers, and Marius Victorinus who, like Prohaeresius, had been honoured with a statue in Rome, were among converts to Christianity.[5] It was probably at this time that

Virgilian centos on biblical subjects came into vogue among Christian aristocratic literati. Faltonia Betitia Proba, the Christian wife of a pagan prefect of the City, wrote such a work to celebrate 'Christ's holy gifts announced by Virgil'.[6] Her programme was one expression of that symbiosis of Christianity and classical culture which also produced the calendar for the year 354, including lists of pagan Roman feasts, evidently being celebrated (and not merely as a traditional romp divested of religious connotations as were the Lupercalia in the time of pope Gelasius I at the end of the fifth century), for a Christian patron.[7] Christianity in the 350s shows very little inhibition about classical literature, and even about the pagan religious traditions of which it was so often the vehicle. The clearest testimony of the esteem in which classical learning was held among Christians is their reaction to Julian's decree of 17 June 362 which excluded them from teaching in the schools.[8] In their eyes it was a manifestation of 'diabolical tyranny'.[9] Not many of them can have felt any consciousness of 'profanity' attaching to the study and the teaching of pagan literature. The pagan Eunapius respected his Christian teacher Prohaeresius as much as the Christian John Chrysostom respected his pagan master Libanius. It was Julian, not the Christians, who thought that the classics and the gospels could not go together.

The opposition between the civilised and civilising *paideia* of 'Hellenism' and the lies, folly and barbarity of the 'Galilean superstition' was Julian's projection onto the cultural life of the 350s and early 360s. It gave currency to an old image which had had its vogue a century, even two centuries before Julian's time.[10] Christians themselves had, at times, been prepared to see themselves in such terms as the upholders of a 'barbarian philosophy',[11] against the godless sophistication of Greek wisdom and secular learning. But the opposition had been losing its relevance since the later third century. Christians were penetrating every level of society and assimilating the culture of educated Roman townsmen rapidly: perhaps even too rapidly, and with too little reserve. The new bitterness of the pagan opposition to Christianity at the end of the third century betrays a growing sense among the classes from which the Roman governing élite was largely drawn of a threat posed to them by Christianity. Men such as Porphyry, the philosopher, disciple and biographer of Plotinus, or Hierocles, who also wrote a work attacking Christianity and is said to have been one of the instigators of the 'great persecution' under Diocletian, saw that Christianity could be heading for a take-over bid in Roman society. It had progressed far in assimilating the current cultural capital even before Constantine. Half a century of imperial favour, of growing respectability and influence certainly did nothing to reverse this.

Julian's hated decree – even some of his pagan admirers disapproved[12] – was the product of his own, anachronistic attempt to polarise two cultures. It tried to drive a wedge into the comfortable *modus vivendi* they had achieved, and to some extent it succeeded. A few of the learned apostatised, among them Hecebolius, Julian's teacher, and the bishop Pegasius[13] who had loved the ancient Homeric sites and taken delight in showing Julian round them. How far such men were convinced that classical culture belonged to paganism, we can only guess: Hecebolius's career, at any rate, gives no grounds for inferring anything but sheer opportunism as their motivating force.[14] Others resigned their posts, including Julian's teacher, Prohaeresius of Athens, and the Christian rhetor, Marius Victorinus in Rome. Victorinus seems to have used his retirement to compose commentaries on the letters of St Paul.[15] Two Apollinarii, father and son, grammarian and rhetorician respectively, turned their learned skills to good use on the Bible: the former composed a Christian Greek grammar, turned the pentateuch into heroic verse and paraphrased the historical books of the Old Testament in the form of dramatic poetry, utilising all the available verse-forms; the latter turned the New Testament into Platonic dialogues.[16]

Julian's death the following year deprived his decree of effect. But the wedge it had driven into the developing Christian classical culture had gone deep, especially in the Latin West. In the Greek East there had never been such readiness to oppose sacred and secular as was always liable to break out in the consciousness of Western – especially of African – Christians. The Greek East recovered quickly from the set-back. The work of the Cappadocian fathers shows how slightly Christianity had been affected by Julian's intervention. On Western Latin culture, however, it left a deeper mark. The social stratification of West Roman society, especially as it had been developing since the time of Constantine, here facilitated the polarisation of pagan and Christian in a way that would scarcely have been possible in the East.[17] The last, repressive, years of Constantius II's and the brief interlude of Julian's reign brought about a crystallisation of deep religious divisions. Under the more tolerant régime of Julian's immediate successors the drift towards confrontation was checked, though only temporarily. From about 380 western churchmen and pagan aristocrats were facing each other from increasingly embattled positions. The unchecked assimilation of classical culture by Christians was now halted, even reversed, for forty years or more. For a few years Pope Damasus (366–384) could continue to adorn the tombs of his predecessors and of the Christian martyrs with versified epigrams, inscribed in fine classical lettering by his friend Filocalus, the calligrapher who had been responsible for the calendar made for a Christian patron in the year 353 (see above, p. 3). But by the end of Damasus's pontificate the world had come to differ starkly from the more easy-going world for which Filocalus had produced his calendar.

The dichotomy between Christianity and classical culture which Julian had tried to foist on Christians was becoming less of an anachronism than it had been when he had tried to give it a new lease of life. In the famous dream in which Jerome found himself accused by his heavenly judge of being a Ciceronian, not a Christian, we have one notorious example of an uneasy conscience in a Christian scholar about his love of classical literature. Perhaps it is easy to take it too seriously: when his enemy Rufinus years later accused him of teaching and copying classical works in flagrant breech of his promise never to open a book of the classics again, Jerome himself pointed out that even the prophets warn us not to take dreams seriously.[18] But Jerome's dream is also reflected in his waking life: his undoubted love of classical literature coexists uneasily with a disapproval of its Christian devotees. 'Even priests of God are seen reading comedies, reciting love poems from bucolic verse, and holding on to Virgil, to the neglect of the gospels and the prophets; guilty of doing voluntarily what children at school have to do under compulsion'.[19] Whether Damasus, the papal poetaster to whom this letter was addressed, was intended to take Jerome's words as a veiled reproof is a question the answer to which Jerome's literary skill has placed beyond our grasp. But it is striking that another famous letter of Jerome's in which he pours scorn on Christian versifiers of biblical subjects was addressed to another Christian poet, Paulinus of Nola. Virgilian centos like Proba's [20] are 'puerile nonsense, like the play of charlatans'; and quoting Horace's *scribimus indocti doctique poemata passim* (*Ep.* II.1, 117 – learned or not we all keep scribbling poems) he pours venom on 'garrulous old women, men in their dotage, verbose windbags' who consider themselves experts in the field of scripture. [21] Whether or not this letter had an overtone which Paulinus was not intended to miss, whether Jerome's disapproval was meant to spill over onto the work of Christian poets of his acquaintance or not, he certainly expressed himself with characteristic force, in the vein of Tertullian: 'what has Horace to do with the Psalter, Virgil with the gospels, Cicero with Paul?' [22]

Jerome was apt to express himself without reservations and to fall, the victim of his own – well-learned! – rhetoric. But if we may entertain reservations about giving his words full weight or about taking his views as more than those of a wayward and idiosyncratic scholar, we need look no further than his younger contemporary, Augustine of Hippo, for much more deeply reflected reservations about classical learning.

Augustine's love of the Latin classics and his heavy indebtedness to the whole rhetorical culture of his day are too well documented to need restating. It is equally clear, however, that a growing ambivalence can be traced in his mind in their regard. The author of the latest and most substantial work on this subject sees a turning point in Augustine's *Confessions*, written by Augustine in his middle forties, some five years after he had become bishop of Hippo. [23]

Hardly any work by a Christian writer breathes such a deep-seated hostility to the old cultural tradition as this manifesto of fanatical religiosity. The bishop turns violently against the reading of the classics in the schools and opposes to it the elementary teaching of reading, writing and counting, whilst he reverses his former valuation of them. He condemns outright rhetoric, to which he has devoted a great part of his life, as 'loquacity fair'. He feigns ignorance when talking of Virgil's once beloved poem (*Aeneae nescio*

6

cuius errores . . .) and the work of Cicero which awakened
his first love of philosophy (*librum cuiusdam Ciceronis . . .*).

Under Augustine's pen poets, orators and philosophers become
the purveyors of lies, inflated verbosity and garrulous argumenta-
tion.[24] It is not difficult to explain such a change in Augustine's
mind exclusively in terms of his spiritual and intellectual biography. It is important, however, to see it in the context of a widespread hardening among Christians towards secular learning and
letters at the end of the fourth century.[25] Augustine and Jerome
were not alone. More significant than Jerome's own malaise
about reading Cicero is the readiness of others – not only his
favourite enemy, Rufinus – to charge him with his crimes in this
respect. More than once Jerome thought it necessary to defend
himself on this score.[26]

By the end of the fourth century the assumptions about Christianity in its relation to pagan Roman society and its culture were
very different from those current around its middle years. The
shift obtrudes in Augustine's account of the conversion of Marius
Victorinus.[27] The process of thought which had brought the
neo-Platonist thinker and Latin rhetor to find in Christianity
an expression of the true philosophy is transformed in Augustine's
account into a dramatic renunciation of a militant pagan past,
and a painful break with the circle of his aristocratic friends.[28]
The passage of nearly half a century has distorted the perspective
in which Augustine saw the conversion of a pagan man of letters.
The image of conversion in terms of crossing from one of the
front lines on a battlefield to the other belongs to the 390s rather
than to the 350s.

Much had changed between Augustine and Victorinus,
between Jerome and Proba, and the change raised the problem of
classical thought and classical literature in an acute form for
Western Christians. Julian's attack on Christianity in the name
of 'Hellenism' had drawn classical learning into the conflict;
and classical learning was itself becoming one of the principal
issues at stake in the polarisation of pagan and Christian attitudes
in the last two decades of the century. This is not easy to infer
from what we know of the actual polemics between pagans and
Christians in these years. To read the various formal set pieces,
the *contra paganos* type of literature from the pens of Christian

apologists, is to enter a world of almost total unreality. We are the spectators of shadow-boxing. The real issues scarcely ever appear, except between the lines. What is said and written is in every sense 'academic'. More than sixty years ago Franz Cumont remarked that the blows of the polemic seem to strike only the dead,[29] and recent studies[30] have only underlined the extent to which Roman paganism, for instance as seen in the attack mounted on it in Augustine's *City of God*, is for all essential purposes the paganism of the late Republic as expounded by Varro, rather than that of the last pagan revival in the Western Empire. This learned antiquarianism pervades not only the reports we have of pagan beliefs from Christians. The pagan polemic is dominated by the clichés familiar from Celsus in the second century, and Porphyry's bitter attack written around 270 still provided a rich quarry for pagan apologists. And Christians were just as ready to make use of old arguments and to copy them from old books.[31] The real issues of the present seem, somehow, to elude these controversialists. The archaism is more than a literary device: it provides a means of debating something which neither side in the debate has quite got into focus. The pagan – or the Christian – had to be refuted; but it was not quite clear just what it was that needed refutation. To an outsider such as the Manichaean Faustus, paganism and Christianity looked only too alike,[32] and more than one pagan was horrified to find Christian monotheism apparently less uncompromising than his own.[33]

The real division between pagan and Christian at the end of the fourth century did not coincide with the old religious division; indeed, it was a recent creation, and not primarily a religious division at root. The attempt, first by the emperor Julian in a Greek form, then by groups of the Roman aristocracy in a more Latin mould, to rally the forces of Roman conservatism to the defence of a tradition transformed the confrontation of religions into a confrontation of cultures. Just as around 360 Julian had claimed the whole classical heritage for his 'Hellenism', to which the despised Galileans were outsiders, so now, the pagan aristocracy of Rome identified itself with a classical past in which Christians were to have no share. Their main ground for repudiating Christianity was its addiction to the pursuit of new-fangled ideas[34] in defiance of a hallowed tradition. In the refrain of their charges, as we can infer them from an exceptionally perspicacious little treatise *adversus paganos* by an anonymous writer, we can catch an echo of Celsus, Porphyry and Julian: Christians are *stulti*, fools.[35]

The old weapons had a new, and sharper, edge. For a brief moment here the debate moves among the real issues. The conflict is between a whole tradition of thought and feeling, imagination and ritual, face to face with the intolerant new order which was closing in menacingly. This short anonymous work is one of the very few literary products of the polemics of these years which brings us into the presence – at least fleetingly – of the conflict which divided, for instance, bishop Ambrose of Milan and Quintus Aurelius Symmachus in the celebrated debate over the removal by the Christian emperors of the Altar of Victory from the Senate house. Here, as in Symmachus' *Relationes* and Ambrose's rejoinders, we get a glimpse of what really was at stake: the claims on men's loyalties of the *mores parentum*, the ancestral traditions, the *usus antiquior* – the old custom, the *instituta maiorum* – the legacy of our predecessors, faced with the brash, intolerantly aggressive novelty. The Roman aristocracy who rallied to the defence of hallowed *vetustas* saw themselves, in the words of Symmachus, one of their number, as the *pars melior humani generis*[36] (the better part of the human race). Their labours in restoring the Senate house itself, pagan temples in Rome and in Ostia,[37] their wealth, prestige and influence are well known to us; their literary interests are equally well attested.

Ammianus Marcellinus, the pagan historian writing at the end of the fourth century, has left us an account of the Roman aristocracy which should serve as a warning against seeing in every senator a man of learning and a patron of scholars. 'Learning they hate like poison', he wrote of one of them.[38] No doubt many of these senators took little interest in anything weightier than Juvenal and Marius Maximus. But this need not have debarred them from sharing that ubiquitous tendency among the literate classes of the late Empire to which M. Marrou has devoted some fine studies: the diffuse beliefs and attitudes which combined to produce the ideal of the cultured man as a religious ideal: 'intellectual culture itself became the true religion'.[39] This religion was certainly more widely diffused than the intellectual culture; and Ammianus' Roman friends were no doubt often boorish dilettanti. But the circle of Symmachus, even though to some extent it was the creation of the free play of Macrobius's dramatic imagination,[40] was something more. Their output of generally trivial, but quite polished, verse, of letters, their interest in history and the classics,[41] were by no means negligible. Macrobius could bring the Virgilian commentator Servius and the fabulist Avienus[42] into their close-knit group: though too young to belong to it, their interests would have made them feel at home in the group assembled at the dramatic date of December 384 around Vettius Agorius Praetextatus.

For these men their pagan religion was part of their traditional Roman culture. This is what gave their circle coherence, despite some variety in the precise shade of their religious affiliations.[43] Praetextatus himself managed to combine quite serious scholarship with ten priesthoods, spanning Roman, Greek and oriental cults; he had undergone the taurobolium and seen to the religious initiation of his wife.[44] His interest in so wide a range of cults appears not to have been shared by Symmachus, who kept to the narrower circle of traditional Roman cults. It may be that there was some shift of emphasis in the religious tastes of the Roman aristocracy, and that Praetextatus' 'oriental' type of religion belongs more to the generation of Julian and its survivors into the 380s, and that Symmachus's more 'Roman' religion is more characteristic of their successors. In any case, however, they are unlikely themselves to have been very conscious of any deep divisions among themselves arising from their different religious tastes. Their religious solidarity is not sheer invention, either by Macrobius, looking back on their circle some thirty or forty years later, or of their Christian opponents. What united them was their veneration of Rome's pagan past, and, the obverse of this veneration, their attitude to the rejection of that past by Christians. Whether these pagans attached much importance to religious rites or not, and whether the rites they favoured were oriental, Greek or Roman in origin, they were all at least as interested in the books about the gods as in the gods themselves. They shared a love of Roman antiquity and treasured the literature which was the principal vehicle of its traditions. What we have here is, in Peter Brown's felicitous description, 'a whole culture running fast to stand still . . . the preservation of a whole way of life in the present, by transfusing it with the inviolable safety of an adored past'.[45] These men have earned their genera-

tion the designation of a 'Theodosian renaissance' by their patronage of a fine classicising style of carving on their ivories, by their
own, assuredly minor, contributions to Latin poetry, *belles-lettres*
and history, and, supremely, by their reading, copying and editing
of the classics, especially of the sacred text of Virgil. Two frag-
mentary manuscripts of Virgil surviving from this period are
produced in the 'majestic lapidary square capital' [46] reserved for
very special purposes. The antiquarianism of these men sometimes
found bizarre expression, as, for instance, in the affectation that
they were reading Virgil (their bible) from the old-fashioned roll,
whereas in fact they were using, as their Christian contemporaries
had long been using for their scriptures, the newer codex form. [47]
In a world of dramatically rapid change these men created a
mirage of the permanence of an older and static order of things.
Their literary culture enabled them to disguise from their own
consciousness the chasm between the Augustan and the Theodosian age.

Their devotion to poetry, above all to Virgil, the creator of
the Roman myth, was proverbial. *Carmina semper amasti* – 'poems
you have always loved' – wrote an anonymous Christian lampoon-
ist, addressing one of them. [48] It is not difficult to appreciate the
reasons that turned Jerome and Augustine against the *carmina
poetarum*: [49] if they were not quite, as Jerome thought, the food
of demons, they certainly were the chief nourishment of these
last pagans. Second to Virgil, Roman history, and particularly
Livy, was another object of their devotion. Symmachus
had planned to edit the whole of the Livian corpus; Virius
Nicomachus Flavianus, the pagan leader who committed suicide
after the defeat of the pagan reaction in 394, is called *historicus
disertissimus* by Quintus Fabius Memmius Symmachus, the orator's
son, on the inscription commemorating Nicomachus as his
wife's grandfather. [50] Both families were active, as we know from
a series of subscriptions in manuscripts of the first decade of
Livy, in editing the text over at least two generations. [51] We can
appreciate why Augustine should have set Orosius to write a
work more properly called *contra paganos* than 'Histories', and
perhaps even more properly to be called *contra livianos*. [52] The real
thrust of the pagan opposition lay in its devotion to a culture
seen as an alternative – indeed as an exclusive alternative – to
Christianity. This is why, if we want to read Augustine's real

answer to contemporary paganism, we need to attend not to what he says about the gods and their worship in the *City of God* and elsewhere, but to what he has to say about secular learning, primarily in his *De doctrina christiana*: for that work is his real *adversus paganos*.

Recent discussions of the prologue to this work,[53] its dating and of the question as to whom Augustine had in mind among the possible opponents he is here referring to, have distracted attention from the plain fact that the work is nothing more nor less than a sketch for a Christian culture and education alternative to the pagan *paideia* of the Roman world. It provides a syllabus for a Christian *paideia* based on the scriptures and aiming, in the end, at deepening the Christian believer's understanding of his scriptural faith. Of course the syllabus includes some secular components; but the terms on which secular learning enters this round of studies and the extremely restricted limits within which its pursuit is sanctioned make this educational programme inhumanly narrow. M. Marrou has devoted some eloquent pages[54] to a defence of Augustine's programme. Perhaps he is right in saying that compared with the artificiality, the antiquarianism, the neatly turned trivialities of Symmachus and the urbanity of Ausonius and their contemporaries, it is Augustine's intransigence that 'really represents the lasting values of humanism at this time'; it may be that we should allow ourselves to be urged by M. Marrou to see Augustine's programme as the expression of his consciousness of the decadence of the ancient world, 'an escape from false values and phantoms without substance'. We may accept the contrast between the new creative energies at work in Augustine's Christian intellectualism and the antiquarian ideals, the triviality of substance and the artificiality of expression characteristic of much in the literary and rhetorical culture of his age. But we must face the fact that neither the formula of his *De doctrina christiana*, nor any possible application of it, could have saved for us more of the Latin classics than we have potted in the pages of Isidore's *Etymologies*.

Jerome, Augustine, Prudentius and Orosius belong to the world of Praetextatus, the Symmachi and the Flaviani: a world in which the age-old tensions between paganism and Christianity were once again as sharply crystallised as they were never again to be. These decades opened a real possibility of a brutal rejection of the whole classical past by a triumphantly aggressive Catholicism. The possibility was not realised, and the christianisation of the Roman aristocracy proceeded rapidly in the course of the fifth century, without, however, involving a break with their secular traditions. Some impressive studies[55] have recently made us appreciate the continuity in the Roman senatorial families in virtue of which 'the secular traditions of the Roman senatorial class, traditions which one might have assumed to be intimately bound up with the fate of their pagan beliefs, came to be continued by a Christian aristocracy'.[56] The débâcle of the pagan reaction in 394 ushered in a new era of reconciliation and saw a continuing drift of the aristocracy into a 'respectable Christianity'.[57] The growing harmony was shattered, temporarily, by the moral catastrophe of the Gothic sack of Rome in 410, and threatened[58] by the Pelagian movement. But neither setback prevented the absorption of the old senatorial families and their traditions by Christianity. In 431 the memory of Virius Nicomachus Flavianus, the pagan leader of 394, was rehabilitated by the Christian emperors on the initiative of his son, now also a Christian and praetorian prefect of Italy. His grandson, who erected a statue in the Forum of Trajan in his honour, also continued the editorial work on the text of Livy begun by his uncle.[59]

The gulf between Christianity and the classics that had opened in the late 350s was beginning to close. The church historian Socrates, writing around the middle of the fifth century, recalling the work of the two Apollinarii under Julian (see above, p. 4) remarked of their labours to construct a Christian Greek grammar and to turn the Bible into Greek verse: 'their work is now of no more importance than if it had never been written.'[60] The stake of Christians in classical learning and their legitimate interest in them for the sake of 'polished speech and intellectual exercise'[61] could again be taken for granted. Socrates spoke for the generation of Christians who grew up after 410. The pious emperor Theodosius II, under whom he wrote, patronised not only church-historians: he also had the work of Cornelius Nepos[62] and Proba's cento (see above, p. 3) copied for him. His wife, Eudocia, daughter of a pagan Athenian, en route on a pilgrimage to the Holy Land, used a verse of Homer as the punch-line of an address she gave to the Antiochenes.[63] In the West, too, where scars healed more slowly, we enter a new world from the second quarter of the fifth century. When Macrobius wrote his *Saturnalia* soon after 431, according to Professor Alan Cameron's wholly convincing dating of the work,[64] it was possible to look back upon the *saeculum Praetextati*[65] as one looks from a changed world at an idealised past. Recalling Praetextatus, Symmachus and their friends, Macrobius could have concurred with the poet of *Little Gidding*:

> These men, and those who opposed them
> And those whom they opposed
> Accept the constitution of silence
> And are folded in a single party.

In his brilliant study Cameron has shown how thoroughly 'the non-militant and sentimentally pagan atmosphere of the *Saturnalia*'[66] is at home in the climate of these years, when the popes were making common cause with the Roman aristocracy in defence of classical architectural traditions.[67]

The conflicts were becoming a distant memory. Another work of Macrobius, his Commentary on the Dream of Scipio, was shortly to be copied by the Christian great-grandson of the pagan orator Symmachus; and his helper in the task was a Macrobius Plotinus Eudoxius, v.c., almost certainly the author's grandson.[68] This Symmachus, consul in 485, appears among the senators whose names were carved on their seats in the Flavian amphitheatre.[69] One of his neighbours there, Turcius Rufius Apronianus Asterius, edited both Virgil's *Bucolics* and the Christian hymns of Sedulius.[70] A descendant of another senator who sat here[71] edited the text of Horace and of the Christian poet of the Theodosian age, Prudentius.[72] He was Vettius Agorius Basilius Mavortius, related to the Avieni and an associate of the learned pope Agapetus.[73] The site of the library intended for the preservation of the Christian classics founded by pope Agapetus, with the help of Cassiodorus, has been identified by M. Marrou with characteristic ingenuity.[74] It was near that very spot that in 534 the last known rhetor of Rome, Securus Memor (Melior?) Felix, revised the text of Martianus Capella, *Christo adiuvante* (with the help of Christ), as he confessed at the end of his subscription.[75] And it was the same rhetor, master Felix, who assisted the consul Mavortius with editing his text of Horace in the year 527.[76] When Sidonius Apollinaris visited the library of a friend, he was delighted to find that Christian and pagan authors were classified together (at least on the shelves near the men's seats; it was still thought proper to segregate Christian devotional works by placing them near the ladies' seats): Augustine rubbed shoulders with Varro, Prudentius with Horace.[77]

In the course of the hundred years or so between the pagan emperor Julian and the Christian aristocrat, man of letters and eventually bishop, Sidonius, the age-old tensions between Christianity and classical culture, after a moment of crisis in the 380s and 390s was, if not resolved, at any rate, forgotten and overcome. The culture which men of Symmachus' circle and generation regarded as the distinctive property of a pagan élite in an increasingly christianised world became the treasured possession of a Christian élite in an increasingly barbarian world. The letters of Symmachus were among Sidonius' favourite sources and models. In Sidonius the values of the Roman senatorial tradition blended with the exclusive Catholicism of the Theodosian age. It is arguable that this accommodation between Christianity and the aristocratic values of late antiquity constituted a *damnosa haereditas* bequeathed by the ancient world to Western Europe; but it has secured for us the survival of what we have of the Latin classics. Perhaps Hobbes was more correct than he could have known when he wrote that 'there was never any thing so dearly bought as these Western parts have bought the learning of the Greek and Latin tongues'.[78] We have looked at the credit side of this balance sheet: its debit-side is the history of the barbarian kingdoms of Western Europe.

Note on the paganism of the aristocracy in the late fourth century

The view put forward by D. W. Robinson in 1915[79] on the nature of pagan aristocratic religious beliefs has been almost universally followed by modern scholars. According to this view, Symmachus' Roman traditionalism in religion was not characteristic of the religious attitudes of the leaders of the pagan revival; the beliefs of the majority of the aristocracy were more strongly tinged with eastern, devotional and initiatory elements. Fr Cumont also stressed the latter facet of paganism, and liked to note the affinity between this 'oriental' paganism and Christianity,

another 'oriental' religion.[80] Pierre Hadot, in his recent book on
Marius Victorinus, drew a related distinction between two types
of pagan neo-Platonic religion which he calls 'Porphyrian' and
'Iamblichean' respectively.[81] For the first of these, followed by
Plotinus, Porphyry, Victorinus and Symmachus, external ritual
is of little significance. What mattered was the philosophic truth
expressed in the form of religious doctrine. The second type,
more passionate, more mystical and more committed to rituals
and initiations, is the religion of Iamblichus, Julian and Praetextatus. M. Hadot's distinction is related to Robinson's, without
coinciding exactly with it. Hadot lays more stress on the common
philosophical assumptions which could lead, for instance, the
platonist Victorinus (according to Hadot's persuasive interpretation) to acknowledge himself a Christian, having found
in Christian belief the philosophy of the *Logos* which liberates the
sense-bound soul for its ascent to the intelligible world. What
Victorinus shares with Symmachus, in Hadot's view, is 'that
enlightened scepticism in religious matters which was always
traditional among the Roman aristocracy and in cultivated
circles',[82] the belief in many ways to 'so great a secret'.[83] Alan
Cameron, accepting the distinction between Symmachus' paganism and that of Praetextatus and most of the others, gives
Macrobius the credit for bringing them all on to a common
denominator.[84]

The situation seems to me both more complicated and simpler
than these interpretations allow. More complicated in that the
evidence for the type of pagan belief held by members of the
Roman aristocracy is in need of careful sifting. The evidence for
Praetextatus is well known, and seems to be reflected in Macrobius' *Saturnalia* (e.g. 1.7.17, 11.1, 17.1, 24.1). The evidence for
Virius Nicomachus Flavianus being a pagan of the 'oriental'
type rests on the so-called *Carmen adversus Flavianum*. The traditional identification of Nicomachus as its target is secure,[85] but
does not finally dispose of all doubts as to the nature of Nicomachus' religion. Of the case-histories collected by Herbert
Bloch,[86] Alfenius Ceionius Iulianus Kamenius (d. 385) stands out
as one of the few pagans surviving into the 380s with markedly
'oriental' religious tastes. Most of the others died in the 370s.
There is need for a re-examination of the question how far the
'oriental' paganism may be a survival from the generation and

circle of Julian rather than of the pagan revival of the 380s and 390s.

Whatever the precise shades of their religious views, however, I find it hard to believe that these pagans did not consider themselves as standing on common ground. Their differences would have appeared to them as alternative specifications of a common genus; and that would have been seen primarily in terms of opposition to Christianity. Late Roman paganism is the paganism of reaction, almost created by Christianity. Hence the 'enlightened scepticism' and relativism in religious matters which M. Hadot ascribes to Victorinus, which paved his way from paganism to Christianity, and would have made it unthinkable for Symmachus to follow him. He knew very well that what he had in common with the 'oriental' religion of Praetextatus was infinitely more important than the affinities between that, and Christianity, another 'oriental' religion. While Macrobius certainly transformed the religious atmosphere of the 380s and 390s in his work, the religious solidarity of the 'circle of Symmachus' is not sheer invention.

Notes

1 Reviewing J. A. Mc Geachy, *Q. A. Symmachus and the Senatorial Aristocracy of the West* in *JRS* 36 (1946), pp. 173–7, at p. 176; reprinted in *Byzantine Studies and Other Essays* (1955), pp. 361–6, at p. 363.
2 A. Toynbee, *The Study of History*, vol. 7 (1954), ch. 6, 2.
3 Generally, see H. I. Marrou, *Histoire de l'éducation dans l'antiquité* (1948).
4 Amm. Marcell., XXI.16.4 and *CT* XIV.1.1
5 On Prohaeresius, see Eunapius, *Vitae sophist.*, 485–93, Boissonade.
6 'Uergilium cecinisse loquar pia munera Christi' – *Cento Probae*, ed. Schenkl, *CSEL*, 16, 570, line 23.
7 The text, ed. T. Mommsen, *Chron. min.* I.13–148, in *MGHAA* 9; the illustrations, J. Strzygowski, *Die Kalenderbilder des Chronographen von 354* (Jb. d. k. deut. archaol. Inst., 1888); cf. H. Stern, *Le Calendrier de 354: étude sur son texte et ses illustrations* (1953).
8 Julian, *Ep.* 36 (Loeb); *CT* XIII.3.5.
9 Cf. J. Bidez in *Bull. de L'Acad. R. de Belgique, Cl. des lettres* (1914), p. 442; quoted in P. de Labriolle, *La Réaction païenne* (1948), p. 374.
10 E.g. Origen *C. Cels.* I.2; III.55, 75; VI.14.
11 Tatian, *Or.* 1; cf. Tertullian, *De idol.* 10.
12 Cf. Amm. Marcell., XXII.10.7; XXV.4.20; but Libanius, *Or.* 18.158.
13 Cf. Julian, *Ep.* 19 (Loeb).
14 On Hecebolius, cf. Socrates, *HE* III.1.10, 13.5–6, 23.5.

15 Suggested by P. Hadot, *Marius Victorinus: Recherches sur sa vie et ses œuvres* (1971), p. 286.

16 Socrates, *HE* III.16.

17 On this see A. H. M. Jones, 'The social background of the struggle between paganism and Christianity', in *The Conflict of Paganism and Christianity in the Fourth Century*, ed. A. D. Momigliano (1963).

18 Jerome, *Ep.* 22.30; Rufinus, *Apol. c. Hieron.* II.6–11 (*PL*, 21.588–92) and Jerome, *Apol. adv. lib. Rufini*, I.30–1 (*PL*, 23.440–4).

19 *Ep.* 21.13.9.

20 See above, p. 3; that Proba's cento is probably the work Jerome had in mind is argued by P. Courcelle, 'Les exégèses chrétiennes de la quatrième églogue', *REA*, 59 (1957) pp. 294–319, at p. 310.

21 *Ep.* 53.7.

22 *Ep.* 22.29.6.

23 H. Hagendahl, *Augustine and the Latin Classics* (*SGLG* 20.1–2, 1967), p. 715.

24 *Ep.* 101.2, *inter multa*.

25 Ambrose, paradoxically, seems to have been an exception in this respect: see an unpublished thesis by Mrs Carole Hill; and Christian teachers seem to have continued working in Rome through the years of confrontation. One such was Endelechius, whose pupil Salustius Crispus copied the text of Apuleius' *Metamorphoses* and *Apology* under Endelechius' supervision in 395; two years later he was continuing his work in Constantinople – had he gone there to seek a more congenial atmosphere? The Christian grammarian Bonifatius who was teaching in the Forum of Trajan at about this time cannot be dated exactly – cf. *CIL* vi.9446 and H. I. Marrou, 'La vie intellectuelle au Forum de Trajan et au Forum d'Auguste', *MAH*, 49 (1932), pp. 93–110. The Hierius who came to Rome in the 380s (Augustine, *Conf.* IV. 14.21–3) is unlikely to have been a Christian, though he may be identical with the Hierius who assisted Domitius Dracontius in copying a manuscript of pseudo-Quintilianic declamations. Cf. Marrou's article, p. 96.

26 E.g. *Ep.* 70; *In Ep. ad Galat.* 3 (*PL* 26.427–8).

27 Cf. Hadot, *op. cit.*, pp. 52f, 235f, for a convincing interpretation of Victorinus' conversion.

28 *Conf.* VIII.2.3–5.

29 Franz Cumont, *Les Religions orientales dans le paganisme romain* (1906), p. 244. On Cumont's rapprochement of paganism and Christianity, see my note on pp. 15–16.

30 P. Courcelle, 'Propos anti-chrétiennes rapportés par Saint Augustin', *RA*, 1 (1958) pp. 149–86; A Mendouze, 'Saint Augustin et la religion romaine', *ibid.*, pp. 187–223, and P. Brown, *Augustine of Hippo: a Biography* (1967), p. 305.

31 For an interesting example, that of Maximus' *Contra paganos* (drawn from Rufinus' translation of the Clementine *Recognitions*, etc.), see M. Meslin, *Les Ariens de l'occident* (1967), pp. 354–6.

32 Ap. Augustine, *C. Faust.* XX.4.

33 Cf. Maximus *ap.* Augustine *Ep.*16; Longinianus, *ap.* Aug. *Ep.* 234.2.

34 Ambrosiaster, *Q. Vet. & Novi test.*, 114.1 (*CSEL* 50, 303, lines 10–11).

35 *Ibid.*, 7 (pp. 306, 307); 15 (p. 310) etc.

36 *Ep.* I.52.

37 Generally, H. Bloch, 'A new document of the last pagan revival in the West, 393–94 A.D.' *HTR*, 38 (1945), pp. 199–244, and 'The pagan revival in the West at the end of the fourth century', in A. Momigliano, *op. cit.*, pp. 193–218.

38 XXVIII.4.14; cf. XIV.6 and A. Cameron, 'The Roman friends of Ammianus', *JRS*, 54 (1964), pp. 15–28.

39 H. I. Marrou, *Mousikos aner: études sur les scènes de la vie intellectuelle figurant sur les monuments funéraires romains* (1964), p. 255.

40 Alan Cameron, 'The date and identity of Macrobius', *JRS*, 56 (1966), pp. 25–38.

41 For a general account, see J. A. McGeachy, *Quintus Aurelius Symmachus and the Senatorial Aristocracy of the West* (1942), ch. 6.

42 Alan Cameron, 'Macrobius, Avienus and Avianus', *CQ*, n.s. 17 (1967), pp. 388–99, has argued that the correct form of his name is Avienus, and that he is to be identified with the Avienus of the *Saturnalia*.

43 See my note on pp. 15–17.

44 *CIL* vi. 1779; Boethius, *De int. ed. sec.* I.289.

45 Brown, *op. cit.*, p. 301.

46 E. A. Lowe, *CLA* I.13 and VII.977. Quotation from Dr Lowe's description of the Sangallensis.

47 Macrobius, *Sat.* V.3.17 with 4.1.

48 *Carmen ad senatorem* (*CSEL* 23, 227, line 4).

49 Augustine, *Ep.* 101.2; cf. Jerome, *Ep.* 21.13.4.

50 *CIL* vi. 1782.

51 O. Jahn, 'Ueber die Subskriptionen in den Handschriften römischer Classiker', *Ber. über d. Verh. d. k. sächs. Ges. d. Wiss., Phil.-Hist. Cl.*, Bd. 3 (Leipzig 1851), no. 6, pp. 335f.

52 Cf. A. Momigliano, 'Pagan and Christian historiography in the fourth century A.D.', in Momigliano, *op. cit.*, p. 99. Augustine's knowledge of Livy has been vindicated, decisively in my opinion, by H. Hagendahl, *op. cit.*, pp. 650–63, against the misguided attempt of Ida Calabi, 'Le fonte della storia romana nel de civitate Dei di sant'Agostino', *PP*, 10 (1955), pp. 274–94.

53 U. Duchrow, 'Zum Prolog von Augustins De doctrina christiana', *VC*, 17 (1963), pp. 165–72, and E. Kevane, 'Paideia and anti-paideia: the *proemium* of St Augustine's *De doctrina christiana*', *AS*, 1 (1970), pp. 153–80.

54 M. Marrou, *Saint Augustin et la fin de la culture antique* (1938), pp. 352–6; quotations from p. 353.

55 P. R. L. Brown, 'Aspects of the christianisation of the Roman aristocracy', *JRS*, 51 (1961), pp. 1–11, now reprinted in *Religion and Society in the Age of Saint Augustine* (1972), pp. 161–82; J. F. Matthews, 'Continuity in a Roman family: the Rufii Festi of Volsinii', *Historia*, 16 (1967), pp. 484–509, esp. at p. 506; and the two essays of A. Chastagnol, 'Le sénateur Volusien et la conversion d'une famille de l'aristocratie romaine

au Bas-Empire', *REA*, 58 (1956), pp. 241–53 and 'La famille de Caecinia Lolliana, grande dame païenne du IVe siècle après J.C.', *Latomus*, 20 (1961), pp. 744–58.

56 Brown, *Religion and Society*, p. 168.

57 *Ibid.*, p. 178.

58 According to Peter Brown's interpretation of the movement in his deeply impressive papers 'Pelagius and his supporters: aims and environment', *JTS*, n.s. 19 (1968), pp. 93–114, and 'The patrons of Pelagius: the Roman aristocracy between East and West', *ibid.*, 21 (1970), pp. 56–72, both now reprinted in *Religion and Society*, pp. 183–226.

59 Jahn, no. 6, pp. 335f.

60 *HE* III.16.

61 *Ibid.*

62 Cf. A. Momigliano, 'L'età del trapasso fra storiografia antica e storiografia medievale', in *Settimane di studio del Centro Italiano di Studi sull'Alto Mediævo*, 17 (1970), pp. 89–118, at pp. 113–14; and 'Popular religious beliefs and the late Roman historians', in *SCH*, 8 (1972), pp. 1–18, at pp. 14–15 on Theodosius II's interest in learning.

63 Evagrius, *HE* I.20.

64 Cameron, 'The date and identity . . .'

65 *Sat.* I.1.15.

66 Cameron, 'The date and identity . . .', p. 36.

67 On this see R. Krautheimer, 'The architecture of Sixtus III: a fifth-century renaissance?', *De artibus opuscula XL: Essays in honor of Erwin Panofsky* (1961), pp. 291–302, now reprinted in *Studies in Early Christian, Medieval, and Renaissance Art* (1971), pp. 181–96.

68 Jahn, n. 11, pp. 347–8. On Eudoxius, see Cameron, 'The date and identity . . .', p. 37.

69 A. Chastagnol, *Le Sénat romain sous le règne d'Odoacre* (*Antiquitas*, Reihe 3, Bd. 3, 1966). esp. p. 50; *CIL* vi.32162.

70 Jahn, n. 12, pp. 348–51; *CIL* vi.32103.

71 *CIL*, vi.32163.

72 Jahn, n. 14, p. 353.

73 Cf. Matthews, 'Continuity . . .', p. 508.

74 Cf. H. I. Marrou, 'Autour de la bibliothèque du pape Agapit', *MAH*, 48 (1937), pp. 124–69, who identifies it as the building on the Clivus Scauri south of the *titulus Pammachii* (= SS. Giovanni e Paolo), a building which originally formed part of Pammachius' reconstruction (on which see A. Prandi, *Il complesso monumentale della basilica celimontana dei Ss. Giovanni e Paolo* (1953), already crumbling by 535. Marrou suggests that the library was incorporated in Gregory I's monastery constructed in and around the house of his father Gordian: cf. the inscription in De Rossi, *ICUR*, II.28, n. 55 (= Diehl, n. 1898, without the [vital] heading). The books, according to Marrou's argument, were probably moved at this time to the Lateran archive.

75 Jahn, n. 13, pp. 351–2.

76 Cf. above, note 72.

77 *Ep.* II.9.4.

78 Thomas Hobbes, *Leviathan,* ch. 21.
79 D. W. Robinson, 'An analysis of the pagan mind of the late fourth century, with especial reference to Symmachus', *TAPA,* 46 (1915), pp. 87–101.
80 Cumont, *op. cit.,* pp. 253–4.
81 Hadot, *op. cit.,* pp. 47–58.
82 *Ibid.,* p. 48.
83 *Ibid.,* p. 236, alluding to Symmachus, *Rel.* 3.
84 Cameron, 'The date and identity . . .'.
85 Despite the attempt to question it by G. Manganaro, 'La reazione pagana a Roma nel 408–9 d.c. e il poemetto anonimo *contra paganos*', *GIF,* 13 (1960), pp. 210–24; cf. J. F. Matthews, 'The historical setting of the "Carmen contra paganos" (Cod. Par. lat. 8084)', *Historia,* 19 (1970), pp. 464–79.
86 In the table at the end of his paper 'A new document . . .'.

II

Decimus Magnus Ausonius: The Poet and His World

Harold Isbell

The dates of birth and death for Decimus Magnus Ausonius are known with only probable certainty. Most authorities place his birth at about A.D. 310, and his death at about A.D. 393. The intervening events of his life, however, can be placed with more certainty by a judicious and careful reading of his works. Because Ausonius had few if any qualms about placing his own person and history in his writings, we know a very great deal about his life and the events which surround it.[1] Ausonius was born the son of Julius Ausonius and Aemilia Aeonia. In the first of the prefatory pieces composed to accompany his works, Ausonius identified himself as bearing his father's name and emphasised that his antecedents, his rank, family, home and native land were all to be found in the works to which the preface was attached.

> Ausonius genitor nobis, ego nomine eodem:
>   qui sim, qua secta, stirpe, lare et patria,
> adscripsi, ut nosses, bone vir, quicumque fuisses,
>   et notum memori me coleres animo.
>
> <div align="right">(I, <i>Praef.</i> 1, lines 1–4)[2]</div>

(Ausonius was our father; I have his name:
  who I am, my class, my stock, household and country
I have written that you, good man, know me whoever you are,
  and when I am known you will cherish me in your memory.)

In his *Parentalia*, a series of elegies for his dead relatives, Ausonius told much about his family. In the first elegy he memorialised his father. This elegy, a part of the longer series, was in reality only one of two pieces composed for his father. In a series of later poems, the *Domestica*, written after his retirement from public life, he again praised his father in what he later considered his favourite poem:

> alia omnia mea displicent mihi; hoc relegisse amo.
>
> (III, *Domes.* 4)

> (Everything else of mine displeases me; this I
> love to read and reread.)

In the prose preface (from which the above is quoted) to this fourth elegy of the *Domestica*, Ausonius identified the poem as an 'epicedion' which he defined in the following manner:

> titulus a Graecis auctoribus defunctorum honori dicatus,
> non ambitiosus, sed religiosus . . .
>
> (III, *Domes.* 4)

> (a term used by Greek writers to honour the departed.
> It is used not out of ambition but out of devotion . . .)

In the later *Parentalia*, Ausonius expressed his respect and love for his father. But it is in the earlier *Domestica* that we learn most of the senior Ausonius. This epicedion, or dirge, was cast in the voice of the subject presumably telling us about himself. Of course it must be remembered that the literary convention would present the subject as already dead and speaking from beyond the grave.

On the one hand, this epicedion tells us a great deal about Ausonius and his family. Not incidentally, it also tells us much about his own good fortunes and the good fortune conveyed to his family, both older and younger generations. The elder Ausonius was born in Aquitania among the Vasates at a place called Cassio Vasatum and later Bazas. He established his home at Bordeaux and became a senator in both towns, though he filled no other office. According to Ausonius, his father was neither rich nor poor. The old man lived in thrift without poverty, and his life-style, table, clothing and habits of conduct, was equally moderate. Though he had little facility at Latin, he found Greek easy enough for eloquence. He freely gave the benefits of his medical skills and he prized the good opinion of other men, though he was his own most severe judge. Recognising the limits imposed by social circumstance, the elder Ausonius extended such kindnesses as the recipients could receive. Avoiding the civil courts, his estate neither grew nor did it shrink; avoiding criminal charges, he accused no one and was always careful never to testify to the peril of another. Free of envy, he avoided greed and ambition. He avoided deceit of every degree as scrupulously as he avoided the giving of false witness and false oaths. He had no patience for factions and conspiracies and he was careful to honour the ties of friendship.

As the dead Julius Ausonius enumerates his many virtues, the reader must hear the paragon of old-fashioned Roman virtue. In every way the elderly parent here depicted is the noble Roman who could well have been addressing us from the distant past. For us, it is difficult to determine what of this portrait is true and what is convention. Clearly the emphasis on tranquillity and peaceful existence could well suggest that Ausonius, the public figure, is passing judgment on his own manner of life as highlighted by the supposed life-style of his parent. As a dirge presumably read over the subject's coffin, the poem gives an intense view of the feelings and attitudes of its author, if not of its speaker.

The mother of Ausonius, the woman with whom his father lived for forty-five years in irreproachable fidelity, is given much less notice. Her elegy (IV, *Parent.* 2) is only eight verses in length and tells us little except that her mother came from Tarbella (the modern Dax, on the Adour in Aquitanian Gaul) and her father was of Aeduan stock.[3] Beyond seeing every wifely virtue in his mother, Ausonius had little to say about the woman.

> morigerae uxoris virtus cui contigit omnis,
> fama pudicitiae lanificaeque manus
> coniugiique fides et natos cura regendi
> et gravitas comis laetaque serietas.
>
> (IV, *Parent.* 2, lines 3–6)

(Every virtue proper to a dutiful wife
    was yours: a famous chastity, hands for spinning wool,
faith to your bridal bed and care for raising your young;
    grave but friendly, you were sober but bright.)

The next relative to be elegised in the *Parentalia* was Aemilius Magnus Arborius, the poet's maternal uncle.

Culta mihi est pietas patre primum et matre vocatis,
   dici set refugit tertius Arborius,
quem primum memorare nefas mihi patre secundo,
   rursum non primum ponere paene nefas.
(IV, Parent. 3, lines 1–4)

(Pious duty required that I say first my father's and mother's names
   yet Arborius cannot take third place:
though an offence to memorialise him first and my father second,
   it is still offensive to keep him from first place.)

According to Ausonius, Arborius had been his teacher. Arborius
was professor of rhetoric at Toulouse and was a man of very
wide and good reputation. The older man took his nephew into
his household, and recognising the boy's talents, won his love
by praise.

tu, postquam primis placui tibi traditus annis,
   dixisti nato me satis esse tibi.
me tibi, me patribus clarum decus esse professus
   dictasti fatis verba notanda meis.
(IV, Parent. 3, lines 19–22)

(You, after I in my youth was given over to your care
   and pleased you, said you needed nothing more.
When you claimed that I was worthy of both my fathers
   and you, you uttered what I would make my destiny.)

The career of Arborius is noteworthy. As a rhetorician at
Toulouse his fame grew and spread until he came to the attention
of Constantine's family. He was first appointed a governor and
then professor of rhetoric at Constantinople. While there he
became tutor to one of Constantine's sons. Arborius was a man
who went from obscure provincial beginnings first to an advan-
tageous marriage and then to the imperial household so that upon
his death in the east he was a wealthy man.

It is interesting to consider the evolution of the fortunes of the
family of Ausonius.[4] Though many lines were devoted to his
father, Julius Ausonius (sixty-four in the epicedion and eighteen
in the first elegy of the Parentalia), what seems a wealth of detail
is in reality a wealth of conventional piety. The heavy insistence
on probity of life would emphasise, if only by exclusion, the

apparent fact that Julius Ausonius had no higher status than that of a country doctor. Ausonius seems always to have been conscious of social position and prestige. Late in life:

> redisset ad patriam, villulam, quam pater reliquerat
> (III, *Domes.* 1)

(he retired to his fatherland and settled down on
the little estate left him by his father . . .)

to write the thoroughly charming verses:

> Salve, herediolum, maiorum regna meorum,
>   quod proavus, quod avus, quod pater excoluit,
> quod mihi iam senior properata morte reliquit:
>   eheu nolueram tam cito posse frui!
> (III, *Domes.* 1, lines 1–4)

(Hail, little inheritance, realm of my elders,
    cultivated by great-grandfather, grandfather, and father
until my father's untimely death left you to me.
    Alas, I had not wanted to own you so soon.)

In a way, these lines also reflect a great deal of the conventional pose. The inheritor must always express regret at the necessity of claiming his inheritance. But his reluctance must be tempered by his ultimate acceptance of the property transmitted by death. Ausonius was no exception. My point, however, concerns his use of the diminutive form in his initial references to the inheritance: '*villulam*' and '*herediolum*'. In a way it is a mark of modesty and good taste as well as eminent practicality to regard one's wealth as slight and insignificant. Yet I suspect that the diminutive here, set among other more conventional sentiments, is something other than convention and probably even truth. Ausonius after his years of public service wished to be rich in virtue if not in possessions.

The ancestors of Ausonius had been humble men. That certain of their descendants eventually acquired wealth and power is to be ascribed not only to a certain wit, but also and more properly to the ability and good fortune to marry well. In the fourth elegy of the *Parentalia*, Ausonius remembered his maternal grandfather, Caecilius Argicius Arborius:

26

Officiosa pium ne desere, pagina, munus:
　maternum post hos commemoremus avum
Arborium, Haeduico ductum de stemmate nomen,
　conplexum multas nobilitate domus,
qua Lugdunensis provincia quaque potentes
Haedues, Alpino quaque Vienna iugo.

(IV, Parent. 4, lines 1–6)

(Do not put down the burden of your pious task, my page:
　after these let us remember my mother's father,
Arborius, whose name came from Aeduan stock
　to combine the nobility of many a house
in Lyon, the land of Aeduan power,
　and in the Alpine lands of Vienne.)

Though his mother's family had suffered exile at the hands of the
tyrant, Victorinus, still his father had clearly married into a family
of higher social status than most physicians from Bazas and Bordeaux might have expected. In this fourth elegy of the *Parentalia*,
Ausonius had gone on to emphasise that Caecilius Argicius
Arborius, his maternal grandfather, though of noble lineage,
was still a relatively poor man in his exile:

tum profugum in terris, per quas erumpit Aturrus
　Tarbellique furor perstrepit oceani,
grassantis dudum fortunae tela paventem
　pauperis Aemiliae condicio inplicuit.
mox tenuis multo quaesita pecunia nisu
　solamen fesso, non et opes tribuit.

(IV, Parent. 4, lines 11–16)

(Then, exiled in that land through which the Adour rushes,
　in the land where Ocean's rage breaks on the shore of Dax,
still fearing the arrows of Fortune which sought him
　he took the penniless Aemilia into his life.
In a while a slight sum gathered with great pain
　brought relief though not wealth to his weary years.)

The heritage of Ausonius was ennobled though not enriched
by this grandfather. Caecilius Argicius Arborius knew and practised
the arts of divination. According to Ausonius, the old man

entered his last years apparently cheered by the expectation of his grandson's future success.

> tu caeli numeros et conscia sidera fati
> callebas studium dissimulanter agens.
> non ignota tibi nostrae quoque formula vitae,
> signatis quam tu condideras tabulis,
> prodita non umquam; sed matris cura retexit,
> sedula quam timidi cura tegebat avi. . . .
> dicebas sed te solacia longa fovere,
> quod mea praecipuus fata maneret honos.
>
> (IV, *Parent.* 4, lines 17–22, 27f)

(You were skilled in the heavenly numbers and in the stars
  which hold the secrets of men's fates.
Not unknown to you was my own life's pattern
  which you had hidden away on a sealed tablet
and never revealed. But my mother's concern revealed
  what a shy grandfather's care sought to conceal. . . .
You might have said that some slight solace was yours
  because of that distinguished heritage that came only to me.)

The son of a physician, the grandson of a seer who though noble was poor, Ausonius represents a significant social fact: it was possible for a man to rise to wealth and power without a military background. At each accretion to the family tree, there was added some quality which could ultimately lead to the success of Decimus Magnus Ausonius. Clearly, the various social classes and sub-classes of fourth-century Gaul were not strictly exclusive. Though it was possible for a man of wit and good fortune like Ausonius to rise to great heights, he still none the less must have remained conscious of his origins. In his lengthy discourse, the 'Gratiarum Actio ad Gratianum Imperatorem pro Consolatu', the 'Thanksgiving to the Emperor Gratian for the Consulate', Ausonius spent the first section extolling the accomplishments of Gratian, emphasising in particular the presumed tranquillity, a reborn *pax romana*, which allegedly emanated from the young man's imperial person. He contrasted the power of the imperial majesty with his own lowliness now raised to consular dignity.

> ista autem sedes honoris, sella curulis, gloriosa pompis
> imperialis officii, in cuius me fastigio ex qua mediocritate

posuisti, quotiens a me cogitatur, vincor magnitudine et
redigor ad silentium, non oneratus beneficiis, sed oppressus.
(XX, *Grat. Act.* 1)

(Surrounded by the pomp of imperial office into the heights
of which you have lifted me from my mediocrity, I am quite
stunned and reduced to silence by the overwhelming
grandeur of that chair of honour, the glorious curule stool.)

Later he wrote in the same piece:

Fecisti autem et facies alios quoque consules, piissime
Gratiane, sed non et causa pari . . . viros nobilitatis antiquae:
dantur enim multa nominibus et est fama pro merito . . .
(XX, *Grat. Act.* 4)

(Indeed, most dutiful Gratian, you have also made and you
will make – though never for similar cause – consuls of
other men . . . men of ancient nobility, for much is conferred
by a famous name which takes the place of merit.)

And again in the same work, he wrote, first quoting Sallust:

'Non possum fidei causa ostendere imagines maiorum
meorum' . . . veteribus ut illis consulibus (excepta, quae tum
erant, bellicarum conlatione virtutum) si quis me conferre
dignetur, seponat opulentiam non derogaturus industriam.
(XX, *Grat. Act.* 8)

('I cannot show portraits of my forebears as pledge of my
surety' . . . if anyone think me worthy of comparison to
those consuls of other times – though he exclude those
martial virtues then but not now requisite – let him deny
for me their opulence without discounting my industry.)

In his striking and very useful essay, 'Social Mobility in the
Later Roman Empire', Professor M. K. Hopkins sees in this
servility of address, 'all the ambivalence of the social riser, the
dilemma of pride and resentment. While he was flattered beyond
measure to have been ranked with the ancient nobility he had not
yet been assimilated, he had not yet accepted their values. It
rankled that others could gain so easily the honours that he had
won through skill and work.'[5] One cannot argue with the

assertion that Ausonius must have understood all too clearly the
achievement that was his. It should be noted, however, that in the
context of a 'Thanksgiving' the relative stature of the two,
Ausonius and Gratian, would dictate a certain humility, a feeling
of indebtedness, on the part of Ausonius towards his benefactor,
Gratian. Given the difference in station, it is only predictable
that the burden of debt would thereby increase proportionately,
and would thus magnify the necessarily subservient attitude of
the recipient.

Admittedly there is some truth in the assertion of Ausonius
that he alone secured by industry what other men had secured
by right of birth. Yet to identify Ausonius as an *arriviste* painfully
conscious of his origins is to overlook the fact that he was a
parvenu in a parvenu court. Valentinian, the father of Gratian,
though himself a tribune had been a man of peasant birth, who
by the accidents of time and place had been catapulted into the
imperial majesty. Though Gratian was now emperor as had been
his father before him, he could point to no previous nobility,
however slight, as could Ausonius. Still, it would seem that the
claims of aristocratic birth counted much less than we might
be inclined to imagine. The real aristocracy, the ancient patrician
and senatorial families of Rome, counted for little in the political
affairs of the day. Indeed, it might even be argued that the extravagant praise of Ausonius could only call attention to the humble
origins of Gratian and thereby point up the relatively noble
antecedents of Ausonius. In the final analysis, however, it is
best to recognise that neither man was of particularly exalted
stock.[6]

In the *Parentalia* Ausonius memorialised various relatives
until he came to his own immediate family. As he turned from
those older than himself who had already died, he recorded the
deaths of his contemporaries as well as those family members
whose deaths he should never have seen. One cannot help but
feel pity for a man who has come to the end of a long life to find
that he is nearly the last survivor, a man who has outlived his
wife, his eldest son, a grandchild, a son-in-law, four nephews and
one niece, as well as a host of his own generation.

Hactenus ut caros, ita iusto funere fletos
functa piis cecinit nenia nostra modis.

nunc dolor atque cruces nec contrectabile vulnus,
coniugis ereptae mors memoranda mihi.

(IV, *Parent.* 9, lines 1–4)

(Until now my dirge has fulfilled its appointed task
by singing of those who were dear by nature's bond.
But now grief and torment and a wound I cannot touch:
I must tell my wife's untimely death.)

The affection with which Ausonius mourned his long-dead wife
cannot fail to touch the reader. To this point in reviewing the
career of Ausonius, it has been entirely too easy to accuse him
of exercising his muse in a banal and sycophantic pose. There is
much in this ninth elegy that has been all too frequently overlooked by the critics of Ausonius. Before it was all too easy to
challenge the sincerity of his utterance of the more public sentiments, but it is difficult to question here the sincerity of his stated
grief. The problem is germane: which of these two or more
voices represents the real Ausonius? Such a question does not
permit the easy answers that have been too frequently given.
Ausonius was not the greatest of poets, despite the contrary
assertions of Symmachus and Theodosius, nor was he a man of
only one appearance. It is too easy to read the collected works
and then conclude that he must have been some kind of literary
dandy, another laureate. In this elegy, written quite late in his
life, there is little of the conventional pose, there is little of
the hollowness observed in something so recent as the first elegy
(to his father) of the *Parentalia*.

This elegy to his wife touches another literary tradition, though
only slightly, that of the abandoned lover:

torqueo deceptos ego vita caelibe canos,
quoque magis solus, hoc mage maestus ago.

(IV, *Parent.* 9, lines 13f)

(Mocked by my widower's state, I pull at my grey hairs
the more I live alone, the more I live in gloom.)

The image of the solitary lover, maddened by unrequited love,
dishevelled and bowed down by pain, is an image to be found in
Ovid as well as in the works associated with romantic love and the

31

courtly tradition. In a way, Ausonius stated sentiments that would come to be identified with the tradition of courtly love. But he adopted the pose with one very crucial difference: he was mourning not merely the absence of his beloved, but the absence of his beloved wife. There is nothing clandestine, and thereby 'romantic', about the sentiments here expressed. Ausonius knew the works of both Catullus and Ovid.[7] To be genuinely in love, according to these authorities, the love must be not only adulterous but also seasoned by the fear of discovery. For Ausonius this was not the case.

There is little reason to think that the last decades of the fourth century showed any unusual regard for marital probity and the practice of domestic virtue. In such a context, one of a quite usual moral indifference, this claim of Ausonius is the more striking. He was clearly arguing for the exercise of old-fashioned virtue, the sort of virtue that characterised, at least publicly, the Republic rather than the Empire. When Ausonius claimed virtue as the characteristic of his forebears, one could say that he was showing at least propriety, for both the elegy and the epicedion properly and rightly say only good things even if such benevolence required an outright lie. But the ninth elegy of the *Parentalia* is really not about his wife, Attusia Lucana Sabina, for Ausonius elegised her only indirectly by detailing the duration and extent of his grief at having lost her love and companionship. It might be argued that this concern for his own feelings and his own unfortunate situation was a mark of a certain callowness, that he cared less for others than for himself. Perhaps this might be true if this elegy were the only reference to his dead wife. Among his epigrams, however, is a much earlier poem of eight verses addressed to his wife.

> Uxor, vivamus quod viximus, et teneamus
> nomina, quae primo sumpsimus in thalamo:
> nec ferat ulla dies, ut commutemur in aevo;
> quin tibi sim iuvenis tuque puella mihi.
> Nestore sim quamvis provectior aemulaque annis
> vincas Cumanam tu quoque Deiphoben;
> nos ignoremus, quid sit matura senectus.
> scire aevi meritum, non numerare decet.
>
> (XIX, *Epig.* 40)

Ah wife, let us live as we have lived and keep
    those names which we first took upon our bridal bed:
let no day ever work change on time
    for I remain your lad and you my lass.
Though I be even more advanced in years than Nestor
    and you surpass Deiphobe, the sibyl of Cumae,
let us ignore the frailties nature gives to age.
    Better to know the worth of age and not its number.)

It is obvious that his epigram recounts an experience quite different from that to be found in the much later ninth elegy of the *Parentalia*. With the exception of what seems a touch of pedantry in his references to Nestor and the Cumaean sibyl, Ausonius detailed an intensity of feeling and precision of experience that seems entirely sincere. These eight lines are simple and un-cluttered, entirely devoid of the mannered evasions and circum-locutions found in so much of his poetry. In many ways, the literary career of Ausonius was as subject to formality and manners as must have been his public career. In this one quite short poem we have, however, a sharp and valuable insight into a young man's appraisal of the love between his wife and himself. Though the romantic convention argues for the eternity of love, that same romantic convention was never prepared to see the flower and vigour of youthful love develop until it transcended the debilities of age.

This epigram, so hopeful and buoyantly optimistic, clearly represents one of the young man's most devout wishes. While young, Ausonius apparently and typically regarded the fact of age and death with at least some detachment and equanimity, though as he aged he pursued or at least accepted the usual antidotes to the awareness of impending death, fame, power and prestige. By the end of his career he looked back over those most remarkable years to see the death of Attusia Lucana Sabina as the only real and enduring sadness of his life. Those years, it should be noted, witnessed the chain of events that would culminate in the sack of Rome in A.D. 410. Still, Ausonius seems to have been largely oblivious to that possibility. Throughout the turbulence of his very last years he maintained in his own feelings and memories a kind of tranquillity.

In Gaul at least, the lifetime of Ausonius witnessed a high

burst of educational activity. With the leisure that derives from the security of wealth, as well as security from invasion and political disruption, the pursuit of literary study could proceed and develop. Centres of learning were established in which there were well designated faculties of scholars hired to expound the various arts and courses of study thought necessary for a man. At the same time Gaul, and particularly Bordeaux in the Aquitaine, was not only a centre of learning but also a very important centre of commerce. By the lifetime of Ausonius, the chaotic events of the third century had been largely forgotten. For Ausonius, Aquitaine, the home of his forebears, was a land of plenty characterised by that peace which is the tranquillity of order. The extensive lands drained by the Garonne were notable for their many and lavish villas where wealth derived not only from the vineyards set on the terraced hillsides, but also from the grain that grew on the valley's floor.

This south-western section of modern-day France was notable for the high degree to which it had been romanised. So well developed was its school that men were regularly appointed from its faculty to positions in the imperial household or court. Both Ausonius and his maternal uncle, Arborius, were typical of this pattern. One significant characteristic of the thought of that time and place was the absolutely unshaken confidence in the stability of Roman law and custom. Ausonius, at least, seems never to have adverted to the pressures building at the frontiers. If Valentinian was 'the last emperor who systematically patrolled and fortified the western frontiers', then the period immediately after the death of Valentinian at the accession of Gratian in A.D. 375 could only be described as a lull before the gathering storm which would break after the death of Ausonius.[8]

That Ausonius was appointed tutor to the young Gratian in c. 364, is even more remarkable in light of the opinion of Valentinian which Professor A. H. M. Jones cites from Ammianus Marcellinus: 'of a violent and brutal temper, and not only un-cultivated himself, but hostile to cultivated persons: as Ammianus tells us, "he hated the well-dressed and educated and wealthy and well-born"'.[9] In spite of Valentinian's prejudices, Ausonius must be the heir's tutor, and the peasant's son must swallow his dislike so that his line could be touched with learning as well as the purple. This event, the appointment of Ausonius as tutor, and the emotional context out of which Valentinian made the appointment, tell us a great deal about the relations obtaining between the learned class and the centre of imperial power. Because there were virtually no emperors who could look to an aristocratic past, the cultivated and the learned found themselves quite estranged from the process of government. In the old days, the patrician class had not only governed Rome, but had also been the learned as well as the cultivated class. This was no longer true except in brief bursts of imperial grandeur. As the sources of governmental vitality derived more from the barracks than from the salons, the relative positions of scholar and politician became more sharply divided. It is within this context that we must consider the *Commemoratio Professorum Burdigalensium*.

It is reasonable to assume that both the *Parentalia* and the *Professores* had been written in the period after the consulate. Presumably he retired

> ad patriam, villulam, quam pater reliquerat
> (III, *Domes.* 1)

(to his fatherland, to the little estate which his father left)

and there busied his still active years with literary pursuits. In this, he was not at all unlike most political figures, both of ancient as well as of modern times. The violent accession of Maximus to the purple in A.D. 383 must only have confirmed the retired status of Ausonius. It is quite probable that the insistence on virtue was a criticism of the social and political mores of the day, though at the same time, Ausonius was also not oblivious to the hope that one day he too might be the subject of some memorial verses.

> Vos etiam, quos nulla mihi cognatio iunxit,
>   set fama et carae relligio patriae,
> et studium in libris et sedula cura docendi,
>   commemorabo viros morte obita celebres.
> fors erit, ut nostros manes sic adserat olim,
>   exemplo cupiet qui pius esse meo.
> (V, *Prof.* praefatio)

(You, too, I will remember not because you were my kin,
   but for the renown you have brought to our fatherland:
your zeal for learning and the industry of teaching
   joined you to me as famous men now dead.
Perhaps it will be that some day another can address
   himself to my ghost in a piety quite like mine.)

This diverse work commemorated the lives and accomplishments of twenty-four rhetoricians and grammarians. Though
praise is the dominant mode, Ausonius was not always free with
unstinting praise. For example, the ninth poem to the memory
of Jucundus is quite blunt.

> Et te, quem cathedram temere usurpasse locuntur
>   nomen grammatici nec meruisse putant,
> voce ciebo tamen . . .
>
> (V, Prof. 9, lines 1–3)

(Though some would say you improperly claimed your chair,
   and think you did not merit the title of grammarian,
still my voice must be raised . . .)

It would seem that Ausonius relied for certain of his material on
the residue of memory which surrounds every academic enter-
prise. These vignettes of the professors of Bordeaux range from
the politely conventional sketch really devoid of any particular
information to pieces which convey salient and quite specific
data. But these men, though obviously important to the life and
times of Ausonius, are relatively unimportant in the larger context
of history.

The importance of this work lies first in the charm with which
Ausonius wrote. In this, the *Professores* and the *Parentalia* have
much in common. The work, however, has a larger significance.
We have, frequently by indirection and inference, considerable
data regarding the nature of education in fourth-century Gaul.
Though Ausonius spent much of his life in the public service,
he remained throughout his life a rhetorician whose proper
activity was teaching. There are many references in his poems and
letters to the process of education. By the time of Ausonius, the
pattern of education had been largely systematised. But this had

not always been the case. In the earlier days Roman education was carried on in the home with the father assuming almost total responsibility for the rearing of his sons. The public ceremony in which the young man was given his *toga virilis* was not unlike the conferment in later times of an academic degree. This individualised education, unschooled as it was, may not have produced an evolving body of speculative knowledge, but it did produce men who wore the robes of manhood with proud though limited distinction.

With the conquest of Greece and the importation of Greek slaves and manners, there began to be found in Rome a fascination with Greek learning particularly evident in a fascination for acquiring the various arts and skills thought necessary for an educated man. Instead of learning from the wisdom of his ancestors, the patrician youngster sat at the feet of a Greek pedagogue. The various subjects of Greek study were variously received in Rome. As Professor T. R. Glover put it: 'Philosophy the Roman reckoned to be verbiage. Geometry was useless. About Rhetoric he was doubtful. Grammar was obviously above suspicion.'[10] As time passed, the utility of learning, particularly Grammar and Rhetoric, became more apparent. In the earliest days the teacher had been an *entrepreneur*, almost a peddler. His financial security was at best haphazard so that he all too frequently relied for payment on his ingratiating ways as much as on his learning and pedagogy. By the time of Ausonius, the position of the professor had achieved a certain defined social and financial status. Though Valentinian had little regard for learning, he still found it wise to retain a famous rhetorician as tutor for his son.

The benefits of education must have been fairly widespread in fourth-century Gaul. In the epicedion for his father, Julius Ausonius, the following verses are placed in the man's mouth:

> sermone inpromptus Latio, verum Attica lingua
> suffecit culti vocibus eloquii.

(III, Domes. 4, lines 9f)

(I lacked ease in Latin speech, but in truth the Attic tongue
 gave me words of studied eloquence.)

It has been noted previously that Julius Ausonius was a relatively humble man of very simple origins. Yet Ausonius took care to note his father's role in local politics. We can only assume that even such men enjoyed certain of the fruits of learning. It is one thing to educate the sons of the rich and powerful, but it is quite another thing to educate the sons of the humble.

In another work Ausonius addressed an exhortation to his grandson, the young Ausonius. This work was enclosed in a letter to the boy's uncle, Hesperius. Ausonius painted for the child a very detailed and, in all probability, accurate picture of the contemporary classroom. He lingered on the fear which the schoolmaster inspires in his young charges, and finally concluded:

> quod fervent trepido subsellia vestra tumultu,
> pompa loci et vani fucatur scaena timoris.
> haec olim genitorque tuus genetrixque secuti
> securam placido mihi permulsere senectam.
>
> (XVIII, *Epist.* 22, lines 31–4)

(though a tumult of fear makes your benches quake, it is only display and painted scenery meant to cause unfounded fear. Both your parents, mother and father, endured this in their day and survived to ease my tranquil and composed old age.)

Though we have no record of the boy's response, the personal touch is not nearly so important as the fact that Ausonius strongly emphasised that both of the boy's parents had also gone to a similar 'grammar school'. In other words, daughters as well as sons could aspire to at least the beginnings of learning. However, it would be folly to regard this phrase as evidence for an equality of men and women. It remained a man's world, politically as well as socially. The portrait of his mother in the *Parentalia* as being dutiful, chaste, industrious, faithful, grave, friendly, sober and bright, is probably true of every good wife of the day. In other words, a woman received such education as would enhance her adult life of service to husband and family.

The *Commemoratio Professorum Burdigalensium* is never far removed from the ambitions and accomplishments of Ausonius himself. The first elegy was addressed to Tiberius Victor Minervius, the orator. According to Ausonius, this man received the honour of first place because he was

primus Burdigalae columen
(V, *Comm. Prog. Burd.* 1, line 1)

(the first eminence of Bordeaux.)

With a metaphor of such extravagance at the beginning, the reader
has little difficulty in ascertaining the thrust of the entire work.
Clearly, the achievements of Bordeaux were to be remembered as
considerable. Still the reader cannot avoid the relentless enthusiasm
with which Ausonius argued the point.

Generally speaking, these elegies for the professors of Bordeaux
follow a threefold pattern. The opening lines usually summarise
the subject's most notable public accomplishments, the middle
lines proceed to a listing of the less well-known aspects of the
man's career and the conclusion of the elegies concerns itself
with certain details of the subject's private life. As a rule, though
not always, this last section is concerned with the subject's
particular virtues. After this rather well defined elegy, there are
final lines which confront the problem of life after death. The
ending of the first elegy is worth note:

> Et nunc, sive aliquid post fata extrema superfit,
> vivis adhuc aevi, quod periit, meminens:
> sive nihil superest nec habent longa otia sensus,
> tu tibi vixisti: nos tua fama iuvat.
> (V, *Comm. Prof. Burd.* 1, lines 39–42)

(And now, if anything survive the final destiny,
you are alive and remembering a life that has passed;
but if nothing is left and your long rest has no feeling
then you have lived and we rejoice in your fame.)

Though there is the hope that the subject has survived the fact
of death, Ausonius carefully noted the possibility that the spirit
might not be immortal. If the soul does not survive, one can at
least take comfort in the continuation of fame. Perhaps this is the
point of the *Commemoratio*: despite the fact that every man hopes
for immortality, there is no absolute certitude that one does in
fact survive death.

The elegies are anything but grief-stricken and heavy; indeed,
the tone generally is one of lightness and good humour. The very
inevitability of death makes possible a comedy not often to be

found in Ausonius. He did not dwell solely on the more obvious kinds of goodness, he detailed as well the particular kinds of activity which identified the individual as unique. Professor T. R. Glover has remarked that 'The Professors of Bordeaux and Toulouse seem to have been on the whole a genial and agreeable set of men, not very great perhaps, nor always very good.' These men of learning represent in their own lives the high mobility characteristic of men like them in the Empire at that time. From east to west, Bordeaux to Constantinople, these 'wandering scholars' travelled, searching always for fame and, lacking that, students. They were the cultivated men of the day and their verbal skills made them social assets. However, they were cultivated men separated from the culture which should have been their nurture and their work. This displacement of Rome's grandeur was much more than a geographical fact. According to Glover, 'Style, polish, grace, neatness were there, but not life, and its absence vitiates all the excellence they attain.'[11]

The twenty-six poems of the *Commemoratio* are cast in a variety of metres. One cannot help thinking that Ausonius set out to commemorate diversity with a diversity of style. Yet the conclusion enjoins on the reader an interesting caution.

> quos memorasse mihi morte obita satis est.
> viventum inlecebra est laudatio: nomina tantum
>   voce ciere suis sufficiet tumulis.
> ergo, qui nostrae legis otia tristia chartae,
>   eloquium ne tu quaere, set officium,
> quo claris doctisque viris pia cura parentat,
>   dum decora egregiae commeminit patriae.
>
>   (V, *Comm. Prof. Burd.* 25, lines 4–10)

> (for the dead it is enough to have been remembered.
> For the living praise is a lure: if the voice only cry
>   their names, those entombed will be at rest.
> Hence, you who read these gloomy pieces ought not to
>   look for eloquent speeches, rather you should
> seek the affection which directs a pious offering
>   to the famous and learned while recalling my country's glory.)

Throughout the corpus of his writing Ausonius habitually adopted a humble and suppliant pose which seems to have disparaged his own production and invited the mocking laughter of his reader. The reader, on the other hand, quite quickly determines the real intent of these remarks. It seems an exercise in vanity; by appearing humble, he invited if not compelled the reader to insist that the poems are not tedious. In the end, however, a charming ingenuosity becomes finally cloying. The stance cannot be genuine; but in this twenty-fifth poem of the *Professores*, the self-disparagement takes a new and perhaps anti-rhetorical tack. Ausonius drew a line between eloquence and affection or feeling. In this, he recalled the ancient bias that for a truly good man eloquence flowed naturally from the fulness of his virtue. In this way, to be a political animal followed immediately upon being an ethical animal. This view of eloquence tended to regard rhetorical skill as a habit of deceit.

It does not seem, however, that we could regard Ausonius as doing anything but adopting a half-serious even mocking pose. Criticism of this poet has traditionally regarded such statements as evidence of an almost overbearing self-confidence. Instead of a virtuous humility which only enhances greatness, it is said that Ausonius reveals himself as having been a man for whom one can have little or no respect. The problem, however, would seem to be larger than the idiosyncrasies of any one man. The fourth century was characterised by unsettled and unsettling conditions. The imperial power, though it took pains to be a party to the religious and cultural activity of the day, was in fact quite removed from whatever traditions there might have been. With the political legitimacy of each reign a matter best left unmentioned, the issues of the day were problems associated with the holding and transmittal of power. In such a context, the man of letters is almost certain to be of ornamental value alone. This must have been the role of Ausonius at the court of Valentinian.

In such a situation, the subtleties of learning and its artful expression could hardly have much real value. As a result, the learned man must become a source of entertainment rather than enlightenment. It was not a great age; those years represented a transition from one political order to another order almost apolitical. In spite of the extravagant praise emanating from men like Ausonius, the empire was dead and collapsing inward in its inability to govern and keep secure the lands conquered over the centuries. When he attempted to achieve a public presence,

Ausonius was little more than vacuous. On the other hand, when he turned his vision to the *minutiae* of domestic existence, he achieved an ease and grandeur quite unlike anything he had done before.

Besides the verses concerning his wife, Ausonius achieved ease and a beautiful simplicity in perhaps only two other works, the series of epigrams done for the girl, Bissula, and the long poem, *Mosella*. The *Bissula* has attached to it an introductory letter and a preface of six verses. Ausonius hastened to disclaim any poetic achievement, protesting all the while that these *poematia* or 'versifications' should remain in the darkness to which he had originally consigned them. He described them, further, as *rudia et incohata* or 'coarse and incomplete' things which must be put to shame by the poems of Paulus, to whom Ausonius was sending the manuscript. In the preface to the work, he again presented an identification for these poems:

> otium magis foventes, quam studentes gloriae.
> (IX, *Biss.* 1, line 3)

(stirring up boredom rather than pursuing glory.)

Ausonius warned his reader to read in a light spirit, preferably a spirit already lifted by wine, so that if by chance the reader should fall into a dream, he might imagine the dream to be the poem.

So much for the good humour. Comedy is one thing, flippancy quite another. It is a charming trifle which describes and praises the beauty of this barbarian serving girl. One must be careful to remember that Ausonius was entirely capable of being casual with his muse, for our romanticised image of the poet was quite foreign to him. To Ausonius, the poet was not only a medium of reflective language, he was also and quite properly a source of entertainment. Doubtless he knew the tradition that surrounded the use of poetry at public functions. Ausonius, in addition, did not have the luxury of an entirely sophisticated audience. Whatever his own abilities might have been, his poems were quite frequently products of his audience and its grave limitations as much as products of his own genius. Gibbon's remark regarding the popularity of Ausonius in his own time has already been too much quoted. To condemn either the man or his times by comparisons of taste is to forget that, after all, matters of taste like matters of fact are not fit subjects for the parry and thrust of disputation.[12]

During his own era and in the years after, it is the *Mosella* on which the reputation of Ausonius has depended. The opening of the poem refers to a journey on which the author passed through a relatively desolate land until he came to the shores of the Moselle. H. G. Evelyn White argues, as do many others, that the journey must have occurred during one of the frontier expeditions which Valentinian conducted to the north and east of the more settled areas of Gaul. Ausonius presented the charm and beauty of the Moselle and the rivers of Bordeaux as contrasted by the bleakness of the Belgian and German countrysides. Though Trier was some distance from Bordeaux, Ausonius was careful to regard both places as part of his homeland.

The poem's four hundred and eighty-three lines can be read as a series of elaborate apostrophes directed to the personified river. This method is not so unlikely as it might first seem, since Ausonius took great care to refer to the many deities and lesser deities normally associated with the land. But the most significant feature of the *Mosella* is the almost tedious devotion to the idea of tranquillity. Clearly, this was intended to be a profound compliment to the emperor whose court resided at Trier on the Moselle. By inference, Ausonius seems to have argued – factual evidence to the contrary notwithstanding – that the goodness and legitimacy of the emperor had an immediate effect on the tranquillity of the land over which he ruled. Because the Moselle had the good fortune to flow past the seat of imperial power, its modest stream became the channel by which the imperial goodness flowed to the outer world. Such a profound respect for the powers of kingship was by no means novel, nor did it die with Ausonius and the Empire.

The most astonishing feature of the *Mosella* and the feature most obvious at a first reading, is the relentless insistence on cataloguing every aspect of the river's detail. The poem is arranged according to a principle of visibility: that is, the description begins with a salutation which encompasses the entire river – its vine-bearing hills, its grassy banks, its ship-bearing depths, its clarity, its springs, its freedom from turbulence by wind or hidden rocks, its straight channel, its boats that move with oars or tow ropes, its sandy shallows and shoreline free of mud and sedge. After this preliminary listing of the river's overall characteristics, Ausonius digressed briefly to repudiate the wanton waste of resources in marble floors, professing to desire only the river's firm sand for his feet. Ausonius returned to his initial description turning his vision to the river's bottom, a feature readily apparent because of the unusual surface clarity. Here Ausonius moved to a detail of vision that might not have been expected: the sandy furrows on the bottom, the water plants swaying in the current, the shifting gravel, the patches of moss. Ausonius then used the shore of Scotland with its tides as a figure for the river's bottom. The shifting tides alternately reveal and hide the beauties of the sea's bottom, so too do the plants by their motion reveal and hide the treasures of the river's bottom.

After exhausting this phase of the description, Ausonius recognised that he must turn to a description of the multitude of fish. However, he found that Neptune forbade him such access because the poet is never a creature of the deeps. The poet recognises that to treat of the fish, he must call on the Nymph who dwells in the river because it is she who properly resides there and knows the stream intimately. Presumably Ausonius intended that this lengthy description (lines 85–149) should be delivered in the voice of the Nymph. This, however, could be only the merest convention intended to maintain the fiction that the poet himself has been unable to probe and study the watery depths. The passage clearly reflects an unwillingness to separate his own person from the poem, whether by style or by the attribution of specific data to the Nymph.

It would seem that Ausonius had at his elbow a carefully drawn list of the various fish to be found in the river. Such a list could not have been far removed from his actual experience. For a man who lived most of his life near rivers, a detailed knowledge of fish and their culinary uses could hardly be unusual. But the gourmet poet is not content with identities alone. He also detailed the habitat of many species as well as the method by which certain of the more tasty are best caught. Such an awareness tells us much about Ausonius himself, as well as the rivers and the fish.

From his discussion of the fish Ausonius turned his eye to the vineyards growing along the Moselle, taking care to note that the richness and profusion of these vineyards was not at all unlike that of other renowned grape growing areas: Gaurus (Monte Barbano) in Campania, Rhodope in Thrace, the Pangaean hills between Thrace and Macedon, Ismarus on the coast of Thrace and most particularly his own vineyards along the Garonne in Bordeaux. From a scene of such pastoral beauty Ausonius enlarged the picture to include the traditionally happy husbandman whose pleasure is found in his work. Jesting with one another, both workman and traveller along this river proceed in a manner both busy and carefree. The beauty of the place coupled with its riches both natural and cultivated engendered only happiness.

This sudden turn towards the pastoral convention is quite interesting. Ausonius the courtier could hardly have been a man who lived in the pastoral manner. For Ausonius, as for all men, the pastoral convention was a life-style which could never have been possible. Men who find themselves caught up in the business of the city inevitably turn to the apparent peace of the countryside as an antidote to the pressures of their own harried lives. But in the last analysis the pastoral as defined by literary convention remains an entirely imagined way of life. That such imaginings are the pastime of the governing classes may tell us more about the state of a society than has hitherto been supposed. Though busy men, Ausonius and his associates were men for whom leisure was guaranteed by accumulated wealth and power. Such leisure could never be the life-style of a man whose meagre livelihood derived from the cultivation of a few grapevines and the care of sheep.

After describing the natural scenery, Ausonius turned (line 169) to imagine the satyrs and nymphs also at play in this place. From this he then continued to describe the sight of the hills mirrored by the stream's surface. Not content with the scene alone, he again invoked the river dwellers and travellers whose games involved these reflected images in a manner both simple and rustic. From this he moved to describe the country men who fish the stream. Before, the people in the poem had been good; now, as they seek out the fish, their actions become sinister and threatening. The figured language which Ausonius used details this added quality: the men are no longer boisterous and playful; they are cunning beings whose strength is suddenly utilised in a coherent act with a specific and entirely planned effect. One man draws his knotted nets through the channel and 'sweeps up' (*verrit*) the fish while another uses seines and yet another uses baited hooks so that when the fish bites, the creature is pulled to the shore so swiftly that the pole hisses

> . . . ut raptis quondam per inane flagellis
> aura crepat motoque adsibilat aere ventus.
> (X, *Mosella*, lines 257–8)

(. . . as the very air rustles and whistles when a whip cracks through empty space and disturbs the air.)

From this discussion of man's violent imposition of himself on other living things, Ausonius proceeded to a discussion of the villas and houses set on the hills along the river. Again we find him turning to other more famous examples, in this case examples of things built by men along a water's edge. He compared these structures to those built by the most renowned architects and builders of antiquity and myth: Daedalus, Philo, Archimedes, Menecrates, Ictinus, Dinochares, as well as many whose names are forgotten but whose works have endured. Such men of genius might well have designed and built the magnificent structures that grace the Moselle. Passing his eye along the river, Ausonius took care to note the more remarkable of these structures. The buildings are presented as active agents which hold their places, it would seem, by their own continuous act rather than by the fact that they are lifeless and unmoving things that rest where they had been built. Once again, however, Ausonius returned to the river as the subject of his poem. This he did by describing first the baths attached to these establishments and then by noting how refreshing it is to go directly from the hot bath to the fresh and invigorating coolness of the river.

From such pleasantness Ausonius moved to a more vexing problem, that of the river's tributaries and the river to which it is in turn a tributary, the Rhine. By his earlier linking of the Moselle to the imperial, Ausonius must ultimately have seen the metaphor become a political problem. Clearly, the emperor was supreme and subservient to no one and the same must be true of the river beside which the imperial court resided. Though the Moselle does have tributaries which swell its progress – a kingly metaphor

– it is a fact that the Moselle in turn flows into a mightier stream. The dilemma is solved quite ingeniously by an insistence that Rome on the Tiber is the true seat of Roman government. No matter where the emperor resided, and it was prudent that Ausonius overlooked the causes for such residence, Rome remained his true home and the true hub of the empire. Later in the poem Ausonius emphasised that of all the Rhine's tributaries, only the Moselle profoundly alters the course and character of the larger stream. After solving the political dilemma, the topo-graphical fact was easily and safely conveyed.

Finally the poet affects fatigue and longs only to praise the glory of the men who live along the Moselle: the farmers, the lawyers, the senators, the governors. But finally he desires to praise not so much the famous men as the river which is the source of all their strength. At last, Ausonius turned his poem to him-self, a man alien to the Moselle who claimed to speak out of love rather than out of genius. When he would finally be retired from the imperial service, he would expect to return to Bordeaux to write more, and again about the Moselle and the culture which he claimed to have observed along the river's banks. These later poems would emphasise the tranquillity which depends on an ordered society. In the end, it became his goal to praise the gran-deur of the Moselle until its fame and reputation – now enhanced by those along its shores – would surpass that of every other river in Gaul.

Ausonius concluded his poem with the fond hope that wherever its verses are to be recited the fame of its subject will be enhanced until all the earth will have heard of the Moselle. At last, at the poem's end, even the Garonne whose stream touched his estates will itself hear and acknowledge the Moselle's eminence. This fame which Ausonius pursued with such singular energy came to him in his own lifetime. Some years after the composition of the *Mosella*, Theodosius wrote to Ausonius who was by then living in retirement.

Amor meus qui in te est et admiratio ingenii atque
eruditionis tuae, quae multo maxima sunt, fecit, parens
iucundissime, ut morem principibus aliis solitum sequestrarem
familiaremque sermonem autographum ad te transmitterem,
postulans pro iure non equidem regio, sed illius privatae

inter nos caritatis, ne fraudari me scriptorum tuorum
lectione patiaris.

(I, Praef. 3)

(Dearest father, my love for you and my admiration for your
very great wit and erudition have caused me to follow the
custom of other princes and send myself a familiar greeting
to ask – not for reasons of kingship, but out of a mutual
affection – that I be not deprived of the chance to read your
works.)

On another occasion, his close friend Symmachus wrote to thank
Ausonius for sending a manuscript of poems.

Merum mihi gaudium eruditionis tuae scriptae
tribuerunt, quae Capuae locatus accepi.

(XVIII, Epist. 1)

(Your erudite manuscript, which I received while
at Capua, gave me very much delight.)

But it is in the epistles that we find something of the diversity
which comprised the man. The letters fall into several categories.
First, there are the letters addressed to certain of his colleagues
and contemporaries. These are the letters to Quintus Aurelius
Symmachus (No. 2), Sextus Petronius Probus, the Praetorian
Prefect (No. 12), Axius Paulus, the Rhetorician (Nos 4, 5, 6, 7, 8,
9, 10), and Ursulus the grammarian (No. 13). The next category
includes letters addressed to those former students who had
achieved some degree of success: Tetradius the rhetorician (No.
11) and most particularly Meropius Pontius Paulinus known to
us as Paulinus of Nola (Nos 23, 24, 25, 26, 27, 28, 29). The next
category includes those letters addressed to various members of
his family: Hesperius, his son (Nos 18, 20, 22); Julius, his father
(No. 19); and Ausonius, his grandson (No. 22). The final category
of letters includes those addressed to Theon the rustic who lived
in Médoc (Nos 14, 15, 16, 17).

In each of these categories, Ausonius displayed a quite different
personality. The letters to his colleagues and contemporaries are
very obviously the products of a public figure addressing another
public figure. The formalised pattern of flattery and tribute are
everywhere present, even when the recipient is being addressed

as 'friend.' In each of these letters Ausonius zealously guarded
his own stance and reputation. Most men who read these letters
rapidly conclude that Ausonius was protesting too much. The
more vigorously he protested his own inadequacy and the poverty
of his muse, the more we are convinced that if the recipient had
acquiesced in such protestations the result would have been fury.

Leaving behind the flatteries and studied inanities of the public
correspondence, the next larger group of letters consists of those
seven addressed to his former pupil, Paulinus, and the one
addressed to another former pupil, Tetradius. This latter had been
separated from Ausonius for many years, but had returned
to the area so that Ausonius sought again the pleasure of his
company. The letter opens with entirely proper compliments
to the younger man's rhetorical abilities and closes with a compliment to the genius and fame of Ausonius himself.

> at nunc – frequentes atque claros nec procul
>   cum floreas inter viros
> tibique nostras ventus auras deferat
>   auresque sermo verberet –
> cur me supino pectoris fastu tumens
>   spernis poetam consulem,
> tuique amantem teque mirantem ac tua
>   desiderantem carmina
> oblitus alto neglegis fastidio?
>   (XVIII, *Epist.* 11, lines 25–33)

> (But now – because you thrive not far away,
>   among famous men in a place
> where the very winds must bear my fame and
>   your ears must ring with talk of me – why do you
> puff up your body with disdain as though to scorn
>   me a poet and consul, one who cherishes
> you, respects you, and hopes to enjoy your verse?
>   I ask you now, is it possible that you
> neglect me with some proud neglect?)

It is a curious pose, yet not inconsistent with what we have seen
earlier. Tetradius was not an intimate; though a one-time student,
he was also a man of stature for whom Ausonius must maintain
his pose which may well have been begun in jest.

The remaining letters of this second group are addressed to Pontius Paulinus. The first of these is a rather trivial note of thanks written on the receipt of several poems by Paulinus. Ausonius in recognising his pupil's great accomplishments spoke with mellowness and fondness of their relative literary achievements. He asked for only two things, that Paulinus send more poems and that he then come himself to visit. That fond wish, however, was not to be realised. A little later Ausonius drafted a brief epistle of fourteen verses to Paulinus. This epistle seems to have been occasioned by nothing so much as fondness and the desire to keep his name before Paulinus. The tone is laudatory and self-deprecating without being unpleasantly obsequious. The concluding lines are worth note:

> cedimus ingenio, quantum praecedimus aevo;
> adsurgit Musae nostra Camena tuae.
> Vive, vale et totidem venturos consere ianos,
> quot tuus aut noster conseruere patres.
> (XVIII, *Epist.* 24, lines 11–14)

(Our wit falls behind you as our age advances before you;
our muse stands in the presence of your muse.
Farewell and live, linking the years together
as did our fathers before us.)

Paulinus responded, it seems, not with a visit but with a gift of some delicacies, first a measure of oil, then later more oil and a Spanish sauce or condiment called *muria*. Ausonius wrote at length to thank Paulinus. This latter gift of oil and *muria* seems also to have been accompanied by a letter and some verses, both of which Ausonius admired though he agreed, at the request of Paulinus, to polish the poem. In another letter, Ausonius wrote to ask the assistance of Paulinus in completing certain negotiations for the purchase and transportation of grain.

But still Paulinus refused to visit. Another, even longer, letter was drafted; a letter more importunate than the preceding. We suddenly begin to hear the querulous voice of an old man now reduced to pleading for the favour of a visit. The obdurance of Paulinus as the younger man pursued his chosen way of life became more and more inexplicable to the older man. In a letter replete with allusion, Ausonius diagrammed the nature of

Paulinus's heartlessness hoping still that he would not be crushed by a younger man's forgetful indifference:

> obruar usque tamen, veteris ne desit amici
> me durante fides memorique ut fixa sub aevo
> restituant profugum, solacia cassa, sodalem.
>   (XVIII, *Epist.* 27, lines 31–3)

(Yet let me be struck down so long as my devotion
to an old friend fails not until at last memory set in time
brings back – idle comfort – my fugitive comrade.)

Ausonius continued to detail his loneliness, recognising finally in the pastoral mode that even the climate and the countryside lacked their normal vigour because Paulinus had been absent:

> te sine set nullus grata vice provenit annus.
> ver pluvium sine flore fugit, Canis aestifer ardet,
> nulla autumnales variat Pomona sapores
> effusaque hiemem contristat Aquarius unda.
> agnoscisne tuam, Ponti dulcissime, culpam?
> nam mihi certa fides nec conmutabilis umquam
> Paulini illius veteris reverentia durat
> quaeque meoque tuoque fuit concordia patri.
>   (XVIII, *Epist.* 27, lines 99–106)

(The year advances unchanging without you.
Rain drenched Spring bears no flower; *Canis Major* languishes;
Pomona confers no Autumn harvest;
Aquarius drenches the winter with dismal rains.
Can you not see your sin, my dearest Pontius?
My confidence remains constant and unchanged,
my concern for the Paulinus of old persists
as our fathers' friendship persisted.)

Though the language has remained lofty, Ausonius has thoroughly substituted the intensity of his own feelings for the conventions of literary friendship. Again, as noted before in the epigram addressed to his wife, Ausonius has revealed a degree of sensitivity and honesty seldom found in his poetry.

Almost immediately Ausonius drafted yet another letter whose burden was to develop the suspicion that Paulinus was being

restrained by his ascetic wife, Therasia. Whether or not this might
have been the case (Paulinus was later careful to deny the assertion), it must be said that Ausonius did not hesitate to indulge in
insult to achieve his end. Yet even here, we must be prepared to
confront another example of courtly irony. A diatribe against
the wiles of womankind, in particular the wiles of Therasia,
can also be read as at least a partial jest the point of which is that
such a man as Paulinus surely could not be subject to such a
restriction, in spite of the appearances. By dwelling on the notion
of uxorious tyranny, Ausonius could well have hoped that Paulinus would demonstrate his freedom by responding to the old
man's plea.

Yet, there was no reply and Ausonius composed finally a fourth
letter in which he argued that response is proper even to enemies
and inanimate nature:

> hostis ab hoste tamen per barbara verba salutem
> accipit et Salve mediis intervenis armis.
> respondent et saxa homini et percussus ab antris
> sermo redit, redit et nemorum vocalis imago . . .
> (XVIII, *Epist.* 29, lines 7–10)

(Even an enemy receives barbarous greetings from his enemy
and 'Hail' rings out between opposing arms.
Even the rocks make answer to men; caves echo
speech and the very woods return our words . . .)

From light-hearted gratitude to a bantering request, to insult
and finally to reproach, the argument and pleading of Ausonius
ran the gamut of possible expression. Paulinus replied at last
stiffly and with reserve to the four letters. His letter as we have
it begins abruptly in *medias res*:

> Continuata meae durare silentia linguae
> te numquam tacito memoras placitamque latebris
> desidiam exprobras neglectaeque insuper addis
> crimen amicitiae formidatamque iugalem
> obicis et durum iacis in mea viscera versum.
> parce, precor, lacerare tuum, nec amara paternis
> admiscere velis, ceu melle absinthia, verbis.
> Cura mihi semper fuit et manet officiis te

omnibus excolere, adfectu observare fideli. . . .
numquam animo divisus agam: prius ipsa recedet
corpore vita meo, quam vester pectore vultus.
                    (XVIII, *Epist.* 30, lines 1–9, 47f)

(You pretend that my tongue maintains unbroken silence
while yours is never still; you assert that I have chosen
idleness in remote places and then you go on about
friendship neglected teasing me the while with fear of my
wife, a tactic which cruelly strikes my heart's love itself. I
pray you, spare your friend these wounds, do not mingle –
as honey and wormwood – reproaches with paternal love.
  My every concern has always been to honour you with
every mark of devotion, to endow you with my fidelity. . . .
In my soul I shall never be away from you; better that life
itself leave my body than your face leave my heart.)

Paulinus wrote more letters, but there is no indication that he
ever saw Ausonius again. For Paulinus, the muses were dead
and he followed instead the call of Christ:

> Quid abdicatas in meam curam, pater,
>   redire Musas praecipis?
> negant Camenis nec patent Apollini
>   dicata Christo pectora.
>   XVIII, *Epist.* 31, lines 19–22)

(Why do you remand the outcast Muses
    to my concern, Father?
Hearts pledged to Christ are closed
    to Apollo and deny the Camenae.)

Though Paulinus expressed every consideration for Ausonius, the
announcement of the closing of his heart to Apollo announced
the opening of a gap between the two which neither was willing
or able to bridge.
  The third category of letters includes those addressed to
various members of his family. The first of these dates from the
early years of Ausonius' marriage and is addressed to his father,
Julius Ausonius, with the request that the older man acknowledge
the birth of a grandson, the son of Ausonius. In the letter Ausonius

demonstrated a profound awareness of paternity as an experience of the continuum of life. Here too, the reader hears a quite different voice:

> annos me nescire tuos, pater optime, testor
> totque putare tuos, quot reor esse meos.
> nesciat hos natus, numeret properantior heres,
> testamenta magis quam pia vota fovens
> exemploque docens pravo iuvenescere natos,
> ut nolint patres se quoque habere senes.
>
> (XVIII, *Epist.* 19, lines 25–30)

(I swear, dearest Father, I cannot count your age
  for I know it only as great as my own.
No son should know his father's years for the anxious heir
  will count them as he counts his inheritance in his heart,
teaching his sons the evil of his ways so that they too
  can one day wish for their father a speedy end.)

In this context Ausonius argued most movingly for the endurance of virtue and probity. In his public life he seemed to have been quite unaware of the pressures of reality. In his private correspondence, he revealed himself as a man who saw no solution to the incredible hazards of the day except in the goodness of the individual. Apparently powerless to reverse the tide of disaster, he had no more authority than even the humblest peasant to alter the course of events. The appeal to individual virtue must be then a pitiful recognition that no one, not even the emperor's intimate, could effect a return to the stability and the tranquillity which properly underlies public order. In his letters to his family, he is a sage and at times avuncular man, in sharp contrast to his public correspondence.

It is in the final group of letters, those addressed to Theon, that the reader finds another manifestation of Ausonius's domestic personality. These letters come to us as burlesques, jokes, almost, at the expense of Theon's rusticity. The first letter is an overly elaborate request that Theon send a selection of poems. Containing a cleverly phrased and measured-out lesson in prosody, the letter purports to tease Theon away from rural pleasures back to his all-too-rustic muse. In another letter Ausonius thanked Theon for a gift of thirty exquisite oysters while complaining that they were no more than thirty. In this same letter Ausonius devoted some thirty lines to stating and restating the number thirty. In yet another letter, Ausonius complained that Theon had deprived him of a visit. The last letter to Theon thanked the peasant for other gifts:

Aurea mala, Theon, set plumbea carmina mittis . . .
(XVIII, *Epist.* 17, line 2)

(Theon, you have sent golden apples but leaden verse.)

Could such a relationship have been a friendship depending on mutual love and trust or was it rather the relationship that obtains between master and servant, a relation requiring not only the lesser man's labour but his laughter and song as well?

To understand the complexities of the correspondence is to reconcile the public appearance with the private man. In seeking the identity of Ausonius, if one condemn the flattery and thereby the man, he must then consider the formal proprieties out of which the flatteries were developed. These men were courtiers in a court whose power was a mitigated thing. In the absence of a strong emperor, the members of the court necessarily conducted their affairs and their lives in a context of such extreme ambivalence that it was essential for even friends to curry one another's favour. This activity, because it constituted an unending assault on individual dignity, could only have debilitated an already shattered body politic. A more profound consideration, however, is the fact that the culture to which Ausonius and his contemporaries were committed had in its earlier transplantation to Gaul lost contact with its origins. Gratian was a Roman in name only. Even Ausonius, in spite of his largely barbarian ancestry, was more properly Roman than Valentinian's son. Despite many and vigorous attempts to restore it, the ancient religion had become a thing of the past. Though Constantine had established Christianity by edict, the fact of its establishment wavered as subsequent emperors wavered in the exercise of their own power.

Though Gratian managed, finally, to inherit the purple at his father's death, such a succession was hardly conventional; Gratian himself was finally overthrown by assassination. The imperial succession and the normal transmittal of absolute power was by usurpation. In such a system of government, the courtier's position necessarily mirrored that of his imperial master. To describe the positions of these men as insecure is a gross understatement of the tenor and tone of their lives. Such a system of government by terror is particularly susceptible to disruption. This turbulence could have come from factions from within the court or army or from sudden pressures on the perimeters of the empire. At the same time, there was constant danger of famine and epidemic disease, any of which would have generated nearly intolerable pressures on an already precarious balance of power.

Although Ausonius and others like him held positions that conferred something like ministerial status, they all unfortunately served at the emperor's pleasure, which was a fickle commodity at its best and at its worst a prescription for disaster. The reverential grandeur which had surrounded the emperor's person in the earliest days of the empire had undergone profound change. This was not so much the fault of individual men – the old days had seen imperial madness and incompetence – as it was a symptom that an era had passed. The division of the empire had been a political necessity which could not have been mitigated by any consideration of its consequences. These observations are made to argue that the stature of Ausonius and the nature of his preoccupations were determined in large part by events over which he certainly had no control and whose magnitude was such that he could not imagine even their existence.

It is not enough to define and then condemn the comparative inadequacies of that period's taste, as Gibbon did. It is more proper to observe the incredible limitations placed on life and leisure and then assess the product in the light of its very narrowed resources. Even if it were possible to engage in calculations of such refinement, the conclusions would remain relatively valueless because they would represent life in its most public and conspicuous manifestations, ignoring all the while the life lived in private. If we had only the public life of Ausonius, we would have only a poor and debased image of Rome's grandeur. It is important that we judge Ausonius for the worth of his life. Few men ever achieve unquestioned glory; even the greatest have pediments of clay. Such is no less true of Ausonius. However, it is in his private and domestic existence that we find a man, rather than the façade erected for his public. A village of Potemkin, perhaps, but all the same a man concerned for his own reputation and integrity. That he succeeded to a lesser degree than he might have hoped is neither more nor less than still another demonstration of the human condition.

Notes

1 The list of relevant titles and authors that might be recommended is virtually endless. The student might well wish to consider the following three in addition to those cited in succeeding notes.
A. H. M. Jones, *The Decline of the Ancient World* (1966).
F. J. E. Raby, *A History of Christian Latin Poetry from the Beginnings to the Close of the Middle Ages* (2nd edition, 1953).
F. J. E. Raby, *A History of Secular Latin Poetry in the Middle Ages*, 2 vols (2nd edition, 1957).

2 All references to the Latin text of Ausonius are to that given by H. G. Evelyn White in his *Ausonius with an English Translation*, 2 vols (1919). The translations given in this essay are my own. For prose translations of the entirety of Ausonius, the reader is referred to the *en face* edition of H. G. Evelyn White; for verse translations of the *Mosella*, 'Bissula', and *Cupido Cruciatur*, the reader is referred to my book, *The Last Poets of Imperial Rome* (1971), pp. 44-68.

3 Samuel Dill, *Roman Society in the Last Century of the Western Empire* (2nd revised edition 1899; reprinted 1958), pp. 167f.

4 M. K. Hopkins, 'Social Mobility in the Later Roman Empire: The Evidence of Ausonius', *CQ*, n.s. 11 (1961), pp. 239-48.

5 *Ibid.*, p. 244.

6 A. H. M. Jones, *The Later Roman Empire, 284-602: A Social, Economic and Administrative Survey* (1964), vol. I, pp. 321-65 and 523-62.

7 The first line of Catullus (I:1) is quoted twice by Ausonius (VII, *Eclog. Lib.* 1, line 1 and again in XVI, *Griphus Ternarii Numeri*). Ovid's *Metamorphoses,* particularly the story of Hermaphroditus at the fount of Salmacis (*Metam.* IV, lines 285ff), is also noted in Ausonius XIX, *Epig.* 75, line 11. This epigram concerns those who have changed their sex. The same epigram also refers briefly to the stories of Tiresias and Caenis which are to be found, respectively, in books III (323ff) and XII (189ff) of the *Metamorphoses.*

8 Peter Brown, *The World of Late Antiquity: From Marcus Aurelius to Muhammad* (p. 119). This title would be particularly useful to a student inasmuch as it contains ample illustrations, a map, a chronological table, and an annotated bibliography.

9 Jones, *The Later Roman Empire . . .* , vol. I, p. 139.

10 Terrot Reaveley Glover, *Life and Letters in the Fourth Century* (1901), p. 105 .

11 *Ibid.*, p. 107.

12 *The History of the Decline and Fall of the Roman Empire by Edward Gibbon edited in Seven Volumes . . .* , ed. J. B. Bury (new edition, 1901), vol. III, p. 134n.

The Letters of Symmachus

J. F. Matthews

I

In the winter of 401/2, Q. Aurelius Symmachus travelled from Rome for the last time, as an envoy of the senate to the imperial court at Milan. His journey, which he briefly described in two letters to his son, was beset by inconvenience.[1] The direct road to Milan was unsafe for travellers, enforcing a laborious detour by way of Ticinum (Pavia). The rigours of the journey itself, always considerable at that time of year, were aggravated by Symmachus' poor state of health; now an old man of sixty, he had for some years been troubled by a bad liver and attacks of gout (which it would doubtless be uncharitable to regard as the natural consequences of an aristocratic life). Arriving at Milan, he was received graciously by the emperor, Honorius, but obliged to await the return of Stilicho, the effective political eminence of the day, before he could present the petition which he had brought from the senate.[2] Symmachus returned to Rome early in 402, the emperor's courtesy fresh in his mind; but he had to inform the court that his health was not restored.[3] From the abrupt cessation of his letters, which were in their most intensive phase during the last few years of Symmachus' life, it is safe to infer his death soon after his return to Rome.

From other sources, we can reconstruct in greater detail the background of Symmachus' visit to Milan. The direct road to the court city was rendered unsafe by no less an event than the first invasion of Italy by Alaric the Visigoth (in 401–2).[4] The absence of Stilicho was caused, according to his propagandist Claudian, by the need to recruit troops and to repel a Vandal incursion in Raetia.[5] Indeed, Claudian would suggest that Milan itself was threatened, and that the return of Stilicho, with the reinforcements that Symmachus too had anticipated in one of the letters to his son, was barely in time to save the city from Alaric: his picture of its inhabitants, crowding the walls for a sight of their returning saviour, lends an entirely new dimension to the anxieties of Symmachus' visit.[6] At the same time, north Italian bishops were prevented by the invasion from attending the dedication of a new church by Gaudentius of Brescia;[7] and when Symmachus returned to Rome, it was to a city recently – perhaps even during his absence – re-fortified by the direct initiative of the imperial court.[8] And finally: had Symmachus survived to visit the court again a year later, he would have found himself travelling from Ariminum, not along the familiar Via Aemilia through Bononia to Milan, but along the coastal road to Ravenna. For the court, thoroughly scared by the previous winter's experiences, had taken its refuge behind the shifting lagoons and marshes that would also, in time, protect the Ostrogothic kings of Italy and the Byzantine Exarchate.[9]

This reconstruction of the last episode of Symmachus' life well illustrates the feature of his correspondence which has caused most irritation among its modern readers: his apparent lack of response to the most pressing political events of his day. Symmachus' later years were overshadowed by the threat of barbarian invasion. He ended his life with the threat realised in actuality – and to meet it, the Roman court of Milan under the control of a half-Vandal regent; yet the course of these events can scarcely begin to be told from the letters of the most prolific correspondent of the time. It had been the same a quarter of a century earlier. In the last months of 378, Symmachus had written to an acquaintance from the imperial court, Eutropius, in the aftermath of the greatest military disaster of the late empire – the battle of Hadrianople, in which the eastern emperor Valens had been killed and most of his army destroyed. Symmachus alluded in his letter to the precarious situation of the Roman state, and to the strenuous efforts of the surviving western emperor, Gratian, to sustain it.[10] Now this was no more than courteous, since it can be shown that Eutropius was himself playing an important role in the crisis – he was involved in the political manœuvres and negotiations that brought the new emperor, Theodosius, to the eastern throne in place of Valens.[11] But Symmachus declined to pursue this topic, consigning it instead to Eutropius' proven abilities as a historian (he was the author of the highly successful *Breviarium*, dedicated to Valens); and he reverted to more intimate concerns – the state of his own health, which had been bad but, Eutropius would be reassured to know, was now improved. This too was an appropriate remark to make to Eutropius, whatever we may think of its suitability to the political events in which he was involved: for Eutropius was known as an expert on medicine as well as on Roman history.[12] Meanwhile, Eutropius was encouraged to assist Symmachus' convalescence by granting him the benefit of a letter from his pen.

These reactions of Symmachus to political events of his day are typical of what can perhaps be called a 'systematic reticence' concerning them: a tendency to evade the unpleasant or excessively dramatic, an unwillingness to allow the surface of his correspondence to be clouded by mention of disturbing events. For he cannot be held unaware of their significance. He was evidently alive to the importance of the battle of Hadrianople – in other letters to Eutropius he recommended men who would soon appear as supporters of the new emperor Theodosius, and he welcomed the imperial victories which he personally was honoured to announce to the senate in 379:[13] nor can he have been unconscious of any of the circumstances surrounding his journey to Milan in the winter of 401/2.

It was confronted by this persistent evasiveness on Symmachus' part that his great editor, Otto Seeck, was moved to comment wryly on his labour, that if an author of such limited talent was likely to find few readers in his own right, yet many might be drawn to consult him on one particular point or another.[14] It is a judgment which, made in passing but allied to an edition of monumental authority, has found few dissentients. The letters of Symmachus have been consistently characterised: as 'words without content', 'the dullest epistles in the Latin language'.[15] 'Never', wrote one critic (by no means the least sympathetic), 'has any man written so much to say so little.'[16] For the disappointed historian, Symmachus simply 'tells us less than might have been expected of the events of his day' – while at the same time, according to the harshest recent opinion, being utterly devoid of literary merit.[17]

It is not difficult to understand these sentiments. Symmachus lived through an age of military crisis and religious diversity, perhaps the most tumultuous (certainly, for a modern student, the most richly documented) age since that of Cicero. Yet he is far from casting Cicero's light on it. In a correspondence of nine hundred letters, extending from the middle 360s to 402, political highlights are few, moments of real personal involvement sparingly offered. Instead of the colour, the variety and descriptive vigour that we might have expected from a contemporary, we are shown the repetitive routine of upper-class life, reduced to its most monotonously undemonstrative: estate administration, the sale and purchase of property; travel with its petty inconveniences, the polite exchange of invitations to stay on the estates of senatorial colleagues or to entertain them on one's own; interminable petitions for the social and political advancement of clients, for their protection in litigation by sympathetic governors, in professional difficulties by indulgent officials. The majority of the letters are notes of a mere few lines, expressed in a language as artificially wrought as it is often tantalisingly allusive. Over a quarter of the nine hundred concern the recommendation of protégés to well-placed acquaintances, brief notes for which the reputation of the writer was clearly of greater significance than anything he actually said of the candidate. Thus, taken at random:

The merits of Sexio, formerly governor of Calabria [cf. *ILS* 790], are well spoken of by many, who have therefore requested that I should recommend him to your patronage (*suffragium*). It is part of the generosity habitual to your nature, to honour with your affection those whom others have found congenial. I ask you, then, that if you find no obstacle against satisfying the wishes of those who make this request, you allow Sexio to draw the benefit of my words and the hopes of his many admirers (*Ep.* II 43, to Nicomachus Flavianus).

I am delighted that my friend Drinnacius has proved acceptable to your judgment: for it conveys very great honour on me also, when our sentiments are in accordance. He will therefore enjoy the richest possible rewards for his blameless integrity of character, having won my affection by his proper attention to social duties, and your respect by the strictness of his professional conduct (*mihi honestis carus officiis, tibi iustis negotiis adprobatus*) (V 42, to Neoterius).

Other letters are formal acceptances or refusals of invitations to attend the public functions of Symmachus' colleagues in official life: many others, the merest occasional courtesies, written for no other reason than that the opportunity presented itself in the form of a willing traveller – a friend, perhaps, on the way to court, or an agent on business:

> An address has to be brief, when it is handed to one in a hurry to be on his journey. So it satisfies the proprieties of friendship (*officio satis est*) as well as meeting the haste of the moment, for me to perform the honour of greeting you (*salutationis honore perfungar*). I am sure that I have no need to exact a reply, which I think will be conveyed to me without any encouragement by our friend, a man most attentive to the duties of friendship (*amicitiae servantissimo*) (II 68, to Nicomachus Flavianus).

> You should not complain of my silence, having never until now honoured me with your letters. But since you await a like greeting from me, receive this as a demonstration of my proper duty (*religiosi officii*), which you must emulate. I will in future be quicker to lay pen to paper, if you inspire me with the fruits of our exchange of greeting (VIII 39, to Dynamius).

Under the guise of a collected correspondence, suggested one writer with such letters as these in mind, we have nothing but a stack of visiting cards, a series of 'polite attentions':[18] to put it otherwise, a museum of late Roman *amicitia* in all its complacency, with its affected rules of etiquette, its repetitive trivialities.

Yet if so, it is fair to observe that there were moments at which Symmachus allowed himself to share these opinions. 'For how long,' he wrote to his intimate friend Nicomachus Flavianus, 'are we to go on pouring out futile words of salutation?' – remarking that the restricted political life of their own day offered nothing to compare with the thrilling events with which their ancestors (meaning of course Cicero) had filled their letters.[19] As for the letters of recommendation which he wrote in such prolific numbers, Symmachus expected his correspondents to distinguish those which were written from mere kindness and sense of duty, from those inspired by genuine warmth of feeling and respect for the abilities of their beneficiaries.[20] In these as in other cases, clearly, much was to be understood by Symmachus' correspondents that was not actually stated in the letters themselves.

Le style, c'est l'homme is, as we shall see, a deceptive principle of interpretation when applied to an age as complex as the later fourth century, and to a society as self-conscious as that of Symmachus. If there has been a certain tendency in his critics to allow literary judgments of his style to slide into historical assessments of his personality, Symmachus can be relieved at least of the worst misapprehensions entertained of him. It is clear, for instance, that the letters were not always intended to say everything that we might expect of them. In some cases, a surviving letter was merely the 'covering note' attached to a *breviarium* or *indiculum* which would have contained detailed news and information.[21] On other occasions, it was left to the bearer of a letter to convey by word of mouth information of a more personal or trivial nature than was appropriately set down in writing.[22] It has been suggested, also, that the process of editing the letters for publication, which was carried out after Symmachus' death by his son Q. Fabius Memmius Symmachus, has led to the excision of the more politically embarrassing among them – those referring, for instance, to his collaboration with the usurper Maximus, or to his conduct under the rebellion of Eugenius in 393–4.[23] Such letters would, of course, have possessed a particular interest to historians of the age of Symmachus: but it is clear that the process of excision, if it in fact occurred, cannot have seriously affected the general character of the correspondence as we now read it. At the same time, it should be pointed out that the circumstantial information which is actually contained in Symmachus' letters can only too easily be under-estimated. Without the correspondence, and particularly the *Relationes*, the administrative reports submitted to the emperor during Symmachus' prefecture of Rome in 384/5, our knowledge of the conditions of aristocratic life, and of the role of the senate and senatorial class in the politics and urban life of Rome in the late fourth century, would be very much the poorer.[24]

But there is a more fundamental level at which criticism of Symmachus has been misconceived. For it may well be that Seeck's invitation to look 'here and there' in the letters for information that might happen to be of interest, has in the end encouraged their misuse. Perhaps partly because of it, Symmachus has rarely been understood in his own terms, his letters for what, in their own time and social context, they were intended to achieve rather than as a quarry, which happens not to be a particularly rich one, of facts for the modern historian to exploit. For Symmachus was an administrator, not a historian or social commentator. His aim was the pursuit and cultivation of *amicitia*: and his letters were primarily intended not to inform but to manipulate, to produce results. In opening a friendship with one correspondent, Symmachus visualised its development very precisely – in terms of the benefits of patronage which it might convey.[25] On another occasion, he used a recent introduction to a court official to support – it appears, successfully – a petition of a delegation of Campanian *curiales* for tax concessions.[26] Once, he felt unable to approach a man of influence at court because he happened not to have first exchanged formal introductions with him, and had therefore to make his way indirectly, through a functionary whom he did know.[27] It is easy to criticise the letters of Symmachus as 'words without content'. What is perhaps harder to appreciate is that without the words, the 'content' as Symmachus saw it – in terms of the accumulation and exercise of patronage – could not have ensued. The relationship between 'style' and 'content' is thus in the case of Symmachus a particularly subtle one, so much of the 'content' lying, as it were, outside the letters themselves: and I shall offer no apology for attempting a reassessment of the letters in terms of a historical discussion of the nature and social context of Symmachus' influence.

At the same time, to cast adverse comment on the style of the letters is in itself to affect a dangerous detachment from the standards of Symmachus' own day. For what is not in doubt is that the publication of the letters was an event of literary importance. Symmachus regarded letter-writing as one of the acknowledged forms of literary activity.[28] Some of his friends collected the letters they had received from him (and of course Symmachus preserved his own copies).[29] He could affect to be afraid of forged imitations circulating under his name, and of the 'highway robbery' of letters from the hands of their bearers.[30] Symmachus' literary reputation, moreover, is recognised by

Sidonius Apollinaris and by a contributor in the *Saturnalia* of Macrobius, both of whom link him with the younger Pliny: and if Macrobius, who matched the two as exponents of the style known as 'rich and ornate' (*pingue et floridum*), was referring to their oratory, Sidonius ought to have meant his judgment of the letters, since he made it precisely in order to introduce his own collection of literary epistles.[31] Sidonius' contrast of Symmachus' *rotunditas* with the *disciplina* and *maturitas* which he felt to be characteristic of Pliny, meets very well our sense of the stylistic 'completeness', combined with the economy, of his writing. Perhaps it was this sense that lay behind the judgment of a twelfth-century critic, Alan of Lille, that Symmachus was 'prodigus in sensu, verbis angustus'[32] – and for this reason, also, that selections of the letters survive, as exemplars of style, in numerous medieval *florilegia*. The latest editor of Symmachus can list no less than forty, from the twelfth to the fifteenth centuries.[33]

By the time that the letters of Symmachus entered upon this late season of glory, the orations – upon which his contemporary reputation was chiefly founded – had been long lost from view. Yet for two historians of the fifth century, Olympiodorus and Socrates, Symmachus was 'the orator' (*logographos*),[34] and it was as *orator disertissimus* that his son (and editor) honoured him in an inscription to his memory.[35] It is clear from references in the letters that Symmachus sent copies of his speeches to his friends for their appreciation.[36] In one letter he cited a phrase of a speech of about 396; and brief quotations of others are made by Arusianus Messius (around 395), and in the early sixth century, by Cassiodorus.[37] In these circumstances, it has not on the whole been to the advantage of Symmachus' more recent reputation, that in the early nineteenth century, quite substantial fragments of eight speeches were detected, written in a sixth-century hand, on a palimpsest from Bobbio (now divided between Milan and the Vatican): three imperial panegyrics, and five speeches on various aspects of senatorial life.[38] If the content of these orations has not seemed to support the judgment held of Symmachus by his contemporaries, at least the circumstances of their survival lend weight to Macrobius' comparison of Symmachus with the younger Pliny; for preserved with them on the Bobbio palimpsest are a few fragments of the *Panegyricus*.[39] Pliny of course can look after himself; but it is one of the more undeserved ironies of Symmachus' fate that his oratory survives only under a Latin translation of the Acts of the Council of Chalcedon.

The link with Pliny is brought out in the arrangement of Symmachus' letters in the edition made by his son. Like those of Pliny, they are set out in ten books, the first nine composed of letters addressed to private correspondents. In the tenth book, the forty-nine *Relationes* immediately evoke the letters of Pliny written to Trajan from Bithynia;[40] preceding them, two letters (X.1–2), addressed respectively to the father of Theodosius and to Gratian, recall the letters written by Pliny in a private capacity to Trajan.[41]

The edition of Symmachus' letters departs from its model, however, in that the letters are classified, not in chronological sequence, but under the names of their recipients. The superficial inconvenience of the procedure will be recognised by anyone who has tried to browse casually in Seeck's edition – the more so, since even within the individual groups of letters there is little attempt to preserve or to restore chronological order. Yet on this last point, it should be observed in defence of the editor, that once the actual sequence of composition of the letters had been disturbed, precisely that stylistic uniformity, brevity and allusiveness of which modern critics have complained, would effectively have forbidden any systematic reconstruction. The defence applies equally to the general arrangement of the letters; given their stylistic character, together with the practical consideration that the edition was constructed (or so it would appear) from Symmachus' own collection of his letters and so reflects his method of classification, the grouping by correspondents seems a natural and satisfactory, not to say the inevitable, solution.

Within this scheme, the groups of letters are arranged after a coherent pattern, one which preserves a fairly steady chronological movement, reflects the main phases of Symmachus' influence, and at the same time allows an appropriate degree of variety within the individual books. At least, this is true of Books I–VII of the collection. Books VIII and IX provide a contrast. These books contain some of Symmachus' most interesting, as well as most elusive, individual letters. Yet the care for organisation and structure, which characterised the first seven books, is conspicuously absent. The most obvious sign of this is in the sheer numbers of correspondents addressed. As against 56 recipients in the whole of Books I–VII, 113 of the 229 letters in VIII–IX (the remaining 116 lack the names of their recipients) are addressed to no less than 74 different correspondents. Of these, 49 are addressed in a single letter, 15 in only two; and in the case of those correspondents who are addressed more than once, scarcely any attempt is made to group these letters together.[42]

The discrepancy between Books I–VII and VIII–IX has led to the suggestion that I–VII were prepared for publication by Symmachus himself, his son's role as editor of the letters being confined to the 'literary executorship' of these books (and the *Relationes*), and to the assembling and publication of VIII–IX in their present disordered state.[43] There is of course no need to doubt Symmachus' interest in the publication of his letters, and it is quite open to suppose that he gave any amount of advice and assistance in its preparation. But the suggestion needs to be handled with care. There is no doubt that the whole edition in its present form is to be attributed to Q. Fabius Memmius Symmachus, since subscriptions commemorating his work, done after his father's death, stand after Books II and IV as well as at the beginning of Book X of the letters.[44] Further, as we have seen, Books IV, V and VII contain the very latest of Symmachus' letters, those relating to the journey to Milan of winter 401/2, shortly after which he died;[45] while the arrangement of the letters in their ten books, after Pliny, seems so fundamental to the entire collection, that the notion of a substantial division of editorial functions between the younger Symmachus and his father would seem to require a very subtle formulation – certainly more subtle than will be found in the evidence.

Since it is generally acknowledged that Books VIII and IX look like nothing more than the 'odds and ends' of Symmachus' files, it is perhaps worth asking what part of the work of editing the letters could not have been achieved by Symmachus' son himself, working from his father's papers. On this assumption the younger Symmachus, finding the majority of the letters preserved with the names of their recipients (possibly even classified by individual correspondents, although this would not fully account for certain features in Books VIII and IX),[46] satisfied himself with arranging Books I–VII in accordance with the main

phases of his father's career. He then put the remainder – mainly
isolated or anonymous letters – into two further books of unequal
length, classifying them only in so far as he put nearly all the letters
of recommendation among them into Book IX, 'continens
commendaticias'. [47] He then returned to order, and to the model
established by Pliny, with the official communications which
comprised Book X. It is difficult to see how in the circumstances
he could have devised a better, or at least a less troublesome,
solution: while the disordered state of Books VIII and IX will
remind us again that in the letters of Symmachus we are reading
what was in essence a working correspondence.

II

The interpretation of the letters of Symmachus can only be
attempted within the horizons – social, political, and stylistic –
which defined their field of operation. The social horizons are
at first sight the easiest to delineate; they were those of the senate
and senatorial class, to which Symmachus belonged and to which
he devoted so many of his ideological and emotional resources. [48]
Symmachus believed that the senate was the 'nobler', quite
simply the 'better part of the human race'. [49] Given the opportunity, he could still represent the political system of his own
day as, at its best, a balanced partnership between the senate and
an emperor mutually respectful and unanimous in their wishes. [50]
More realistically (since in these terms, the political system of the
fourth century was very rarely at its best), he thought it the specific
function of the prefecture of Rome to defend the rights of senators: [51] in this as in so many ways, senatorial breeding, as Symmachus neatly put it, 'recognised itself'. [52] Four of the eight
speeches, of which fragments are preserved, directly concern
the enrolment, the status or public functions of senators; and
the letters themselves show us nothing less than the senatorial
life in action. In defending the claims of litigants with the expectation of favour before governors and officials, [53] in petitioning
for tax relief on the estates of a financially straitened senatorial
lady, [54] in getting governors in office to look after the interests
of absentee landowners, [55] no less than in supporting representa-
tions against the imposition of military levies upon senatorial
estates, [56] Symmachus was speaking as a member of a class which,

with quite unconscious selfishness, would preserve its economic interests and prejudices through the impoverishment and collapse of the western imperial government. [57] Symmachus could summon up the traditional Roman attitude to Greek infirmity of character, in exhorting an acquaintance of Greek origin not to resign public office prematurely: let him recall that he was now enrolled in the 'tribes of Romulus' and sustain the burden of responsibility, at least for a year or two. [58] He could bring to bear the moral authority of a senator, as well as the public duty of a Roman priest, in asking a Vestal Virgin to confirm or deny rumours that she intended to give up her office before the regular time; [59] and in pressing a colleague not to call off a marriage arranged between his daughter and a young friend of Symmachus, he suggested that he ought not to sacrifice his *fides* as a senator to a mere change of mind. [60]

It is within the imaginative limits of a Roman and a senator that we must interpret Symmachus' personal attitudes and sensitivities. His evidently deep sense of bereavement at the deaths of relatives and colleagues must be set beside his anger when a group of Saxon prisoners committed suicide to a man, rather than grace his public games by fighting as gladiators. 'But what could be expected from a race of men more vile than Spartacus', he wrote to Nicomachus Flavianus – drawing consolation from the attitude of Socrates to misfortune, and turning instead to the Libyan antelopes which he hoped to exhibit in their place. [61] Again to Nicomachus Flavianus, who as praetorian prefect at the time held administrative authority over Illyricum, Symmachus wrote asking for his help in securing twenty strong young men, again for the games – since slaves were easily come by on the frontiers, and the price was usually not extortionate. [62] He could even say to the younger Flavianus that nothing had happened at Rome worth speaking of, except that an apartment block had collapsed, crushing all the inhabitants and enforcing the resignation of the governor: [63] contrast his attitude to a colleague who, having suffered some mishap to his person or property from the river Po, received from the leisure of Symmachus' Praenestine retreat an elaborately contrived letter of sympathy, denouncing the treacherous insolence of a river that had dared to incommode a senator! [64] or to the fall from his official carriage of a suffect consul at a public ceremony, as a result of which he had been carried off, dressed in the cloak of office and full consular regalia, with a broken leg. Shocked by the mishap, and disturbed by the ill-omen, which was only the worst of several recently witnessed by the city, Symmachus declined to narrate it at length.[65]

These expressions of attitude are taken from widely separated passages and different contexts in Symmachus' letters: but they are like the isolated outcrops of an imaginative sensibility so deeply aristocratic that one doubts whether Symmachus was even aware of its existence. It would of course have been inconceivable to have found it otherwise: Symmachus was no more capable than his senatorial predecessors (or many of his critics) of feeling any real sympathy for the passions and misfortunes of the lower classes in Roman society, nor of questioning his own right to the privileges which he enjoyed as a senator. But, at the same time, Symmachus enables us to see that the real situation was far more complex than his stated attitudes would imply. Perhaps more than any other writer of his class, he gives an insight into the relationship between the senators and people of Rome, as one of a complexity and intensity that are not always fully appreciated.

This was particularly true of the fourth century. The absence of the emperors, devoted to the protection of the military frontiers from which they themselves originated, had left the senators of Rome as masters in their own house. They visibly dominated the material and public life of the city – attended in the streets by columns of servants, the halls of their luxurious mansions crowded with clients and dependants, or else echoing with the sounds of banquets, music and dancing.[66] Committed to an outright policy of conspicuous expenditure, they celebrated their public offices by providing spectacular games, and left their names over Rome as the founders and restorers of monuments and public amenities. The prefects of Rome, who were in normal circumstances drawn from senatorial families, were responsible for public order, for the physical well-being of the city and the regular distribution of its supplies of corn, oil and wine.[67] The influence of the senators extended through patronage beyond their own class, to the urban guilds and corporations: beyond Rome, to the communities of the Italian countryside and, further afield, to North Africa, where they possessed many of their estates.[68]

Many episodes show the intimacy of the relationship which, in the emperors' absence, had developed between the senate and people of Rome. The death of the great pagan senator, Vettius Agorius Praetextatus, as consul designate late in 384, was followed by intense public mourning. The people, as Symmachus reported in a *Relatio* to the imperial court, in a quite unusual demonstration of grief refused to pursue its regular pleasures in the theatre, assembling there instead to express its respect for Praetextatus' memory in a series of acclamations.[69] (It is a view of the event which contrasts strikingly and sympathetically with that of Jerome, for whom the great pagan was now consigned to the darkest depths of Tartarus, rather than the shining heavenly palace of his widow's fancy: but what Jerome brings out no less strongly than Symmachus, is the sheer public impact of Praetextatus' death).[70] Earlier, in happier circumstances, the father of Symmachus had, as prefect of Rome in 364–5, inaugurated the building of a new bridge over the Tiber, 'to the great gladness of the citizens'.[71] In recognition of the personal popularity achieved by his action, Symmachus was permitted to perform the dedication of the bridge after laying down the prefecture: so he is described on the dedicatory inscriptions as 'ex-prefect of the city'.[72]

Peace went with plenty. In times of shortage, when the corn ships were delayed or held back by adverse winds, the relationship between the people of Rome and the senators might quickly turn sour. Rioting might ensue, and senators be forced to leave the city for safety, while their urban mansions rose in flames behind them.[73] This had happened, again to Symmachus' father, in 376: he had been heard to say, during a severe wine shortage, that sooner than sell the surplus wine from his estates at a reduced price to the people, he would use it to mix concrete![74] As has only recently been recognised, he was referring to a technique, described in Pliny's *Natural History*, for making a particularly hard, waterproof variety of concrete known as 'maltha', used especially for lining fish-ponds and bathing-pools.[75] His remark was then far from frivolous; it was a particularly provocative assertion of senatorial privilege at a time when it was most out of place. Symmachus himself, who wrote letters to his father, perhaps at just this time, reporting on the family's luxurious building operations in Campania,[76] formally thanked the senate, in his speech *Pro Patre* (*Or.* IV), when later in 376 a delegation sent by it had invited the old man to return to Rome.

Much the same experience happened to Symmachus himself late in his life. He was forced to leave Rome when a food shortage due to the withholding of the African corn ships was attributed by the people to a political action taken by him (at the initiative of the court, Symmachus had successfully proposed to the senate that the African rebel Gildo be declared a public enemy);[77] yet before long, the people 'turned to repentance' and made known its wish – again by public acclamations in the theatre – that he should return to Rome.[78]

From such episodes, which could be multiplied from Symmachus' letters and from other sources, it is clear that the relationship between the people and senatorial class of Rome was a complex and volatile one; it was certainly not one of aloofness on either side. For the city prefect, an adverse wind could mean the difference between the success and failure of his administration;[79] while for the senators in general, their standing in the eyes of the people of Rome was more important than the expressed social attitudes of Symmachus might suggest. It was not necessary to develop, as some senators did, a personal taste for the pleasures and haunts of the lower classes.[80] Symmachus' letters show to particular effect the strenuous efforts made by him to ensure the success of the public games which he provided to celebrate his son's quaestorship and praetorship (in 393 and 401); indeed, commentators have tended to find these, from a circumstantial point of view, the most interesting of the letters.[81] Symmachus appears in them, writing to otherwise unknown landowning colleagues in Gaul and Spain,[82] to provincial governors and to perhaps most of the important court officials of the day, invoking their assistance in collecting exotic beasts to display at the games: horses from Spain, lions from Africa, bears from Dalmatia, antelopes, crocodiles, Scottish dogs (and in 393, with the results already noted, Saxon gladiators). He petitioned Stilicho for the easing of restrictions of expenditure, so that the people should not have to go without a spectacle of which they were especially fond.[83] The whole correspondence is not merely a splendid affirmation of the effectiveness of the links of friendship and patronage which Symmachus had patiently developed throughout his adult life; with their references to the popularity of some of the particular forms of display prepared by Symmachus, and his evident anxiety that the games should be a success with the people,[84] the letters on this subject are a standing proof of the importance to senators of their good relations with the *populus Romanus*.

The 'social horizons' of the letters of Symmachus, then, turn out to possess more varied contours than at first anticipated. Behind their assumptions of privilege, their often patronising complacency, their absorption in upper-class attitudes, lies an intense, volatile relationship with the people of Rome, and a real awareness that the opinions of the people were important and needed to be fostered. The 'political horizons' of the letters need similarly close scrutiny. Symmachus was a politically active senator, at least in so far as he pursued a full career of the 'senatorial' type, culminating in the prefecture of Rome in 384–5. What is not so clear is the relationship between this career and the sort of influence which the letters show him to have exercised. To help define this relationship it is necessary to review briefly Symmachus' political career – the more so since it illustrates the general nature of the participation of the senatorial class in the political life of the later fourth century.[85]

Symmachus' first public offices were the quaestorship and praetorship. These offices in themselves reflect the political evolution of the fourth-century senate. In the early empire, they had been stages in distinguished careers, leading to legionary commands and ultimately to governorships in the military provinces of the empire. In the fourth century, with military commands and governorships in any case no longer in the hands of Roman senators, the urban offices had suffered a diminution in their significance, being now held by young senators on the threshold of their public careers.[86] The actual functions of the quaestorship and praetorship are obscure; their most significant feature was, indeed, strictly incidental – the obligation incumbent on the young senator's father to provide the public games, upon which we have seen Symmachus exert so much energy and influence on his son's behalf.

Symmachus' first administrative post fell in 365: the governorship of Lucania and Bruttium.[87] Symmachus held the post at the same time that his father was prefect of Rome; and letters to

Nicomachus Flavianus, written at this time, show that Flavianus was at the same moment governor (*consularis*) of Sicily: this was another regular post in a traditional senatorial *cursus* of the late empire. Symmachus advised his friend to secure his position after leaving office by making an exact inventory of the number of animals he had employed, what he had spent on the upkeep of his official residences, and the amount of tax which he had succeeded in gathering.[88] Another letter concerned the case of some arrested court officials whom Flavianus had asked should be transferred from Bruttium to Sicily, but whom the prefect of Rome – Symmachus' father, perhaps hoping to save his young colleagues from embarrassment in a case concerning *palatini* – had claimed for his own jurisdiction.[89]

Next for Symmachus, after an interval of eight years, came the proconsulship of Africa (373/4); here again, Symmachus was moving in the regular pattern of a senatorial career. Nothing is known of his administration, except an obscure affair in which Symmachus was deprived by 'envy' of the honour of a public statue;[90] nevertheless, in a couple of letters, Symmachus recalled his affection for Carthage (where the proconsuls had their chief residence), and mentioned praises expressed by an African acquaintance for his conduct there.[91] It can be suggested that, after leaving office in the early summer of 374, Symmachus remained in Africa for a time, perhaps travelling along the coast to Mauretania Caesariensis, where he possessed estates, and where he formed, or renewed, a friendship with the distinguished (but ill-fated) *magister militum*, Theodosius.[92] At least, by 375 Symmachus was back in Italy, as is shown by several letters written at this time; and either now or before his departure for Africa as proconsul, came his marriage to Rusticiana, the daughter of a former prefect of Rome, Memmius Vitrasius Orfitus.[93]

Another interval of eight or nine years separated Symmachus' proconsulship from his prefecture of Rome, the culmination of his administrative career. A letter to the emperor, included among the *Relationes*, expressed Symmachus' gratitude for the honour, which came to him at the regular age of about forty-five.[94] He held the office for barely six months before, stricken by the death of Praetextatus and depressed by the other troubles of his administration, he wrote again, requesting his release from it.[95] His tenure was thus a short one; but it should be emphasised

that the prefecture of Rome was rarely, and only in special circumstances, held for much longer than a year.

These three posts – the governorship of Lucania and Bruttium,
the proconsulship of Africa and the prefecture of Rome – are
the sum total of Symmachus' administrative duties in a public
career of more than forty years. In this, and in the distribution
of his offices, he was representative of his class. It was precisely
in the areas where their social influence was most pronounced –
in Rome itself, in central and southern Italy, Sicily and North
Africa (especially Proconsularis and Numidia) – that senators were
accustomed to hold governorships. This regional coincidence of
the social and of the political distribution of senatorial influence
is a matter of fundamental importance, which must underly any
discussion of the nature of the political role of the late Roman
senatorial class.[96]

The consulship, which Symmachus received from Theodosius
in 391, was the result of circumstances quite beyond the reach of
prediction or calculation. It was in fact quite rare for it to be held,
in these days, by a member of the senatorial aristocracy, and
Symmachus' tenure of it leads to discussion of the other aspect
of Symmachus' official career: his relations with the imperial court.

This was essentially a 'diplomatic' relationship. Symmachus'
first, and most protracted, visit to the imperial court took him,
as a young man of about thirty, to Trier as a senatorial representative: his function was to convey the *aurum oblaticium*, the 'contribution' made by the senate to commemorate the fifth anniversary of the reign of Valentinian I. From the time of his stay
at Trier, in 369–370, survive three of his orations, of which
substantial fragments are preserved: they are panegyrics, two
of them (*Or.* I and III) addressed in February 369, respectively
to Valentinian and his young son Gratian, the third (*Or.* II)
again to Valentinian, at the opening of 370.[97] The highly-wrought
and compressed, somewhat 'bulging' style of these speeches has
on the whole attracted unfavourable comment from modern
critics; but their use for the historian, particularly in their allusive
precision, should not be under-estimated. Symmachus' references
in *Or.* II to skirmishes against Alamanni, to the reception of
Burgundian embassies to Valentinian, and in particular to the
emperor's personal inauguration of the building of a new fort
on the far bank of the Rhine, suggest a fascinating comparison

with Ammianus Marcellinus' descriptions of just such events;[98] while an allusion to Alta Ripa (Altrip-bei-Speyer) can be used to date Symmachus' visit precisely, by a law issued there by Valentinian on 19 June 369.[99]

Symmachus' sojourn at Trier was notable especially for new acquaintances made there; particularly for the friendship then formed with the poet Ausonius, who was at Trier as tutor of the young Gratian (and later, as *quaestor sacri palatii*).[100] Symmachus probably accompanied Ausonius on the imperial journey described in the opening lines of Ausonius' best-known and finest poem, the *Mosella*; and in a letter written after his departure, he recalled with pleasure his stay 'at camp'.[101] Ausonius' virtuosic list of the fishes which inhabited the Mosel gave Symmachus the occasion to remind his friend of the dinners which they had enjoyed together at Trier.[102] In a later letter, he referred to the office of *quaestor* which Ausonius received after Symmachus' departure from the court; and in return, Ausonius alluded to the rank of *comes ordinis tertii* with which his friend left Trier.[103] The honour was a delicate compliment to Symmachus' presence 'with the standards'; but Symmachus' stay at court has the air of an organised tour of the frontier region of the empire rather than serious campaigning, with a minor clash with the barbarians, Burgundian legations and the building of the new fort carefully 'laid on' for the occasion – and for Symmachus to report back to a senate which would want to be assured that its quinquennial contribution was not being frivolously spent. Symmachus' stay at Trier was thus salutary for its widening of his experience – and of his range of acquaintances. For it is likely that not only Ausonius, but the *magister militum* Theodosius, to whom Symmachus later wrote after their meeting in Africa, first became known to him at this time.[104]

Symmachus' later contacts with the emperors can be more summarily described. After his return from Trier, it was some years before he next approached the court; but his contacts became more frequent in the later years of his life – this reflecting his increasing prestige within the senate itself. It is an error to suppose that the third *Relatio*, on the altar of Victory, was personally presented by Symmachus to the court of Valentinian II. It was sent like the other *Relationes*, as an official dispatch (and it is hard to imagine how a serving prefect of Rome could

leave his office for a visit to Milan); but Symmachus refers in
it to a senatorial legation of 382 on the same subject, of which he
had been a member. [105] In 387, he attended the consular celebrations of Valentinian II; and in 388, those of the usurper Maximus.
If this turned out in the event to have been an error of judgment,
it was one shared by the senate – for Symmachus was undoubtedly acting as senatorial delegate on that occasion. [106] It
is likely that Symmachus' own consulship was held at Rome,
inaugurated by the usual public games at the beginning of 391;
he wrote to contacts at the court concerning the preparations,
though the letters cannot now suggest the real scope of the
arrangements. [107] His behaviour during the usurpation of Eugenius
and the pagan revival which attended it (393–4) was scrupulously
discreet though courteous; at least, Symmachus refrained from
anything that might look like direct association with the régime,
contenting himself with the due performance of social civilities. [108]
From the middle 390s, senatorial embassies are mentioned in the
letters, with which Symmachus was concerned without himself
participating in them; but he visited Milan at the beginning of
400 for the consular celebrations of Stilicho, and again in the
winter of 401/2, on the last journey with which this survey
opened. [109]

Symmachus' increasing contact with the imperial court during
the last years of his life reflects a relationship between senate and
emperor which was actually becoming more intimate in these
years, and would continue to do so after Symmachus' death. [110]
This development can be measured in the letters; but in general
terms, it is not a simple matter to draw the connections between
Symmachus' official public career, as just described, and the nature
of his influence. Related to this problem is the question of
senatorial attitudes to the holding of office.

If Symmachus himself is any guide, senators were not openly
ambitious for office. His letters repeatedly express what can perhaps be termed an 'ideology of leisure' – a studiously affected
distaste for the cares and responsibilities of office, as opposed
to the quiet charms, the leisured equanimity of private life.
Office was a reward for merit, it provided status and title, opportunities to advance the interests of one's friends. In office,
senators were expected to – and to judge, not least from Symmachus' *Relationes*, did – conduct themselves conscientiously;

while the cares of office were one of the few accepted justifications for the less than strict performance of the social obligations of friendship. At the same time, it was made quite clear that senators undertook office as a matter of public duty, to satisfy the needs of the state and not their own ambitions; and their retirement was seen as the overdue restoration to private life of men who had never wished to leave it.[111]

The literal sincerity of these attitudes need not be taken for granted. They were shared, for instance, by Petronius Probus, of whom Ammianus Marcellinus wrote that he was like a 'fish out of water' when not holding office, pining away when not in possession of the prefectures which his family forced him to hold in order to defend their private interests.[112] When Probus was recalled to office by Valentinian II, to assume his fourth and last praetorian prefecture (in 383), he received a letter of sympathy from Symmachus, expressing regret at the interruption of his leisure. Probus was urged to be tolerant of the burden imposed upon him, remembering that repeated labours were the price of virtue, and that in calling again on his services, the emperors had considered more his abilities than his desires.[113]

Symmachus' attitudes are important in a more general sense; for they suggest a complex and somewhat ambivalent view of public office – a view in which office was valued only in relation to a declared preference for private life. To put it differently: public office was a function of the private status of senators; it was not the other way round.

One might be inclined to dismiss this view as a mere affectation, were it not consistent with certain features, which have already been noted, of senatorial office: short tenures of governorships, with intervals of several years between them – and equally important, the distribution of these offices in regions where senators already, as private individuals, possessed property and the economic and social influence which derived from it. It is not always easy to draw a clear line between the 'public' and 'private' comportment of senators in office – as for instance when they used it, as they often did, to foster and perpetuate links of patronage with provincial communities, which had been founded by their own ancestors, holding the same office in previous generations. Hence the *patroni originales* of Italian and African communities:[114] and when a prefect of Rome paraded around the streets of his city in an official carriage, receiving the cheers and applause of the populace,[115] was he doing so in his capacity as a public official, or as a senator who already possessed influence there? In such ways, it seems clear that the position of senatorial governors in their provinces cannot be defined merely by reference to a set of precise functions and powers ascribed to them by their letters of office: also involved was a whole range of sources of influence deriving from their position as wealthy landowners with personal and inherited connections in these provinces.

In these circumstances, the relationship between public office and the exercise of private influence as we see it in Symmachus' letters, will not have been a simple one, the influence deriving directly and solely from the office. There is no need to doubt, though the letters do not clearly show it, that Symmachus did derive private influence from his tenure of governorships. His letters leave no question that the offices of Symmachus' friends provided him with the opportunities to acquire benefits and advantages, and it would be unreasonable to deny that Symmachus used his own offices to convey benefits upon others. Although the vast majority of the letters show influence which cannot have derived in this way, it should be observed that they only concern the cases which Symmachus passed on for others to take action: they cannot give any idea of the number of occasions on which Symmachus might have exercised his own discretion in favour of a client, or responded directly to an approach made to himself.

In these respects, the almost total lack of reference in Symmachus' letters to his own public offices, and so to influence deriving from them, may be deceptive. But in general terms, it would be difficult to show a direct link of dependence of influence upon office, for a precise reason: that Symmachus' administrative career, no less than his relations with the imperial court (which in practice provided most of Symmachus' actual opportunities to exercise patronage), themselves derived from deeper sources, as the consequences, or rather the direct expressions, of his prestige as a senator. It was this prestige, since it also lay behind Symmachus' public career, which was the real basis of his patronage and influence.

And finally, the actual nature of Symmachus' influence should dissuade us from an excessively 'political' interpretation of its sources. For it was an influence with few, if any, moments of real impact at the highest levels of government policy, and lacking significant ambition in this direction. It was, rather, an accumulation of particular, often quite trivial, advantages which, however tedious to the modern reader of the letters, were clearly appreciated by Symmachus and the colleagues and clients who benefited from them, and are much more central to an understanding of his position. It is misleading to regard the senate of the late empire simply as a forgotten class, deprived of political power and inhabiting a neglected backwater of late Roman life: equally so, to attempt to redress the imbalance by attributing too much to the senators in terms of direct political influence over the imperial government and participation in its institutions.[116] There is a wide middle ground of senatorial influence, practical, cumulative and as unspectacular as it was durable. It is this influence which is illustrated by Symmachus, and within these horizons that his letters, with their style and social etiquette, their repetitive courtesies and 'polite attentions', must be understood.

III

Symmachus' mature years, as we saw, were lived against a background of military insecurity culminating, at the time of his last journey to Milan, in the first Visigothic invasion of Italy. It was, equally, a time of great social fluidity, and within the upper classes themselves, of a religious and cultural diversity unprecedented in the history of the Roman empire. I would suggest that, paradoxically, it is against this background of insecurity, movement and change, that the letters of Symmachus are best understood.

There might seem little support for this view. Symmachus' letters are notable more for their immobility, their careful observance of precise rules of etiquette, than for any qualities of variety, movement or spontaneity. A man leaving on a journey is expected to write first, to inform his friends of his progress and safe arrival.[117] He will never miss an opportunity to greet his friends, nor fail to respond to a letter received. He will satisfy these obligations at the acknowledged cost of writing letters with no content except the *salutatio* which they were designed to convey (and of course, the obligatory demand for a reply):[118] he will even reply separately to two letters from the same correspondent which happen to have been brought simultaneously by different bearers.[119] (This is less absurd than might appear, when we remember that the replies might be carried by widely different routes, and that the bearers would normally be travelling in the pursuit of some business of their own, which would scarcely be hindered by a friendly word from Symmachus.) Letters were supposed to avoid the inclusion of news – such as ill-health or personal distress, as well as unwelcome political events – that might be disturbing to their recipients, or too trivial to be enshrined in literary form; as we saw, such matters were attached on separate sheets, or entrusted to the bearer for verbal communication.[120] Silence was excused only for certain specified reasons, for instance grief in bereavement, the occupations of office, illness (to avoid conveying bad news), or the most pressing family business.[121] Lack of opportunity, in the absence of travellers to remote parts, was also considered valid: in one letter, Symmachus implicitly contrasted the frequency of travellers to the Rhineland during an imperial visit to the region, with their extreme rarity after his departure; and his contacts with a friend in Spain were limited by distance and the seasons to an annual exchange of letters.[122]

Such rules were made, it goes without saying, in order to be broken (to defy etiquette by writing first to a departing acquaintance in itself offered an appropriate *sententia* with which to open a letter);[123] and they involved, in many cases, the elevation into principles of etiquette of the most prosaically obvious necessities. How could one do otherwise than regard the absence of letter-carriers as an excuse for not writing, or not recognise the difficulties, in ancient conditions of travel, in contacting friends who were actually on journeys? Yet it is precisely this translation of practicalities into principles that is most characteristic of the language of 'Symmachan' *amicitia* in general. The social attentions just described were, for Symmachus, nothing less than the 'religiones, quibus iure amicitia confertur';[124] and in this term, *religio*, with its companions *munus* and *officium*, we can see defined most clearly the nature of this 'friendship' and the qualities of character and social conformity which were exacted by its satisfactory performance. As everyone knew, the term 'religiosus' implied not merely respect for the sanctity of the gods, but attention to social obligations among men.[125]

In these conditions, it is not surprising to find that the degree of spontaneity which Symmachus permitted himself in his letters was carefully measured. Writing to his son, he admired the wit, the sparkling *sententiae* of his letters, but advised him to add variety to his style with something 'maturum et comicum', even a touch of negligence.[126] Friends were sometimes encouraged to drop the severe mode of address, with full names, ranks and titles, that was appropriate for strangers or distant acquaintances, in favour of a more intimate and informal manner.[127] (The letter mentioned earlier, in which Symmachus complained to Nicomachus Flavianus of the lack of interesting material with which to fill correspondence, was elicited by an error on the part of his own *librarius*, who had inserted Flavianus' full name and title at the head of an earlier letter to him.)[128] Such stiffly conventional forms of address were an affectation of archaism ('*archaismos* scribendi'), which Symmachus appreciated, while himself preferring something more contemporary in style.[129] Nor did Symmachus profess much liking for letters thin in content but artificially drawn-out in length. He preferred 'Laconian brevity' to 'Nestorian expansiveness' – while on other occasions welcoming the promise (or rather, regretting the failure to materialise) of 'litterae largiores' from certain friends.[130]

Within these conventions, Symmachus' letters are perhaps the more remarkable for their allusive sensitivity. We have already seen this quality in the second *Oratio*, delivered at Trier at the beginning of 370.[131] In letters addressed to Ausonius after his departure from the court, Symmachus referred with delicate brevity to his sojourn 'in comitatu': in a single phrase, 'cum aeternorum principum . . . signa comitarer', he recalled the visit itself, his presence 'on campaign' and the rank of *comes tertii ordinis,* acquired to mark it.[132] He described his reaction to Ausonius' *Mosella* in a letter almost swimming with pun and allusive metaphor to the poem and its subject;[133] and in a letter to Julianus Rusticus, a friend both of himself and Ausonius, Symmachus neatly pointed the relationship by quoting a phrase from a letter of Ausonius to himself, which happened to mention Julianus.[134] We have already noted how, in a letter of a mere few lines to Eutropius, Symmachus could evoke his correspondent's reputation both as a historian and medical writer, as well as the political crisis in which he was currently involved.[135]

But perhaps the most impressive instance of Symmachus' allusive skill is in his letters to Vettius Agorius Praetextatus. In a formidable alliance of intellectual and spiritual capacities which has made him in modern eyes one of the outstanding personalities of late Roman paganism, Praetextatus established his reputation both as a philosopher, whose work on Themistius' commentaries on Aristotle would be known to Boethius,[136] and as a religious *dévot* – and activist. For he not only became initiated into the 'Oriental' cults in vogue among the aristocracy at Rome, and as proconsul of Achaia (361–4) into the leading mysteries of Greece;[137] he used each of his senior official positions – the proconsulship, the prefecture of Rome, and the praetorian prefecture (384) – to win significant concessions on behalf of paganism from the Christian emperors.[138] Praetextatus' wife, Aconia Fabia Paulina, who shared her husband's religious tastes, after his death commemorated his achievement in an epitaph, in which he was said to have devoted his erudition to the complex mystery of the divine nature ('divumque numen multiplex doctus colis');[139] while in Macrobius' *Saturnalia*, he was made to define his religious convictions in terms of a syncretism, the gods of the Classical pantheon being seen as functions of the Sun.[140]

Symmachus, whose respect for Praetextatus is evident from the letters addressed to him, acknowledged his friend's tastes when, having once broached a topic, he abandoned it to the 'disputations of philosophers': in another letter, he referred in an impressive phrase to Praetextatus' spending his leisure at Baiae, 'taming his mighty intellect' in peace and solitude.[141] Once, when Praetextatus was ill, Symmachus anticipated his return to health when the gods permitted the 'reconciliation of the forces of his mind'; and the recovery of Paulina, on another occasion, was attributed to the restoration of the 'pax deorum'.[142] As prefect of Rome in 367–8, Praetextatus had restored the 'porticus deorum consentium' in the Forum; there is no need to doubt that Symmachus' expression was a precise allusion to the nature of Praetextatus' theological beliefs.[143]

To judge from such cases as these, it would appear that behind the studiously observed conventions and uniform language of Symmachus' letters lies, at need, an allusive repertoire of some precision and delicacy. Equipped with this repertoire, Symmachus was able to adapt his tone to meet particular circumstances (though as we have seen, he could on occasions express himself very directly),[144] and bend himself to the tastes of individual correspondents. At the same time, it is possible to suggest that the conventions and style themselves satisfied a complementary and equally important, function: they could serve, in certain conditions, to shield Symmachus from disruptive intrusions of reality. I propose, in conclusion, to indicate how this could be so, taking into account two facets of Symmachus' activity: first, his relations with the usurping régime of Eugenius in 393–4; and second, and more general in scope, his approach to the issue of religious diversity in the society of his time.

The political embarrassment which had followed Symmachus' involvement with the rebellion of Maximus may be expected to have encouraged in him a sense of caution, when in 393 Eugenius, who had been proclaimed emperor in Gaul the previous summer, brought his armies over the Alps and settled at Milan: and particularly so when, presented with the opportunity to turn the rebellion into a gesture of defiance against the Christian emperor, Theodosius, Symmachus' close friend Nicomachus Flavianus inspired and organised what has become known as the 'last pagan revival' in the west.[145] There is, indeed, little sign that Symmachus allowed himself to become deeply involved with the régime. He was not certainly implicated in the pagan ceremonies revived by Flavianus during a visit to Rome in the spring of 394, nor did he himself attend Flavianus' consular celebrations, held at Milan at the beginning of the year.[146] After the suppression of the rebellion by Theodosius and the suicide of Flavianus (September 394), Symmachus was able to approach Ambrose of Milan, on behalf of Marcianus, a senator whom Eugenius and Flavianus had appointed proconsul of Africa,[147] and in due course defend the younger Flavianus from penalisation by the court. As prefect of Rome during his father's rebellion, Flavianus had been prominent in the physical restoration of temples and other monuments, which accompanied the pagan revival.[148]

Yet Symmachus was far from breaking off all contact with the

régime. It was four or five years earlier that the younger Nicomachus Flavianus had entered Symmachus' family as his son-in-
law; and precisely in 393 that Symmachus' own son, Q. Fabius
Memmius Symmachus (the editor of the letters), celebrated
his quaestorian games.[149] Symmachus did not hesitate to write
to the elder Flavianus, praetorian prefect under Eugenius, and to
other officials – even including a 'Theodosian' proconsul of
Africa, appointed and addressed from Constantinople – to gain
their assistance in assembling beasts and performers for the
games;[150] while after their completion, he duly sent to Flavianus
the usual offerings of diptychs and small gifts in celebration of
the occasion.[151] To Eugenius himself, Symmachus sent a special
diptych, set in a golden frame; and to other friends at court
presentation writing-tablets of ivory, and silver caskets.[152]
Further, when Flavianus assumed the consulship at the beginning
of 394 – not of course recognised by Theodosius – Symmachus
did not refrain from conveying his pleasure, in the persons of
friends invited to Milan for the ceremonies.[153] Still more intrigu-
ingly, he recommended to Flavianus one Alypius, whose
attendance at the consular celebrations represented a reconciliation
after an earlier difference between the two men. The reconciliation would be especially worthy of note if, as is usually
supposed, Alypius was Faltonius Probus Alypius, a member of
the Christian Anician family – and a recent prefect of Rome
of Theodosius.[154]

Yet it seems that this contact with the usurping régime did not
affect Symmachus' subsequent relations with the imperial court.
A period of withdrawal from public life may reflect his grief
at the death of his old friend and ally;[155] but otherwise, Symmachus could take up the cases of the proconsul (and apostate)
Marcianus, and of the younger Flavianus, rehabilitated by 399;[156]
and already by the very first months of 395, he was able to support
the petition to the imperial court of a legation of Campanian
notables, who were seeking tax concessions on their estates.[157]
In all this, we can see that there was a recognised distinction
between active support for a usurping régime, and the regular
conduct of due social courtesies with its members: a respect
for etiquette which allowed for the functioning of normal, and
necessary, social relations through times of political disturbance.

A similar success for etiquette over a potentially divisive

issue in late fourth-century society is shown in a wider field, in the role of religion in the letters of Symmachus. It might at first sight appear that the comparative rarity of overt religious allusions in the letters gives the lie to Symmachus' reputation, acquired from his involvement in the affair of the altar of Victory, as one of the last defenders of Roman paganism. This, of course, he was; but it was a reputation that was clearly not allowed to interfere with the smooth functioning of his correspondence.

Symmachus' open references to paganism are strictly limited, both in their distribution among his correspondents, and in their content. The great majority of such references occur in letters to Symmachus' known pagan allies, especially Praetextatus and Nicomachus Flavianus; and they concern, almost exclusively, the public conduct of the old state religion – what Symmachus, in a phrase used to Praetextatus which admirably reflects the nature of his own preoccupations, calls 'pontificalis administratio'.[158] So he can be seen, writing again to Praetextatus of his concern at the failure of the priests to expiate a portent observed at Spoletium, or to his own brother on behalf of an agent despatched by the college to do business concerning its estates in Africa:[159] deprecating the current neglect of the gods, and attributing to it a serious food shortage, or the lack of conviction of Romans, as shown by their inclination to swim with the tide by absenting themselves from the altars:[160] on occasions, even, persuading evidently reluctant colleagues to attend meetings of the priestly colleges.[161] We have noted his reaction to the Vestal Virgin who was reported to wish to give up her office before the regular time: perhaps better known is his attempt to persuade certain officials (unfortunately anonymous, although the prefect of Rome seems prudently to have evaded responsibility) to punish a Vestal, whom an enquiry of the college had pronounced guilty of adultery.[162] The affair shows Symmachus in an unsympathetically severe light as a religious legalist – as indeed does his opposition to a proposal made to the college that the memory of Praetextatus be honoured by a statue dedicated by the Vestals, as against all tradition and precedent.[163]

In other letters, Symmachus mentioned the festivals of Vesta and Minerva, and on a single occasion to Nicomachus Flavianus, the public cult of Cybele, the Mother of the Gods;[164] while he was delighted to report, in a letter to his father (therefore before

377) the pagan loyalties of the citizens of Beneventum. [165] Yet, if only a relatively small proportion of Symmachus' letters was concerned with contemporary paganism, Christianity – as indeed we should expect – is still more fleetingly represented. The new religion is never mentioned by name in the letters, nor directly referred to: though on two occasions, Symmachus found himself recommending bishops – one, Clemens of Mauretanian Caesarea, from a town where he himself had connections. [166] On each occasion, Symmachus took pains to anticipate his correspondent's surprise by emphasising his respect for his protégé's personal merits, as independent of those of his 'sect' – as Symmachus, with deliberately pointed objectivity, styles Christianity. [167] Another letter refers with tantalising obscurity to a legal dispute involving an intervention of 'priests' (*antistites*), leading to a clash of interest between 'justice and innocence' on the one hand, and 'religion' on the other. [168] Symmachus' personal distaste is clear, and there can be little doubt that the 'priests' in question were of the Christian persuasion: but beyond this, his allusion is obscure beyond the possibility of recovery.

Symmachus' practical attitude to Christianity in his correspondence is perhaps more typically represented by his letters to Ambrose of Milan. These letters (III.30–7) contain only a single reference to Ambrose's episcopal office, and none to his religion: not surprisingly, the one reference is a plea to Ambrose not to employ episcopal jurisdiction, as Symmachus clearly suspected he was about to, against a protégé of Symmachus – 'there are laws, there are courts and magistrates which a litigant can make use of, without endangering your conscience'. [169] Yet Symmachus could also recommend for protection to Ambrose the former proconsul of Eugenius, Marcianus, as well as a doctor who would later appear as a minor character in the *Saturnalia* of Macrobius; [170] and perhaps as significant as any is another letter, from which it appears that Ambrose had sent to Symmachus two men with a single letter between them. Without questioning their merits, Symmachus suggested that it would be more in order if he were to receive a separate letter for each individual. [171] Clearly, even Ambrose was expected to observe the normal conventions of Symmachan *amicitia*; and otherwise, Symmachus can address Ambrose precisely as he addresses regular court officials with patronage and influence. Indeed, it may be that in these letters we catch a glimpse of the Ambrose whom Augustine found so difficult of access – a man preoccupied by everyday concerns, surrounded by the crowds of 'busy men, whose infirmities he served.'[172]

This ascendancy of practical interest, even of the niceties of etiquette, over such a potentially divisive issue as religion in late Roman society, is for the historian one of the most important aspects of the correspondence of Symmachus. It might have been anticipated that such a correspondence, with its 130 named recipients, would have served as a 'sounding board' for the religious state of Roman society in the late fourth century, sensitive to its diverse tastes and enabling the progress of Christianity in this society to be measured with some finesse. In fact, this is not so: it turns out to be impossible to make any systematic or substantial classification of Symmachus' correspondents, as between Christians and pagans among them. The fullest attempt to perform such a classification was not a success;[173] and its failure is significant, less for the reason that the circumstantial evidence is so often lacking with which to carry out the identification of religious tastes, than because the letters themselves scarcely ever provide any criteria for distinction between the two groups. The inference from this should be clear; it was a prime purpose of the idiom of Symmachus' letters precisely to elide the distinction, to make it possible for his *amicitia* to function across the boundaries of religious difference (just as it also crossed the racial boundaries presented by the barbarian generals at court, whom Symmachus could equally address with no change of tone or sign of embarrassment).[174] At least, Symmachus' use of religious expressions – always excepting the letters to his close pagan colleagues such as Praetextatus and Nicomachus Flavianus – pays little or no attention to such boundaries. So, for instance, he could employ a series of stylistic formulae to invoke the 'gods' in letters to demonstrably Christian correspondents – 'dii modo optata fortunent', 'deos precor, ut tua secunda proficiant', 'praefata ope deorum' and other such phrases[175] – while on the other hand referring to 'divina miseratio', or 'dei venia', when writing to a friend usually taken to have been a pagan.[176] One metaphor in particular, deriving from pagan initiation ceremonies, was used by Symmachus in introducing a protégé to the friendship of the younger Nicomachus Flavianus, 'tamquam mystagogus';[177]

yet he did not find the metaphor inappropriate in addressing a Christian praetorian prefect known also to St Martin of Tours, and other court officials whose Christian belief is not in doubt.[178]

It would be laborious to catalogue such expressions through all their stylistic variations. The conclusion would not be affected – that they amounted to little more than harmless formalities, emptied of religious content; that neither Symmachus nor the friends whom he addressed set much emotional store by them, and that Symmachus made no attempt on this basis to adapt his tone to the religion (assuming that he knew it) of a particular correspondent. They are a manner of speech, containing nothing to provoke contention or give offence: nothing to weaken the elaborately contrived façade of unanimity affected by Symmachus and his senatorial colleagues.

If there should remain any doubt as to the significance of this feature of Symmachus' style, it may perhaps be resolved by a brief survey of his relations with one particular correspondent, Fl. Rufinus. This was an acquaintance formed at the moment of Symmachus' greatest political uncertainty – Theodosius' suppression in August 388 of the usurper Maximus, to whom Symmachus had delivered a panegyric.[179] There are possible signs of the delicacy of Symmachus' position in the letters to Rufinus. From one, which refers to the recent promotion at court of Symmachus' friend Nicomachus Flavianus, it appears that Rufinus, writing to Symmachus, had alluded to the supporters of Maximus as 'men of bad faith' (*inprobi*).[180] In reply to this scarcely veiled hint, Symmachus suggested that it was no new or unprecedented thing, but quite habitual to Theodosius to choose men after fresh and careful examination of their merit, and never to rely on the passive acceptance of reputation – a suitably innocuous sentiment by which Symmachus cleverly diverted attention from the personal implications of Rufinus' remark. On another occasion, Symmachus took especial care to excuse his attendance at the consular celebrations (in 390) of the Emperor Valentinian II, writing not only to Rufinus but also to other court officials to explain that the invitation had arrived too late for him to be able to arrange the journey to Milan.[181] Yet again, Symmachus referred to a reproach which he had incurred for failing to offer Rufinus his condolences on the death, which had occurred at Rome, of a 'distinguished citizen' (*civis emeriti*).[182] Here too,

Symmachus neatly 'turned' the rebuke by pretending – as Rufinus had clearly given him the opportunity to – that it had not been delivered in full seriousness.[183] Symmachus suggested that he had wished to avoid offending Rufinus by appearing to write with too great alacrity upon the death of one with whom he could not claim to have enjoyed close or harmonious relations; in such cases, he observed, if one could not show genuine grief, one had best show due reverence by maintaining silence. If the 'distinguished citizen' in question was indeed Petronius Probus – whose death, after baptism, and burial in the family mausoleum at St Peter's, cannot have occurred far from this moment – then Symmachus' comments are an interesting reflection on the courteous and sympathetic letters with which he had himself addressed Probus.[184]

From these examples it appears that, at a time of political unease for himself, Symmachus was able by various artifices of style and sentiment to divert possible causes of embarrassment between himself and the court. Yet perhaps of wider significance, from the present point of view, than the political differences between Rufinus and Symmachus, was their total incompatibility in matters of religious taste.

Rufinus was a Gaul from the town of Elusa (Eauze) in the south-west, who had joined the eastern court of Theodosius and accompanied the emperor to Italy on the campaign against Maximus: his first encounter with Symmachus was as *magister officiorum* during Theodosius' visit to Rome in the summer of 389.[185] Upon his departure, Symmachus, consciously breaking normal etiquette, wrote to Rufinus first, recalling their recent acquaintance and admiring the friendliness and civility which Rufinus had displayed at Rome.[186] In a slightly later letter, referring to apparent resentment at court at Nicomachus Flavianus' promotion to high office, Symmachus mentioned the similarity of virtues of Flavianus and Rufinus as conducive to a spirit of concord between them.[187] We could never guess from such allusions that Rufinus had left Rome, not merely with Symmachus' acquaintance fresh in his mind, but possessing relics of the Roman saints, Peter and Paul, which he had acquired from pope Siricius. These relics he was to install, upon his return to the east, in a martyr's shrine which he founded at Chalcedon – and adjoining it, a monastery populated with monks from

Egypt.[188] Further, Rufinus' sister-in-law was to embark on a pilgrimage to the Holy Land and Egypt, in the course of which she met the elder Melania and Palladius, author of the *Lausiac History* in which the encounter was mentioned;[189] while, upon Rufinus' assassination in November 395, his widow and daughter took themselves to live with the ascetic circles established at Jerusalem.[190]

If two worlds as diverse as these can be linked in the correspondence of Symmachus, it can at least be said not to have lacked a certain practical effectiveness. But I would go further than this, in suggesting that it is precisely in its ability to obscure the contentious and evade potentially divisive issues that this correspondence, with its equability of style, its religious and emotional opacity, its careful observance of etiquette and its polite attentions, is seen at its most persuasive; and that only within the context of its actual functioning in the society of Symmachus' own time, can its interpretation be properly undertaken. The impression of the fourth century as an age of 'conflict' between paganism and Christianity has offered a vein of interpretation richly exploited by modern scholars. It is perhaps equally important to appreciate how men who lived in this age were able to limit the scope of this and other sources of conflict, in order to make the normal conduct of social relations possible for themselves, their colleagues and those dependent upon them. In this process, the letters of Symmachus are a document of fundamental significance.

Notes

The following documentation, though extensive, is selective in that it bears mainly upon Symmachus himself, and only secondarily upon the historical background against which the article does, in fact, attempt to place him. The letters themselves are referred to, in the simple form VII.13, V.95, etc., from the edition of Otto Seeck, in *MGHAA*, VI.1 (1883, repr. 1961: cited throughout as Seeck, *Symmachus*); though we may welcome the appearance of the first volume (1972) of a Budé edition, by J. P. Callu, containing Books I–II (for the *Relationes*, see below, note 24). In addition, the Chicago dissertation of 1942 by J. A. McGeachy, *Quintus Aurelius Symmachus and the Senatorial Aristocracy of the West*, is cited as McGeachy, *Q. Aurelius Symmachus*, and A. Chastagnol, *Les Fastes de la préfecture de Rome au bas-empire* (1962) as Chastagnol, *Fastes*.

1 VII.13–14, cf. VII.2 and V.95 (to Helpidius).
2 IV.9 to Stilicho presents the 'amplissimi ordinis petitiones'. For the

position of Stilicho, see Alan Cameron's chapter on Claudian in this volume (p. 134).

3 IV.13, cf. V 94, 96 to Helpidius; 'sanitatis ... quam labefactavit peregrinationis iniuria et hiemalis asperitas'.

4 *Chron. Min.* I, p. 299 (18 November 401).

5 Claudian, *De Bello Getico* (of 402), esp. 314f.

6 Claudian, *op. cit.* 450 f, cf. Symmachus VII.13; 'vir cuncta praecelsus ... mox cum praesidiis validissimis adfore nuntiatur'.

7 Gaudentius, *Tract.* 17.1f, cf. 13.21 (*CSEL* LXVIII, pp. 141, 120).

8 Cf. *ILS* 797, with Chastagnol, *Fastes*, p. 256.

9 The first law issued there was dated 6 December 402 (*CT* VII.13.15). For Symmachus' connections with Ariminum, cf. IX.120, 'Ariminum saepe praeteriens', IX.48.

10 III.47.

11 See *Latomus*, 30 (1971), pp. 1076-7.

12 Marcellus, *De Medicamentis*, praef. (ed. Helmreich, Teubner 1889, p. 1).

13 I.95; III.18. Cf. Seeck, *Symmachus* CXI.

14 Seeck, *Symmachus* LXXIII; 'scriptorem ingenii tam pauperis pauci certe lecturi sunt, sed multi hic illic inspicient, ut singulas res excerpant'.

15 Respectively M. Schanz, *Gesch. der römischen Litteratur*[2] (1914), vol. IV.1, p. 127 ('Worte ohne Inhalt'); F. Homes Dudden, *The Life and Times of St Ambrose* (1935), p. 39.

16 G. Boissier, *La Fin du paganisme* (1891), vol. II, p. 183 (cf. his review of Seeck's edition; in *Journal des Savants* (1888), pp. 402-10, 597-609, 712-26).

17 A. H. M. Jones, *The Later Roman Empire* (1964), vol. I, p. 155; F. Paschoud, 'Réflexions sur l'idéal religieux de Symmaque', *Historia*, 14 (1965), p. 215.

18 S. Dill, *Roman Society in the Last Century of the Western Empire* (1899), p. 153.

19 II.35; 'quousque ... dandae ac reddendae salutationis verba blaterabimus, cum alia stilo materia non suppetat? at olim parentes ... etiam patriae negotia, quae nunc angusta vel nulla sunt, in familiares paginas conferebant'.

20 E.g. II.82; VII.87; IX.60, 90, etc.

21 E.g. II.25; VI.48; VII.82.

22 I.46, 90; II.38; III.30; VI.12; IX.116, etc. (cf. for the avoidance of unpleasant news, I.85; II.49; VI.65; VIII.33, etc.).

23 Seeck, *Symmachus* XXIII; developed by J. A. McGeachy, *CP*, 44 (1949), pp. 222-9.

24 See below, pp. 68f; and esp. McGeachy, *Q. Aurelius Symmachus*, and A. Chastagnol, *La Préfecture urbaine à Rome sous le bas-empire* (1960). The *Relationes* are now translated and commented by R. H. Barrow, *Prefect and Emperor: the Relationes of Symmachus, A.D. 384* (1973).

25 VII.42; cf. V.84; IX.18, 35, 102, etc. For the recipient of VII.42 as Hadrianus, *magister officiorum* in 399 (and later praetorian prefect), see R. J. Bonney, 'A new friend for Symmachus', forthcoming in *Historia*.

26 IV.46 (apparently satisfied by *CT* XI.28.2, of 24 March 395); cf. IV.35 for the formation of the acquaintance.

27 V.66.5–6, cf. IX.88; 'diu officium scribendi per verecundiam distuli, ne in aula positum viderer ambire'.

28 VIII.69.

29 IV.34, 64; V.85–6: see below, pp. 67f.

30 II.12, 48 (not to be taken too seriously).

31 Macrobius, *Sat.* V.1.7; Sidonius, *Ep. No. I.1.1.*

32 Cited by J. P. Callu, *Symmaque: Lettres* (ed. Budé, 1972), introd., p. 26.

33 Callu, p. 55f.

34 Olympiodorus, *fr.* 44 (Müller, *FHG* IV, p. 67); Socrates V.14.5.

35 *ILS* 2946.

36 Cf. I.44, 52; 78; 96, 105; III.7; IV.29, 45; 64; V.8; VII.58. Cf. Seeck, *Symmachus* VI–VII.

37 IV.49; Arusianus Messius, ed. Keil (*GL* VII), pp. 458, 489; Cassiodorus, *Variae* XI.1. Compare Symmachus' influence upon Ennodius; Seeck, *Symmachus* V, n. 4.

38 Seeck, *Symmachus*, 318–39 and introd., VIII–IX. For the palimpsest, see E. A. Lowe, *CLA* I (1934), Nos 26a–31 (Vatican); III (1938), Nos 26a–31 (Milan): also – since the palimpsest is the unique source for Fronto's letters – J. van den Hout, *M. Cornelii Frontonis Epistulae* (1954), pp.ix–xvii.

39 R. A. B. Mynors, *XII Panegyrici Latini* (OCT, 1964), ix.

40 This seems to me fundamental; see Alan Cameron, *CQ*, n.s. 15 (1965), at pp. 295f. But I still believe that Book X may stand in its original form (contrast Cameron, p. 296; Callu, pp. 19–22); and I am not convinced by Seeck's hypothesis (*Symmachus* XVIf, cf. Callu, pp. 17f) that the *Relationes* had been published separately by Symmachus himself. The arguments are somewhat technical.

41 Viz. X.1–14, 'the private letters', followed by 15–121, 'the Bithynian letters': see A. N. Sherwin-White, *The Letters of Pliny* (1966), pp. 556f.

42 E.g. to Marcianus, VIII.9, 23, 54, 58, 73; to Pacatus, VIII.12; IX.61, 64. On the other hand, certain groups clearly belong together; VIII. 71–2; IX.147–8; 138–9, and many letters on the praetorian games at the beginning of IX. See also n. 46 below.

43 H. Peter, *Der Brief in der römischen Litteratur* (1901), pp. 144f; accepted, in my view too firmly, by McGeachy, *Q. Aurelius Symmachus*, p. 25 and in *CP*, 44 (1949), p. 222.

44 In the form 'editus post eius obitum a Q. Fabio Memmio Symmacho v.c. filio'. See the apparatus of Seeck's ed., pp. 70, 124, 276.

45 Above, nn. 1–3.

46 Viz. the inclusion of letters to Patruinus (VIII.18–19) and to Probinus (IX.60) – assuming these to be the same as the recipients of VII.102–28 and V.67–71 respectively. Further, IX.126 is usually assigned to Probinus and IX.112 to S. Petronius Probus (cf. I.56–61). In addition, the letters to Licinius (V.72–7) include two (74–5) to Limenius. But such errors might equally be ascribed to Symmachus' *librarius* (cf. II.35).

47 Accurately so styled, if taken as a broad rather than exclusive description of contents: Book VIII contains practically no *commendaticiae*.

48 See esp. H. O. Kröner, 'Die politischen Ansichten und Ziele des Q. Aurelius Symmachus', in *Politeia und Res Publica* (*Palingenesia* IV, 1969), pp. 337–56, esp. at pp. 346f.

49 I.52; 'pars melior humani generis', cf. *Or.* VI.1; 'nobilissimos humani generis'.

50 See esp. *Or.* IV.5f (of 376); and on the circumstances, A. Alföldi, *A Conflict of ideas in the Late Roman Empire: the Clash between the Senate and Valentinian I* (1952), pp. 84f.

51 *Rel.* 48.1; 'praefecturae urbanae proprium negotium est senatorum iura tutari', cf. Cassiodorus, *Variae* VI.4.1 ('Formula praefecturae urbanae'); 'grande est quidem procerem esse, sed multo grandius de proceribus iudicare'.

52 *Or.* VIII.3; '. . . boni sanguinis, qui se semper agnoscit'.

53 E.g. II.10, 91; V.41, 66; VII.46, 89, 94, etc.

54 VII.126; cf. IX.40, opening with a definition of Symmachus' ideal of justice – 'ratio quidem semper habenda iustitiae est, sed circa nobiles probabilesque personas plus debet esse moderaminis, ut perspiciatur in discretione iudicium'.

55 IX.6; cf. I.74; IV.68; and (concerning Symmachus himself) VII.66.

56 Cf. Seeck, *Symmachus* LXVIII for the letters (below, n. 109).

57 Cf. *JRS*, 60 (1970), at pp. 92f.

58 VIII.41; cf. *Latomus*, 30 (1971), at p. 1081.

59 IX.108; 'quare officio pontificis, fide senatoris admoneor', etc.

60 IX.43.

61 II.46; 'ferunt Socraten, si quando excidit cupitis aut destinatis, id sibi utile, quod evenerat, aestimasse', etc.

62 II.78; 'quoniam servorum per limitem facilis inventio et pretium solet esse tolerabile', etc.

63 VI.37.

64 IX.83; 'accusato vernula tuo flumine, cuius turbidos meatus et infidum agmen expertus es' (by flooding?).

65 VI.40.

66 Cf. Amm. Marc. XIV.6.16f; XXVI.3.5, etc.

67 See Chastagnol, *Préfecture urbaine, passim,* and esp. pp. 459f on the wider aspects of the senators' position.

68 For such connections in Symmachus, cf. I.3 (Beneventum); IV.46 (Campanians); VIII.27 (Naples); IX.58, 136 (Formiae); 131 (Caieta); 138–9 (Suessa); I.17 (Sicily, cf. *CIL* X.7017); I.64 (Mauretanian Caesarea); IX.51 (Hippo Regius). Compare IX.103, 105; *Rel.* 44 (*mancipes salinarum*).

69 *Rel.* 10, cf. 11–12.

70 Jerome, *Ep.* 23.3; 'non in lacteo caeli palatio, ut uxor conmentitur infelix, sed in sordentibus tenebris continetur'.

71 Amm. Marc. XXVII.3.3; 'magna civium laetitia'.

72 Cf. *ILS* 769; Chastagnol, *Fastes,* p. 162.

73 E.g. Amm. Marc. XXVII.3.8f. According to Ambrose, *Ep.* 40.13 (*PL* XVI, cols 1105–6), this was a frequent experience of prefects of Rome.

74 Amm. Marc. XXVII.3.4.

75 J. Rougé, 'Une émeute à Rome au IVe siècle', *REA*, 63 (1961), pp. 59–77, esp. at pp. 63f. See Pliny, *NH* XXXVI.181; Palladius, *Op. Agr.* I.17.

76 I.10, 12; ascribed by Seeck (*Symmachus* LXXIV) to late 375.

77 See esp. IV.5 to Stilicho; Seeck, *Symmachus* LXIX. On the whole episode, see Alan Cameron's discussion in this volume (pp. 139f).

78 VI.61, 66; VIII.65.

79 E.g. the case of Tertullus; Amm. Marc. XIX.10.1f.

80 E.g. Olybrius; Amm. Marc. XXVIII.4.2 (cf. XIV.6.19f; XXVIII.4.9, 21, etc.).

81 Cf. Seeck, *Symmachus* LXXI–II. According to A. H. M. Jones, *op. cit.*, vol. II, p. 560, this was 'the one subject on which he shows enthusiasm'.

82 See esp. IV.58f; IX.11–12, 18, 20–4, etc.

83 IV.8, cf. 12.

84 E.g. II.76–8 (esp. 78; 'avidus civicae gratiae'); IV.8, 12 ('leopardorum cursus . . . cui iustior plausus et laeta vocum suffragia debeantur'); IV.60.3; VI.42, etc.

85 For the career see Seeck, *Symmachus* XLVf; more briefly (and with some improvements), Chastagnol, *Fastes*, pp. 218f.

86 See esp. Chastagnol, 'Observations sur le consulat suffect et la préture du bas-empire', *RH*, 219 (1958), pp. 221–53.

87 *CT* VIII.5.15 (25 March 365); Chastagnol, *Fastes*, p. 220.

88 II.27.

89 II.44.

90 IX.115. The snub is sometimes ascribed to the influence of his successor, who happens to be known as a Christian (*ILS* 1287; Salona); but there is no evidence for this interpretation.

91 VIII.5, 20.

92 X.1; see *Historia*, 20 (1971), pp. 122–8. Theodosius was executed shortly after his victory over Firmus (Jerome, *Chron.* s.a. 376).

93 Chastagnol, *Fastes*, p. 219; cf. (on Orfitus), pp. 139f.

94 *Rel.* 1; 2 – respectively to Valentinian II and, with scrupulous protocol, to the eastern emperor, Theodosius.

95 *Rel.* 10.3.

96 Below, pp. 78f.

97 Seeck, *Symmachus* CCX–XI.

98 *Or.* II.4; 13; 18f; cf. Amm. Marc. XXVIII.2.2f (fort); 5.9f (Burgundians).

99 *Or.* II.4; *CT* XI.31.4.

100 I.23.3; cf. Ausonius, *Praefatiunculae* (*Opusc.* I Peiper), i, 35; *Gratiarum Actio* (*Opusc.* XX), II(11). etc.

101 I.14.3f (below, p. 82).

102 I.14.4.

103 I.23.3; cf. I.32.4 (Ausonius to Symmachus).

104 X.1; cf. *Historia*, 20 (1971), p. 127. Theodosius was at court at the time (Amm. Marc. XVIII.3.9; 5.15; XXIX.3.6, etc.); and his son, the future emperor, was known to Ausonius (*Opusc.* I.iii–iv).

105 *Rel.* 3.1.

106 Symmachus delivered a panegyric to Maximus; II.30/31, cf. Socrates V.14.4f.

107 Cf. II.64; V.15; IX.149: at Rome, IV.58, 60.

108 Below, pp. 84f.

109 Seeck, *Symmachus* LXIII (cf. IV.31; VII.8; VIII.21, etc. – all of 39 9/400) For the other embassies, cf. IV.18, 52; VII.12, 22, 26 (in 396); VI.52, etc. (Seeck, *Symmachus* CLXIV; 397); VI.58, 62; VII.54, 113–14 (398; cf. *CT* VII.13.13).

110 Cf. *JRS*, 60 (1970), 92.

111 E.g. I.42.2; II.17.2; VI.38; VII.50; VIII.13, etc. Cf. McGeachy, *Q. Aurelius Symmachus*, 45f.

112 Amm. Marc. XXVII.11.3.

113 I.58; '. . . debitam operam solve principibus, qui rationem magis meriti tui quam voluntatis habuerunt'.

114 See L. Harmand, *Le Patronat sur les collectivités publiques, des origines au bas-empire* (1957), esp. pp. 188f, 202f, 285; Chastagnol, *Préfecture urbaine*, p. 461; M. T. W. Arnheim, *The Senatorial Aristocracy in the Later Roman Empire* (1972), pp. 155f.

115 Cf. Cassiodorus, *Variae* VI.4.6; 'carpento veheris per nobilem plebem, publica te vota comitantur, favores gratissimi consona tecum voce procedunt' – words as applicable to the late fourth century as to the early sixth.

116 Thus the work of M. T. W. Arnheim, *op. cit.,* is more limited in its implications than its rather ambitious title might suggest.

117 E.g. IV.23; V.70; VI.60 (departures): II.5, 8; III.8, 65; IX.73, etc. (arrivals). See E. Wistrand, 'Textkritisches und Interpretatorisches zu Symmachus', *Symbolae Gotoburgenses* 56 (1950), pp. 87f [= *Opera Selecta*, Stockholm, 1972, 229f]; McGeachy, *Q. Aurelius Symmachus*, p. 123.

118 II.58; III.78; VI.13; VII.5; VIII.4, 12, and *passim*.

119 E.g. I.76; IV.22.

120 Above, p. 63.

121 E.g. I.83; IV.17; IX.68 (bereavement): I.85; VII.77; VIII.54–5, cf. 31 (illness); I.18, 26; 95; III.2; 28; VII.117; VIII.25, etc. (*occupationes*).

122 IV.28, cf. 30, 33; IV.58; 'annuos gaudii fructus ex litteris tuis capio', etc. Cf. on lack of carriers, I.39, 42; VIII.34; IX.27, etc.

123 E.g. III.3, cf. 84; V.30.

124 VII.129.

125 Festus, p. 348 Lindsay; 'religiosus est non modo deorum sanctitatem magni aestimans sed etiam officiosus adversus homines'. Cited by Wistrand, *op. cit.,* 88.

126 VII.9.

127 IV.30, 42.

128 II.35 (above, p. 62).

129 III.34.

130 I.14; III.11; I.23, 45, cf. III.10.

131 Above, pp. 75f.

132 I.14.3, cf. Ausonius to Symmachus, I.32.4.

133 I.14.2; 'volitat tuus Mosella per manus sinusque multorum . . . sed tantum nostra ora praelabitur', etc.

134 III.6.1, cf. Ausonius to Symmachus, I.32.1.

135 Above, pp. 59f.

136 See the preface to his *Commentary on the De Interpretatione, ed. sec.* (ed. C. Meiser (Teubner, 1880), pp. 3–4).

137 For the evidence, see Seeck, *Symmachus* LXXXIII–VIII; Chastagnol, *Fastes,* pp. 171f Note esp. *ILS* 1259 (his epitaph); *CIL* VI 1778.

138 As proconsul he secured the relaxation for Greece of legislation against nocturnal sacrifice (Zosimus IV.3.2f; cf. *CT* IX.16.7, of 364); as urban prefect, prohibited the abutting of private houses upon temples (Amm. Marc. XXVII.9.10); as praetorian prefect, provoked an enquiry into the unauthorised removal of valuables from temples (Symmachus, *Rel.* 21.3, 5).

139 *ILS* 1259 (p. 259, v. 15). For the religious tastes of Paulina, *ILS* 1260.

140 *Sat.* I.17.1f.

141 Respectively I.48; 47.

142 I.45; 48.

143 *ILS* 4003; cf. H. Bloch, 'A new document of the last pagan revival in the west, 393–394 A.D.', *HTR,* 38 (1945). pp. 207f; Chastagnol, *Fastes,* p. 173.

144 Above, p. 69.

145 See esp. H. Bloch, *op. cit.,* pp. 199–244, and 'The pagan revival in the west at the end of the fourth century', in *The Conflict between Paganism and Christianity in the Fourth Century* (ed. A. Momigliano, 1963), pp. 193–218. But cf. my reservations on Flavianus' activities in 'The historical setting of the "Carmen contra Paganos" (Cod. Par. Lat. 8084)', *Historia,* 19 (1970), pp. 464–79, esp. at pp. 473f.

146 *Historia,* 19 (1970), p. 478.

147 III.33; cf. *Carm. c. paganos* (Riese, *Anth. Lat.*², I, pp. 20–5), v. 86.

148 He inspired Bloch's 'new document' – restoration by the *praefectus annonae* of a temple of Hercules at Ostia (= *AE* 1948, 127) and, in my suggestion, restored a temple of Venus at Rome (*Carm. c. Paganos,* 112f with *Historia,* 19 (1970), p. 477).

149 Seeck, *Symmachus* LII; LVIII: J.-R. Palanque, *REA,* 33 (1931), 353–5.

150 E.g. to Flavianus, II.46, 76–8 (above, pp. 69, 72f); cf. V.20–2 (to Magnillus, *vicarius* of Africa); V.59 (to Aemilius Florus Paternus, proconsul in 393; cf. *CT.*19.14 with *JTS,* n.s. 18 (1967), pp. 442–3); VII.117. For an invitation to attend the games, V.46.

151 II.81.

152 II.81; 'praeterea domino et principi nostro . . . auro circumdatum diptychum misi'; cf. VII.76; IX.119.

153 II.84–5.

154 II.83; cf. Chastagnol, *Fastes,* pp. 236f (*proefectus urbi* in 391). Alypius was probably the recipient of Ambrose, *Ep.* 89; cf. *Latomus,* 30 (1971), p. 1081.

155 ?Cf. IX.10; 68; 78: Seeck, *Symmachus* LIX.

156 For Marcianus, above, p. 84; Flavianus (many letters), Seeck, *Symmachus* LXXI.

157 Above, n. 26.

158 I.51 (cf. I.47; 'pontificalis officii cura'). See *JRS*, 63 (1973), 175–95.

159 I.49; 68.

160 I.51 (referring also to 'tanta sacerdotum neglegentia'); 'nunc aris deesse Romanos genus est ambiendi'.

161 I.51, cf. 47; II.34 (to Nicomachus Flavianus), cf. 53.

162 Above, p. 69; IX.147–8.

163 II.36. Compare *ILS* 1261, a statue set up by Praetextatus' widow in his Esquiline house to the Vestal Coelia Concordia, and referring to a statue earlier dedicated to her by Praetextatus. But see *JRS*, 63 (1973), 192, n. 111.

164 II.34

165 I.3.4; 'amantissimi litterarum morumque mirabiles. deos magna pars veneratur', etc.

166 I.64; for the circumstances, *Historia*, 30 (1971), at pp. 126f.

167 I.64; 'causa istud mihi, non secta persuasit. nam Clemens boni viri functus officium', etc; cf. VII.51; 'fratrem meum Severum episcopum omnium sectarum adtestatione laudabilem'. *Rel.* 21 refers twice to 'Christiana lex'; *Rel.* 3, on the altar of Victory, does not refer to Christianity by name.

168 VI.29; 'neque enim iustitiae et innocentiae deferri plurimum potest, cum illis reverentia religionis opponitur'. For the usual meaning of 'religio' in Symmachus, see above, pp. 81f with n. 125.

169 III.36; 'sunt leges, sunt tribunalia, sunt magistratus, quibus litigator utatur salva conscientia tua'.

170 III.33; 37, cf. *Saturnalia* I.7.1; VII.4.1f, etc., with Alan Cameron, *JRS*, 56 (1966), p. 34.

171 III.32.

172 *Conf.* VI.iii(3); 'secludentibus me ab eius aure atque ore catervis negotiosorum hominum, quorum infirmitatibus serviebat'.

173 J. A. McGeachy, *CP*, 44 (1949), p. 226 n. 26; producing, on what criteria is not clear, 54 pagans or probable pagans, 33 Christians or probable Christians, 47 indeterminate.

174 Viz. Ricomeres (III.54–69); Bauto (IV.15–16); and of course Stilicho (IV.1–14). For other generals, cf. III.70–3; 74–80 (Timasius and Promotus).

175 Respectively I.57 (Petronius Probus); VII.68 (Alypius, cf. above, n. 154); V.13 (Fl. Manlius Theodorus – the Christian Platonist known to Augustine).

176 V.90, 95 to Helpidius – presumed a pagan on the evidence of V.85 (referring to the festival of Minerva). The formulae 'praefato divinitatis favore', 'divinitatis honore praemisso', attached to general invitations to his son's praetorian games (VIII.71–2) might be thought deliberately non-committal.

177 VI.25.

178 IX.9 to Fl. Vincentius (cf. Sulpicius Severus, *Dial.* I.25.6; 'in domus tuae sacrarium tamquam mystagogus induco'). Cf. V.64 to Aemilius

Florus Paternus (above, n. 150); VII.45, to Hadrianus, as argued by
R. J. Bonney, *op. cit.* (n. 25) – and if so, a Christian; also IV.40; IX.64.

179 Above, p. 77.

180 III.81; 'sed quod ais exclusis inprobis spem bonis redditam', etc.

181 III.85; cf. V.34 (Hephaestion); 38 (Neoterius).

182 III.88; 'silentium meum . . . lepidissimo argumento momordisti', etc.

183 *Ibid.* (cont.); 'nam quid excogitari facetius potuit suppressi a me nuntii,
quam ut Caelii montis habitator adventiciis litteris Romae ⟨gesta *vel sim.*⟩
cognoscerem . . . utinam saepe epistulas ioco scribas, quas negas serio'.

184 I.56–61 (above, p. 78). For the circumstances of his burial, and the
recovery, *c.* 1450, of his epitaph (cf. *CIL* VI.1756) and sarcophagus,
see G. de Rossi, *ICUR* 2, pp. 229, 347–9.

185 See *PLRE*, Rufinus 18 (p. 778).

186 III.84; 'sequor te litteris', etc.

187 III.86.

188 Callinicus, *Vita S. Hypatii* 66 (ed. Teubner, 1895, p. 18; *Sources Chrétiennes* 177, pp. 98f).

189 *Lausiac History* 55 (ed. C. Butler, *Texts and Studies* VI (1904), p. 148).
See esp. E. D. Hunt, 'St Silvia of Aquitaine', *JTS*, n.s. 23 (1972),
pp. 351–73.

190 Zosimus V.8.2.

IV

The Two Worlds of Paulinus of Nola*

W. H. C. Frend

The last century of the Roman empire in the west has exercised a fascination on generations of historians since Gibbon. Why did the Roman provincial system that had brought vast areas, such as the Prefecture of the Gauls, under a single administration that held sway from Hadrian's Wall to the mountains of the Rif, give way to the divisive régimes of the Germanic kingdoms? From the effects of military defeat and economic and social ills, the search for factors that led to the western empire's collapse has returned to the psychological and personal, the failure of will among the potential governing class in the west to fulfil its traditional role in the empire's service. Gibbon's charge against 'Christianity and barbarism' as the villains of the piece has been heard again. [1]

The career and literary work of Paulinus of Nola might be put forward to justify this accusation. [2] Paulinus as much as any of his contemporaries may be said to reflect the change of mood which seems to have overtaken members of the western aristocracy in the last two decades of the fourth century, and his writings provide many clues why he opted out of Gallo-Roman society and a tradition of service to the Roman empire. His renunciation of a career as an imperial governor and his position as a wealthy, aristocratic and supremely talented literary figure, for the comparative seclusion of the shrine of St Felix near Nola caused a sensation and also some bitter recrimination. Ambrose, Bishop of Milan, wrote in 395, 'I have ascertained from reliable sources that Paulinus, whose rank in Aquitaine is second to none has sold both his properties and those of his wife . . . and has bidden farewell to home, country and kindred to serve God more zealously. And he is stated to have chosen a retreat in the city of Nola where he may pass his life in seclusion from the tumult of the world.'[3] But Ambrose also believed that there would be plenty of leading men who when they heard, would denounce Paulinus' act as a shameful deed. Both the action and the reaction were signs of the times.

Meropius Pontius Paulinus was born about A.D. 355 into a wealthy land-owning family in Aquitaine. Their estates also included land at Fundi in Campania near Nola, at Ebromagus in north-east Spain, and near Narbonne as well as near Bordeaux. These holdings were vast in extent and could be described as 'kingdoms' (regna) by his friend and fellow-aristocrat Ausonius.[4] Paulinus' father was a senator and he was trained as a lawyer so as to be able to take his place in the senior administration of the empire. It may be assumed that he studied rhetoric at the university of Bordeaux. There, owing to his father's influence, he met the poet Ausonius, who became his mentor. Having practised law for a short time, in 378 he was appointed consul suffectus the year before Ausonius himself attained the Consulate. Paulinus later attributed his success to Ausonius.[5] In 381 he moved from Rome to Campania where he had been appointed consularis (governor). In this relatively prosperous and peaceful province he had his foot firmly on the first rungs of the administrative ladder.

Paulinus, however, was a Christian, and so was Ausonius, though Ausonius had been born circa 310 before Constantine's victory at the Milvian Bridge. This raises some questions about the christianisation of western Gaul, for the life Paulinus was to reject was not paganism, but the same type of conventional and non-assertive Christianity that had driven Jerome from his native town of Stridon circa 373 to semi-solitude and asceticism on an island in the Adriatic.[6] Paulinus' education had been as rooted in the Scriptures as in the classics. One finds perhaps a trace of early influences in his prayer to 'the almighty creator of all things' for 'a contented mind not given over to base gain' to personal purity and rejection of 'lewd jokes'[7] and hope for a beloved wife and children and the tranquillity of the countryside.[8] To be moderate in food and dress and dear to friends and in good health filled his horizon. His object was a quiet life, but there was no hint of rejection of his obligations. Indeed his prayer was for the *patrias virtutes* of his station in life.[9] Ausonius too was a

Christian, punctilious in his observance of Easter celebrations at Bordeaux, if little else.[10]

How and when had formal observance of Christianity replaced formal observance of the cult of the Roman and Gaulish gods? The picture is not clear. Ausonius has left some celebrated character-sketches of his colleagues among the professors at Bordeaux.[11] There was Minervius the *rhetor* who came from Rome and Constantinople to teach at Bordeaux, a 'second Quintilian' Ausonius calls him, two thousand of whose pupils entered the senate.[12] Two others rose to provincial governorships like Ausonius himself. A wide variety of religious opinions were represented. Association with the Druids and the Romano-Gallic gods was regarded as a mark of distinction, and Ausonius' friends wrote verses in honour of Jupiter and the pantheon.[13]

Christianity, however, including the extreme asceticism of the Priscillianists from Spain, was gaining ground in the 370s. We hear of Euchrotia, the wife of a celebrated pagan lawyer, Delphidius, and her daughter who became Priscillianists and were executed under Magnus Maximus (383–388).[14] From the middle of the fourth century there had also been a noticeable movement towards Christianity among the people of south-western Gaul. Thus Hilary of Poitiers testifies (*c.* 356), 'Every day the believing people grow in numbers and multiply the profession of their faith. One abandons pagan superstitions and the vanity of idols. Everyone moves along the road to salvation.'[15] Allowing for exaggeration, it looks as though the 350s saw the trickle of converts grow into a stream. The usurper Magnentius would hardly have chosen the Christogram as the device for his coinage in his final fling of defiance to Constantius in Gaul in 352–353, had Christianity not had a large and influential following in the Gallic provinces.

At first Gallic Christianity was not an intolerant creed. Ausonius' appointment by Valentinian I as tutor to his son Gratian *circa* 365 reflects perhaps the open policy of that emperor, pro-Christian but not aggressively so. His officials in Britain even lent their aid in building the great temple to Nodens near Lydney in 364–67.[16] While he ruled (he died in 375) Christianity in the west tended towards the same slow absorption of pagan culture that characterised its progress in the east. Only the North African Donatists still maintained the traditional western rejection of any alliance between Church and empire. For the rest, Christianity in western Europe seemed destined to continue and build upon the religious and philosophical traditions of the past. Martin of Tours in his cell was far away from the mind of the writer of the *Moselle*.

During the next generation the picture changed dramatically. Ausonius' influence waned while that of Martin of Tours increased beyond belief. Indeed, in his old age Ausonius was to sense that his grandson Paulinus of Pella would be following the example of Martin. The goal of the ambitious young provincial was tending to become less a position in the public service than a bishopric or the monastic cell. Religious orthodoxy supplemented aristocratic connections as the road to a high career in the imperial service. Relics of saints would be regarded as equally effective defences against the barbarian invaders as military skill. Augustine of Hippo was one of the very few North Africans to make good at the imperial court. [17] Despite his provincial origins, and we may assume his provincial accent, in 384 he had become at the age of thirty the official spokesman at the court of Valentinian II and Justina at Milan. On his mother's arrival in Milan the choice before him had defined itself clearly as one between a great administrative career backed by an Italian wife and estates in north Italy, combined with a non-asssertive commitment to Christianity, or dedication to lifelong service of the Catholic Church in ascetic retreat in his native North Africa. Such were the real issues behind the famous conversion scene in the Milanese garden in August 386, and victory went to the call of religion. The empire was robbed of its most promising younger representatives, and for Augustine's circle of friends, the judge Alypius, the *agens in rebus* Evodius and the remainder, the same choice was made. In the reign of Theodosius 379–95, the claims of Church and State were beginning to look like two competing and contrasting alternatives.

In many respects Paulinus' course was to resemble that of his friend, Augustine, and like Augustine he was to persuade others to follow his example. There was Aper, also a lawyer and former provincial governor, Sanctus, Amandus and Desiderius among his correspondents. Others such as Victricius, Bishop of Rouen, and Sulpicius Severus, Martin of Tours' biographer, had already come to the same conclusion. [18] The Aquitanian clergy with whom

Paulinus corresponded were pietists like Bishop Delphinus and the presbyter Amandus, men to whom events in the outside world meant little. Even as the barbarians were sweeping across Gaul, Paulinus' correspondents were writing about the erection of new churches and monasteries and their aspirations towards the monastic life. Their escape from the realities of the world was complete. The change of outlook which was affecting the higher reaches of provincial society in the 380s was to spread even to the old Roman aristocrats in the next two decades. The will to resist the barbarians had been eroded years before Radagaisus and Alaric invaded Italy.[19]

The steps by which Paulinus abandoned his career as provincial governor and devoted himself to a dedicated religious life under the protection of St Felix of Nola may be followed closely. His was not the single crisis of Augustine's conversion. There seem to have been a series of small but cumulatively significant incidents that persuaded him ultimately to make a complete change in his life. Felix's shrine appears to have been located on or near part of Paulinus' family estates. He had visited it as a boy and been awestruck by the services in the saint's honour.[20] Felix himself was reputed to have been the son of a Syrian immigrant and to have been martyred probably during the Decian persecution of 250-1. The shrine had been set up by the Christians of Nola in remorse for the mistreatment the saint had suffered at the hands of their fellow-citizens during the persecution. When he was governor of Campania Paulinus had had the road from Nola to the shrine repaired and a new hospice built for pilgrims.[21] Perhaps at this period or on his return home he may have visited Ambrose at Milan and imbibed some of the enthusiasm the bishop felt for the ascetic way of life.[22] Only ten years before, Ambrose also had been a provincial governor.

Paulinus' return to Gaul may however have been connected less with religious convictions than with violent political changes which occurred in the summer of 383. At that time Magnus Maximus, the commander of the troops on Hadrian's Wall, made a successful bid for power. The Emperor Gratian was captured and murdered at Lyon on 25 August. The whole of the Prefecture of the Gauls fell to the usurper. In Italy the vacuum was filled by the arrival in Milan of Valentinian II and his mother Justina. Able diplomacy by Bishop Ambrose stayed Magnus

Maximus on the western approaches of Italy. It may be assumed that Paulinus' return to Gaul in 384 was connected with the political changes there as well as family affairs. [23] Ausonius as Gratian's tutor and ex-consul was suspect to Magnus Maximus and Paulinus was a close friend of Ausonius. On his return, he retired to his estates, and soon after married the Spanish heiress Therasia. The match extended his already wide holdings beyond the Pyrenees, and more important even, it brought him a relationship with the wealthy and pious Melania the Elder and through her to the doyen of Roman Christian families, the Anicii. [24]

Therasia too, was a resolute woman and a convinced Christian who from now on was to be the predominant influence in his life. For a year or two, however, Paulinus was content to manage his estates and maintain friendly contact with fellow-landowners. His earliest verses follow in the footsteps of Ausonius. He writes to his friend Gestidius partly in prose and partly in elegant verse thanking him for his gift of fish and oysters. In return, he sends him wildfowl and looks forward to their meeting. [25] There was nothing ascetic in the presents or exchange of good wishes. Nor, in the fragment of composition which Paulinus sent to Ausonius, can one detect anything more than half-hearted condemnation of Egyptian mysteries, 'wizards of vain mysteries', which Ausonius might have made himself – 'quique magos docuit mysteria vana Nechepsos et qui regnavit sine nomine moxque Sesostris' (*Carmen* III = Ausonius *Ep.* 23). He was developing into a narrative poet with a sense of the epic. His interest lay in Rome's remote past, and the pride he felt in her history was reflected in the long poem on the kings of Rome which he sent to Ausonius. The latter was enthusiastic. Paulinus had compressed three books of Suetonius into a single 'longe iucundissima poema', he wrote. In the fluency of his style and the natural cadences he produced in his lines Paulinus excelled all youthful Roman rivals. Paulinus too, was seized with a sense of the grandeur of the Latin language. [26] In a passage, preserved by Ausonius, where he dwells on Sallust's inclusion of Libya as an apanage of Europe, he had written that fame had blotted from her page the uncouth names of the Libyan kings which could not be perpetuated in Roman speech. [27] His master had every reason to be proud of his pupil.

Meantime, however, events were gradually drawing Paulinus

towards a more intense commitment to Christianity. First, he came into contact with Martin of Tours, then at the height of his fame. Shortly before, Martin had destroyed paganism in northern Gaul in a swift succession of missions and then in 384 had defied Magnus Maximus in an effort to save Priscillian from execution. Paulinus, afflicted by a disease of the eyes, met the great man at Vienne and was cured;[28] and there he also met Victricius, future Bishop of Rouen, who like Martin himself had renounced his military career for service in the Church.[29] His example was not lost on Paulinus. Soon after, perhaps in 388, occurred the first of two family tragedies that left an indelible mark on his memory. His brother was murdered. Years later, Paulinus still felt the weight of accusation on his conscience.[30] In all probability he was innocent, for he received the condolences of Delphinus, Bishop of Bordeaux, and his presbyter Amandus. Both remained his firm friends. Momentarily he was in serious danger. In his poured-out confidences to Felix he recalls how his lands and his life were threatened. The public assessor had already come to view his possessions prior to putting them up to auction.[31] The incident, together with the executions on the grounds of Priscillianism that struck the intellectuals in Bordeaux, highlights the insecurity that prevailed in Aquitania in the last years of Magnus Maximus' reign.

The effect of these tribulations was to deepen Paulinus' religion. The two earliest of his surviving letters, Letters 35 and 36, are addressed to Delphinus and Amandus at Bordeaux.[32] To Delphinus he writes briefly thanking him for his affection shown towards him after his brother's death and hoping his prayers would be answered. His real grief was not so much that his brother had died but at his spiritual indifference. He was 'more anxious about the anxieties he had to abandon here than of the cures he could look forward to in heaven'. Clearly Paulinus had already marked out his own future career as that of one dedicated to the Christian religion, and in his slightly longer and more intimate letter to Amandus he leaves no doubt of this. Paulinus asks the presbyter to 'be his brother in the Lord', i.e. prepare him for baptism, and in a letter containing no less than thirty-one Scriptural quotations hopes that he himself will not die untimely so that he must face the awful 'Lord our Judge' while still a Christian only in name. In this frame of mind he took the decisive step of baptism at the hands of Delphinus at Bordeaux in 389, and the same year left with his wife for Spain. Despite Magnus Maximus' overthrow he had no wish to resume his official career, and he bade farewell to Aquitaine where such deep tragedy had befallen him.

The group of six poems (*Carmina* IV–IX) which may reasonably be attributed to the next few years show Paulinus profoundly Christian in his outlook but still enamoured of the joys of country life and his home in the new setting of his wife's estates.[33] 'Adsit laeta domus epulisque adludat inemptis', he writes (*Carmen* IV, line 15). He came to enjoy and admire Spain with its combination of wild country, rich agriculture and fine cities,[34] valuable evidence for the continued prosperity of parts of the province on the eve of the barbarian invasions. His mind, however, was turned towards God. God was still addressed in somewhat Vergilian terms in *Carmen* IV as 'omnipotens genitor rerum, cui summa potestas' (compare *Aeneid* X, line 100, 'pater omnipotens rerum cui summa potestas'), and in the neutral Constantinian invocation, 'summus pater' (*Carmen* VI), but familiar classical lines were being imperceptibly transformed to carry new Christian meanings. Thus in *Carmen* VII Paulinus uses the theme of Horace's second epode, that rural life is to be preferred to soldiering, trade or a public career, to express his own distaste for public life. The iambics,

> Beatus ille qui procul vitam suam
> ab inpiorum segregarit coetibus
> et in via peccantium non manserit
> nec in cathedra pestilenti sederit
> sed corde toto fixus in legem dei
> praecepta vitae nocte voluit et die
> mentemque castis institutis excolit
> (*Carmina* VII, 1–6)

(Happy is he who has separated his life far from the crowds of the ungodly and has remained not in the way of the sinners nor has sat in the seat of pestilence, but having fixed his whole mind on the law of God and desiring (to keep) His commands each night and day of his life, ennobles his mind with chaste injunctions.')

may be paralleled by Horace's second epode

Beatus ille qui procul negotiis,
ut prisca gens mortalium
paterna rura bobus exercet suis
solutus omni faenore

(Happy is he who, far from business cares, like the ancient
race of mortals, works his ancestral acres with his steers,
from all money-lending free.)

Already, however, Paulinus was contrasting the lot of any of
those who relied on worldly success with those who fixed their
hopes on God alone. The impious would not rise to glory. They
would be judged and consumed in the flames. The poem ends
significantly,

Vias bonorum laetus agnoscit deus
at inpiorum pronum iter delebitur.

(A joyful God acknowledges the ways of the just but the
downward path of the impious will be destroyed.)

Therasia did not have to drag her husband from pagan altars,
but Ausonius may have been right in suspecting that 'Tanaquil'
as he calls her had influenced her husband's withdrawal from his
old love of the classics and from Ausonius himself. Between
390 and 394 contact between the old tutor and pupil slackened
and then lapsed. Maybe part of the fault was simply communications, for though Ausonius wrote four letters at least to Paulinus
in these years, Paulinus points out that four summers had passed
since he heard from him, when at last three letters arrived at the
same time.[35] Ausonius had written movingly, seeking to persuade
Paulinus to return to Bordeaux. 'What more shall I not righteously
call down on thee, O land of Spain! May Carthaginians ravage
thee . . . Here dost thou, Paulinus, establish thy robe consular
and Roman chair and wilt thou bury thy native honours?'[36]
Gradually, however, the truth was dawning on the old man.
'We are shaking off a yoke, Paulinus, which its tried equableness
once made easy . . . which mild Concord used to guide with even
reins.'[37] It was Therasia who was responsible for this change.
'Let thy Tanaquil know nought of this',[38] he urges, 'Let Paulinus
baffle his inquisitor, and let him abandon his solitude and the

gloomy delusions of a Bellerophon, and return to the "men of
Roman name"[39] and the world of Latin literature that he had left
behind at Bordeaux.'

It was the summer of 394 before Paulinus replied in two letters.
By this time he had had his fill of the classics and the death of his
infant son had thrown him into despair. In 393 he had reopened
correspondence with Delphinus and Amandus after four years,[40]
telling them of his desire to devote himself to Christ. 'I am planted
in Christ and am Christ's dark toil', he tells Amandus.[41] Thus he
was in no mood to heed Ausonius. In the first letter, he defends
himself against the reproach that he had shaken off the yoke that
had bound him to Ausonius in the common pursuit of letters.[42]
That was never the case. He could not match Ausonius' graceful
verses. He was unworthy of his master's praise. 'If thou dost
match calves with bulls or horses with wild asses . . .' he writes.
He would always be yoked in love to his old friend, but it would
be a love between souls, 'linked together in worship of Christ'.
In the emphatically Christian view of friendship Paulinus was
reflecting the difference between his generation and that of Ausonius. The second letter finds Paulinus in a more sombre mood.
Ausonius' three letters contained 'things sweet though somewhat
soured by manifold complaints', and these hurt him. None the
less he would write first in light iambics to repay his master his
debt of words, but the more serious reproaches made against
Therasia and himself must be answered in the 'sterner metre of
hexameters', the 'avenging heroic metre'.

> Ista suo regerenda loco tamen et graviore
> vindicis heroi sunt agitanda sono.

Then to quote:

> Why dost thou bid the deposed Muses return to my affection,
> father? Hearts consecrated to Christ give refusal to the
> Camenae, are closed to Apollo. Once there was accord
> betwixt me and thee, equals in zeal but not in power – to
> call forth deaf Apollo from his Delphic cave, to invoke the
> Muses as divine, to seek from groves or hills the gift of
> utterance by the god's gift bestowed. Now 'tis another
> force that rules my heart, a greater God that demands

another mode of life, claiming for himself from man the
gift he gave, that we may live for the Father of life.

> (*Carmen* X = Ausonius *Ep.* 31, lines 20–32,
>   tr. H. G. Evelyn White)

The new life demanded renunciation of empty business and
pleasure, and idle tales of literature

> vacare vanis otio aut negotio
> et fabulosis litteris . . .
>   (lines 33–4)

The alliteration and play on words conceals Paulinus' resolve.
It was God's will that he abandon the tradition in which he had
grown up. In terms which he was to use more than once in his
letters from Nola, he stressed the utter incompatibility of ordinary
service to the world and obedience to the commands of Christ.

> . . . de vanis liberat curis
> otia amant strepitumque fori rerumque tumultus
> cunctaque divi inimica negotia donis
> et Christi imperiis et amore salutis abhorrent . . .
>   (lines 165–8)

(They love repose void of empty cares and shun the din of
public life, the bustle of affairs, and all concerns hostile to
the gifts of Heaven, both by Christ's command and in the
desire for salvation.)

>   (tr. H. G. Evelyn White).

Let Ausonius blame the Creator if he did not like these commands.
Paulinus repudiated the charge that he wished to live as a solitary
in desert places. His was not the disturbed mind of a Bellerophon.[43] Therasia was no Tanaquil, but a chaste Lucretia,[44]
and there was more to Spain than craggy heights and ruined
cities. It had its Saragossa, its pleasant Barcelona and Tarragona
looking down from majestic heights to the sea.[45] To live for
Christ was not perversion but delight, and indeed the only way
to avoid the certainty of 'the severe wrath of the heavenly
Judge'.[46] 'If thou dost approve', he ends, 'rejoice in thy friend's
rich hope; if otherwise, leave me to be approved by Christ.'[47]
Together, the two letters bade a solemn farewell to his old

tutor and to the outlook that he represented. It was to be many generations before the Classical world and Christianity would come to terms again in the west.

Rejection apart, we may perceive two main aspects of Paulinus' intellectual evolution which affected his religion. First, the nostalgia for a primitive rural golden age, derived originally from Vergil's *Georgics* and Horace is heightened and provided with a Biblical background by reference to the first chapters of Genesis and the life of John the Baptist. Second, Paulinus was becoming ever more influenced by the sense of approaching Judgment. In *Carmen* VI written as a Panegyric of John the Baptist one finds both elements and also examples of how Paulinus was converting Biblical texts into Latin hexameters. Thus, 'Behold I shall send my messenger before thy face' (Isaiah 40: 3–4) becomes

Mittam, ait, ante tuos oculos, o nate, ministrum
(line 309)

Primitive nature corresponded to God's handiwork and was good. The superstructure added by man was the cause of evil. The values of the pagan world were thus turned upside down.[48] John, Paulinus urged, had forsaken the wretched crowds of milling individuals for the wilderness. His garments of camel hair protested against the luxury of the world. His innocence cried out at the intrigues of the secular age. And, perhaps in a flash of anguished memory of his sufferings in Aquitaine, Paulinus expatiated on human violence and strife that merited God's eternal condemnation.

Hinc odia, hinc lites, hinc fraus, hinc livor et irae,
Caedes, arma, cruor, conflictus proelia mortes
Hinc offensa dei quam tartara saeva piabunt
(lines 244–6)

(Hence hatreds, hence lawsuits, hence fraud, hence envy and hatred, murder, arms, blood, strife, battle and death. Hence the offence against God which they will expiate in savage hell.)

Judgment, indeed, was vividly impressed on his mind. He feared that his soul would be 'shackled with paltry cares for the body', he told Ausonius, 'and weighted with a load of business, if perchance the awful trump should peal from the opened heaven, it should fail to raise itself' to meet the Lord.[49] This was another feature which divided Paulinus and his age from that of Ausonius. Judgment was beginning to play the same overwhelming part in western European religious thought that it had always played hitherto in North African Christianity. The onset of the barbarians seemed to believers such as Paulinus more of an irrevocable sign of the approaching end than a military challenge to be overcome. The fall of empires was in the nature of Providence, but to save one's soul was the duty of every individual.

At some stage Paulinus had made contact with Jerome far away in Palestine. In 393/4 he had received from him the latter's works *Against Jovinian* with their exuberant defence of asceticism as the sole means of approach to God.[50] Now he determined to sell his estates and those of Therasia. This must have become public knowledge in Barcelona. The estates of a newly ordained presbyter were supposed to pass to the church in which he was ordained. At Christmas 394 Paulinus found himself forcibly ordained 'through the sudden compulsion, of the crowd'.[51] As at Thagaste in 411, when Pinianus, reputedly the richest man in the west, took up residence and Alypius schemed for his ordination, Barcelona believed itself on the brink of a massive windfall.[52]

Paulinus, however, was not to linger in Spain. For some months he hesitated. On the one hand, early in 395 he wrote the first of a series of thirteen *natalicia* or commemorative poems for the anniversary of Felix' martyrdom reputedly on 14 January (*Carmen* XII). At the same time he allowed himself a final, perhaps self-revealing panegyric[53] devoted to the Emperor Theodosius following his victory over the alliance of aristocratic Roman paganism and barbarian Arianism on the river Frigidus on 6 September 394. The work is lost. It praised, however, Theodosius' (orthodox?) legislation as a model for future ages. Jerome to whom he sent a copy was enthusiastic in his praise; the work reflected Ciceronian diction and often that master's sentiments, but he also told Paulinus he was 'only a beginner' in Christ's service.[54] If he continued, however, he foretold that he would outshine every hitherto Latin Christian writer, pungently criticising each from Tertullian to Hilary.[55] He urged him to progress in his reading of the Scriptures and turn his genius exclusively towards their understanding. 'I will not be satisfied with any mediocrity in you. I shall look for complete perfection'[56] – a life, that was, devoted to asceticism and scriptural study. Writing was to be in the medium of God's word, not Cicero's.

This may have given Paulinus the final impulse he needed. Previously, he had written to his friend Sulpicius Severus, himself an Aquitanian landowner who had fallen under the spell of Martin of Tours and become his biographer. Paulinus had sent, replete with Scriptural quotations, a long and fulsome letter (*Ep*. I). He praised him for abandoning secular affairs, and justified his own decision to do likewise, but finally invited him to spend Easter with him. It was after all only eight days' journey from his estates at Eauze (Elusione) near Narbonne to Paulinus' home. The Pyrenees were less formidable than their name.

Severus did not come. Not long after, Paulinus and Therasia sailed for Italy, making for Nola by slow stages. The trend of Paulinus' thought may be revealed from a later letter to Sulpicius (*Ep*. 5.4). Physical frailty had taken the edge off enjoyment of pleasures: secular life was full of troubles and trials. These taught him 'to hate what perturbed me and increased my practice of religion through my need for hope and fear of doubt. Finally, when I seemed to obtain rest from lying scandal and from wanderings, unbusied by public affairs and far from the din of the forum I enjoyed the leisure of country life and my religious duties.' These had made it possible for him to advance still further towards obedience to Christ's command. He had opted out. Augustine might have written the same from Cassiciacum. Arrived at Milan the couple were welcomed by Ambrose and Paulinus was invited to accept enrolment among Ambrose's clergy. He declined reluctantly. At Rome, however, his welcome from Pope Siricius was icy. The Pope and his clergy refused to see him. No satisfactory reason has been found to account for this. It has been suggested that Siricius feared that Paulinus might be a Priscillianist or that he just disliked aristocrats turned ascetics, or that Paulinus' association with Jerome prejudiced him. Perhaps a simpler explanation is that Paulinus had been a provincial governor and had been ordained presbyter. In the tradition-inspired minds of Siricius and even the more worldly-wise Innocent I (401–417) tenure of such an office could debar the holder from the priesthood, because it would normally involve him in bloodshed through his responsibility for ordering the punishment of criminals.[57] Paulinus makes the point of stating that during his office he shed no blood.[58] He found the rebuff he suffered at Rome mortifying. In the autumn of 395, the party at last reached Nola and there Paulinus was to spend the remaining thirty-six years of his life. Part of his remaining patrimony he devoted to building a magnificent new basilica in honour of Felix, which was dedicated in 403. Five years later Therasia died, and in 409 following the death of the Bishop of Nola, Paulinus was consecrated in his stead. The calm of his existence was ruffled briefly by the appearance of numbers of refugees from Rome fleeing from Alaric's forces as they pressed southwards after capturing Rome. He died in 431 without ever returning to Gaul, and he was buried in the church of Felix on which he had lavished so much of his energy and wealth.

For more than a quarter of a century, however, Paulinus maintained a thriving correspondence with like-minded Christians throughout the western world. He had friends and correspondents from the Channel coast of Gaul to Jerome's cell in Palestine. They included such opposites as Jerome and Rufinus, Augustine and Pelagius, Alypius and Julian of Eclanum. There were writers such as Sulpicius Severus, practical missionary bishops such as Victricius of Rouen and Nicetas of Remesiana in Illyricum, devout clergy such as Delphinus and Amandus of Bordeaux, pious laymen such as Aper and Amanda, Sanctus and Eucher and his relative Jovius, a man of letters and probably a pagan, the only link with his life at Bordeaux.[59] Between 395 and 415 Paulinus had placed himself in a unique position to influence Latin Christianity and Christian literature at a crucial period. It is unfortunate, perhaps, that he had so few ambitions in that direction. He was neither a speculative thinker nor a controversialist. He accepted orthodoxy as he had learnt it and criticised known heretics like Apollinaris with more vigour than understanding.[60] He failed, however, to think through his own position and draw conclusions from his religious experience. In the crisis of the Pelagian controversy in 416–18 he allowed his deference to Augustine to get the better of his judgment. The power of grace he acknowledged fully, but it had been 'assisting Grace'[61] (*adjutorio divinae gratiae*) and his life had been directed by the same search for perfection through personal endeavour that inspired Pelagius and his friends.[62] His also was the cult of the serious, and his aim, like that of Pelagius, was to avoid the penalties of Judgment due to failure to use his free-will aright. Though he accepted the fact of Original Sin he shared the Pelagian ideal of personal approach to God through imitation of Christ as revealed in Scripture, and he took a positive view of the virtues of the pagan ancestors of his friends. 'We see the seeds of light sparkling out of the darkness of unpious minds,'[63] he writes of the forebears of Melania the Elder. He alone had the prestige to uphold the position of his south Italian colleagues when confronted with the full force of Augustinianism in 416. Had he risen to the occasion, western Christendom might have been spared the final fateful injection of theological rigorism from North Africa.

Paulinus' genius, however, lay in personal relations. He was a superb liaison-officer, able to act as a clearing house for the exchange of opinions and books, and contact between personalities. He had a gift for friendship and an ability to enter into a sympathetic bond with like-minded people whom he had never seen.[64] Even Augustine admired his friendship with Pelagius.[65] Paulinus believed that personal relationships were predestined and in many respects Alypius and Augustine whom he never met became as much his friends as Severus and Delphinus whom he had known in Gaul.

Forty-five of Paulinus' letters survive from the period of his stay in Nola, all except one fall within the span 395–413 – the last letter in the series, No. 51 to Eucher, the future bishop of Lyon and Galla, may be as late as 421–3.[66] Little significance, however, may be attached to this apparent gap, as a great deal of Paulinus' correspondence has not survived. Most of the letters are written to his old friends in Gaul, no less than thirteen to Sulpicius Severus, to Delphinus five, Amandus six, Sanctus two, Jovius one, and Victricius of Rouen two. Significantly perhaps, those to Severus are the only group which are not signed jointly by Paulinus and Therasia. Was there perhaps some deep jealousy that prevented Therasia even associating herself with any reminder of Paulinus' earlier years in Aquitaine?

Severus held a special place in Paulinus' affections. Like him he had been a lawyer, and from the leisured existence on his estates with his aristocratic wife had turned towards a religious life.[67] The correspondence extends over ten years (395–404) and some of Paulinus' letters are lengthy documents, a type of composition that one finds in other western Christian authors of the day such as Augustine and Jerome. As we have seen, before he left Barcelona, Paulinus had invited Severus to stay with him and compared his conversion to the ascetic practice of Christianity with the similar experience of his friend. By the summer of 396 Paulinus wrote again, another long and intimate letter (*Ep.* 5). This time he invited him to visit Nola. There is much mutual congratulation that each had found a similar service to Christ. Paulinus wondered indeed if the coincidence of recent illness does not prove the completeness of their mutual harmony. Finally, there is an interesting and revealing account of Paulinus' reception at Rome the previous year (*Ep.* 5.14), and the writer does not hesitate to call the Roman clergy envious and hate-inspired. Fortunately, their influence did not extend to the clergy in Campania nor to Africa whose bishops had sent two couriers to him since his arrival at Nola.

This letter is typical of much that Paulinus wrote to his more intimate friends. It is wordy, introspective and moralising, but also sincere and in its way moving. Paulinus does not hide his feelings. It contains also considerable information about the life and thought of western Christian intellectuals at the time. Incidentally, these letters to Gaul reveal something of the silent religious revolution which was taking place there and of which Paulinus himself was a prime example. The Christianisation of the rural areas was evidently proceeding apace. In another letter to Severus written *circa* 402 (*Ep.* 32) he congratulates his friend on building two basilicas and a baptistery in the village of Primulaicum (Premillac in Perigord) where he owned an estate. He elaborated on the symbolism of the twin-roofed basilicas representing the Church with its two Testaments[68] and enquired after the relics of the saints and the fragment of the Cross brought back by Melania from Jerusalem, and which he had sent.[69] In a spirit of competitive holiness Paulinus went on to describe the basilica he was building in honour of Felix at Nola, a vast building which he described to the last detail of the choice of inscriptions to be painted on the walls for purposes of meditation, an unconscious but priceless aid towards understanding the features of early fifth-century Christian architecture.[70] Elsewhere one may detect the quickening interest in the monastic vocation among the one-time leaders of Gallic society. Aper and Amanda his wife followed Paulinus' example, shrugged off the cares of high office and accepted the ideal of religious poverty.[71] For Paulinus the 'bustle of the churches' was almost as worldly as the crowds in the forum.[72] Devotion to religion implied also a solitary's existence. In the final letter in the collection, to Eucher and Galla, he praised his correspondents' decision to betake themselves to a monastic settlement on the islands of Lerinus off Marseille which was being organised by the presbyter Honoratus. He goes on to name three other young men who intend to follow suit. This was the means of perfection and of avoiding the penalties reserved at Judgment for the unrighteous.

Paulinus also shows considerable interest in missions to the heathen. His letter to Victricius of Rouen (*Ep.* 18) demonstrates, however, more than simple enthusiasm for their conversion. He associated Christianisation with pacification. In this he found himself at one with Ambrose of Milan for Ambrose had written to Queen Fritigil of the Alemanni asking her to use the influence of her Christianity to persuade her husband to live in peace with the Romans.[73] Paulinus praised Victricius for having rendered the Channel coast safe by spreading Christianity among the still unconverted Nervii,[74] and similarly the Morini, more picturesquely than accurately described as dwelling 'at the edge of the world battered by a deafening ocean', had also abandoned their barbarous ways. Again, in a poem addressed to Nicetas of Remesiana he praised the latter for having preached successfully to the barbarous Bessi who dwelt round Nish. Now these men 'harsher than their winter snow were led as sheep into the hall of peace'.[75] Barbarism and aggression against the Roman empire were to be cured by acceptance of the Christian faith, a missionary strategy that came too late.

Paulinus' letters to his Gallic friends throw light on his ultimate thoughts and attitudes. The more public aspect of his life at Nola is illustrated by the correspondence he maintained with members of the Roman nobility, such as the senator Pammachius and the African episcopate, and notably Augustine. Thanks very largely to the researches of P. R. L. Brown it is becoming evident that Paulinus' relationship (through marriage ?) with Melania influenced his friendships and activities.[76] It drew him away, for instance, from the powerful patronage of Jerome and though, so far as we may judge, Paulinus took no part in the Origenist rumpus, it placed him alongside Rufinus and the most powerful of the senatorial Christian families, the Anicii.[77] This in turn drew Pelagius into his circle. Pelagius, Brown believes, may have come to know the contents of Augustine's *Confessions* from Paulinus,[78] and Paulinus' library may have been where Julian of Eclanum studied Augustine's anti-Manichaean works in preparation for launching the great controversy that occupied the last fifteen years of Augustine's life.[79] Certainly Pelagius and Paulinus were on good terms and corresponded about the year 404, and his friendship with Julian of Eclanum and his family is well-known. Paulinus, however, revered Augustine. His were 'verba caelestia'.[80] If Alypius was 'his brother,' Augustine was 'his master'.[81] Pierre Courcelle has been able to trace an exchange of 36 letters between Paulinus and Augustine spread over the years 395–421[82] and of these Paulinus' surviving contribution consists of 4, 6, 45 and 50 from his collection of letters and 24, 25, 30, 94 and 121 from Augustine's correspondence. He had first heard of Augustine from Alypius, who, impetuous as usual, had sought contact with Paulinus very soon after his arrival at Nola.[83] He had written asking him to borrow for him a copy of Eusebius of Caesarea's *Chronicle* translated by Jerome which he knew to be in the possession of Paulinus' relative Domnio in Rome, and eventually sent him the corpus of Augustine's anti-Manichaean works in exchange.[84] Paulinus was greatly impressed and opened a correspondence with Augustine which lasted for more than a quarter of a century. A friendship was established which was proof against differences of opinion and interest, and even the dire suspicion about 400 that Augustine might after all be a secret Manichee.[85]

This was an example of instant and lasting understanding; not surprisingly the question has been asked how far Paulinus influenced Augustine to write the *Confessions* and dictated, as it were, the form these took. The *Confessions* are unique in Latin literature. Augustine in 396–97, imagining himself on the verge of old age although he was only 42–3, wrote a stylised autobiography divided into periods representing the six ages of man,[86] in each of which he believed he saw God's guiding hand moving him towards the ultimate haven of rest in Him. It was a long prayer poured out by one who believed himself saved only by the overwhelming power of God's grace. Previous Christian autobiographies there had been: Perpetua's self-revealing account of her thoughts in prison awaiting martyrdom at Carthage in 203, Cyprian writing to his friend Donatus, *circa* 245, about his conversion, Gregory of Nazianze communing with himself in his *Poemata de Seipiso*, but none of these combines the prayer and sense of divine Grace that permeates the *Confessions*.[87] In Paulinus' early writings, however, one may detect the germ of a similar approach. Augustine retained Paulinus' letters and in the heat of the Pelagian controversy quotes an interesting passage back at him in order to show that he too had been conscious of the depth of his sin. Erubesco pingere quod sum: non audeo pingere quod non sum; odi quod sum sed non sum quod amo (I blush to depict what I am. I do not dare depict what I am not. I hate what I am but I am not what I love). The passage is almost Augustinian both in introspection and in its style.[88]

Paulinus' early poems also take the form of prayers addressed to God. He did not shun self-criticism. The long reply to Ausonius and the earlier letters to Sulpicius Severus already discussed are deeply self-revelatory, and he was interested, as he indicated to Alypius, in hearing of the spiritual experiences of the others.[89] In Alypius, too, he found someone who was ready to oblige but then despite Paulinus' pressure drew back.[90] Augustine's *De Utilitate Credendi* written *circa* 390 already contained autobiographical aspects, written to justify his one-time adherence to and his rejection of Manichaeism. Now, in 396 as his old friends left the monastic surroundings of Thagaste to take up duties as Catholic bishops in Numidia, Augustine felt the solitude. Paulinus' suggestion to Alypius caught his own mood.[91] Augustine told Paulinus he would set down how he too 'had been made separate' by God.[92]

Paulinus may be included therefore among the major influences that had led Augustine to write the *Confessions*. His remaining correspondence with his contemporaries is less significant. Prolix and rhetorical, replete with good spiritual advice, it is often more interesting for what it omits than what it says. References to the growing political and military crises that threatened Italy from Alaric and Radagaisus, and of the battles that were being fought in north and central Italy are absent. The religious vocation, prayer and the attitudes necessary for the soul's salvation, avoidance of sin, advice regarding temperance and humility, and above all attention to the text and interpretation of Scripture filled his pages. As Walsh points out, even when writing to political figures like Pammachius and the elder Melania's son, the senator Publicola, his words were directed to their souls and not to their activities in Rome.[93] Even so, the style is in the ornate late-classical tradition, and though no longer admitted, it continues to be modelled on the authors of the past. Paulinus revels in his account of Victricius' renunciation of his military career in favour of that of dedication to Christ, writing more like a hagiographer of the previous century as he described Victricius' defiance first of his commanding officer and then of the general himself.[94] Now, to transform Rouen 'into the appearance of Jerusalem' and convert it into a place of crowded churches (*Letter* 18.5) was comparably greater service than defence of the frontier in the Roman army.

On the other hand, Paulinus tells his readers a good deal about his life at Nola. It has been pointed out that this was austere rather than ascetic.[95] His library was well stocked. There were lively exchanges of books with Jerome and with his friends in Gaul. There were no exaggerated privations. Paulinus and his family fasted until 3 p.m., and then had a simple meal with wheaten bread, vegetables, wine served in vessels of pottery and boxwood, but the wine was a vintage product from his remaining estates near Narbonne.[96] He had brought servants with him. Some of these, such as Julianus who acted as his emissary to Alypius and the North African clergy (*Letter* 3), were quite important people capable of negotiating on behalf of their master. Another courier was the presbyter Vigilantius, who was entrusted with a message to Jerome at Bethlehem. He became disenchanted with asceticism and had sufficient independence of mind to accuse Jerome of Origenism and write a criticism of a whole range of what he considered useless and superstitious practices. He has been preserved for posterity in Jerome's vitriolic *Contra Vigilantium*, written *c.* 403.[97] Other servants named in the correspondence as couriers to and from Nola were humbler but equally colourful individuals. There was the monk, Victor, originally a disciple of Martin of Tours, who carried letters annually between Paulinus and Severus. He tried to put Paulinus on a more rigorous diet than wheaten bread and Paulinus describes the horrible concoctions he prepared and still more horrible smells that emanated from his kitchen.[98] Victor and Bishop Delphinus' servant Cardamas provide an element of comic relief in Paulinus' correspondence. Cardamas,[99] an actor turned exorcist who drank heavily and purported to terrify demons, foreshadows similar characters in mediaeval monastic life.

Solitude also was a relative term only. Nola was the centre of conferences and discussions. Paulinus craved company. He was anxious for his friends to visit him. On several occasions he pressed Severus to do so and similarly Nicetas of Remesiana twice stayed at Nola, in 398 and 402. In 404 occurred a notable family gathering of Melania the Elder and her relations under Paulinus' roof. Locally Paulinus was on excellent terms with the bishops of Campania including of course Memor and his son Julian of Eclanum. Every year too, the family journeyed to Rome partly on pilgrimage to the shrines of Peter and Paul but also on semi-diplomatic business involving visits to Christian senators and to the successive Popes, Anastasius I and Innocent I. Altogether his life at Nola bore little comparison with those of adherents to a monastic rule.

The heart, however, of Paulinus' existence was Felix's shrine. For nearly a decade (395–403) he devoted all his zeal and energy to constructing the great complex of buildings that replaced the original shrine.[100] Nothing, not even respect for poor people's property, was allowed to stand in the way. The saint's aid, usually invoked to counteract natural calamities, was called upon to bring down fire to consume a peasant's hut that stood in the way. The owner had declared himself readier to die than give in! The occupant of another was so harried that he destroyed his dwelling in disgust and moved away.[101] Felix was not an unmitigated blessing to the community. When it was complete, however, the memorial to the saint must have been an imposing sight. The new church had been built to join the east end of the original basilica erected over the tomb of Felix so that there was, as Paulinus pointed out, a view from one church into the other, in order that worshippers could also look upon the saint's tomb. There was a baptistery adjoining and in front extended a court in which fountains played, and a hospice for pilgrims and guests.[102] Not surprisingly the upkeep, especially the water supply, was more than the town of Nola was willing to undertake. Paulinus, however,

was proud of his handiwork and in 402 before it was completed
he was describing to Nicetas in a style reminiscent of Statius'
description of villas in the first century A.D. a walk through the
porticos to the church, mentioning on the way the useless vege-
table patch the fine building had replaced. [103] At heart, Paulinus had
little feeling for the hard grind of peasant life. Everything he did
had the stamp of the aristocrat born to have his way.

Poetry was always Paulinus' true medium of self-expression. [104]
Some of his letters, like those of Ausonius, break into verse, and as
we have seen, it was through alteration of metre that he expressed to
his master his change of mood and meaning. Elegiacs denoted
a lighter vein, hexameters were reserved for a more serious
message. There is far more classical allusion and far more imitation of the Classics in the poems than in the letters. After his
conversion he might assert that the Muses were closed to him
but he made ample use of the arts he had learnt from them. He
felt no impropriety about continuing to write poetry or of deriving pleasure from this, but the aim was now to fix the reader's
mind on Christ or on his saving mercy through his servant Felix.

Of thirty-three surviving poems, thirteen written between 395
and 407 commemorated the *natalicia* of Felix, and a few fragments
of others on the same theme have survived and are collected in
Carmen XXIX. In general these are long and rather tedious works
designed by Paulinus to be orated to the great concourse drawn
from all classes including numerous peasants who came to the
shrine each year on the occasion of the *natalicia*. There were good
classical precedents for this type of poem. Vergil put into Aeneas'
mouth the wish to observe the anniversary of his father's death
(*Aen.* V.49ff), and significantly Paulinus imitated this passage
(*Carmen* XXVII, lines 148–50). Ausonius also had written one
such commemorative poem. Paulinus, however, transformed completely this literary tradition to serve his purpose of honouring
Felix and of reaching the widest possible audience in language
most calculated to impress it. In North Africa, Augustine had
exploited the popular type of alphabetical poem to win maximum
propaganda effect at the outset of his campaign against the Donatists in 393. [105] Paulinus without a controversial motive wished to
leave his hearers no doubt as to the sanctity and power of Felix
and his own debt to him. Felix's miraculous career was described
in detail, how during the Decian persecution he found safety in a

ruin concealed behind a spider's web and then in a cistern between two houses where he was fed by an old woman for six
months.[106] In another poem, the theme was Felix's funeral, his
assumption into heaven and the building of his tomb. Declama-
tory addresses are frequent. In the two poems devoted mainly to
Felix's career, speeches are given to the ailing bishop of Nola,
Maximus,[107] and a rapid-fire question and answer between pur-
suers of Felix[108] and his well-wishers. The power of the saint is
brought home to the rustic audience by descriptions of his
recent miracles. A thief who tried to steal a cross is paralysed, lost
cattle are returned to a farmer and a pig makes its way to the shrine
after having been left behind by the herdsman because it was too
fat.[109] Paulinus tells even of a cow that had fled the sacrificial
altar returning of its own accord.[110] Behind the miracle stories
lies the fact of the conversion of the Campanian countryside by
the influence of the saint's shrine. Henceforth there would be
the intimate relationship between the rural population and the
cult of the saint. Old forms were not abandoned. Now, however,
the saint was on the side of the rural community. The 'public
enemy' could be depicted in vivid terms as the local big-wigs
at Nola who refused to sanction water-supply for the baptismal
cella. In the course of a few years, paganism had been conquered
for good. Felix was installed as patron saint and protector of
the whole area, sovereign alike against the power of the invading
Goths and the ordinary hazards of farming life.

At heart Paulinus would have liked to apply to himself the
advice he gave to his kinsman Jovius. 'Be a Peripatetic for God and
a Pythagorean as regards the world. Preach the true wisdom that
lies in Christ, and be silent finally towards what is vain.'[111] This
may be shown from poems which seem to follow the classical
traditon most faithfully. At a date between 401 and 404 Paulinus
blessed the marriage of the young Julian, son of Bishop Memor,
to Titia, daughter of Bishop Aemilius of Beneventum (*Carmen*
XXV). The occasion could have come straight out of *Barchester
Towers*. The first decade of the fifth century saw the emergence
of at least one clerical dynasty in south Italy allied to an aristocratic Christian household in Rome with Nola as the focus of
their religious life. Paulinus' *Epithalamium* written for the happy
events adopts the form but reverses the message of its classical
model. While his contemporary Claudian, in 398 writing the

Epithalamium of the most Christian emperor Honorius to Maria, could still depict the bride as 'not ceasing under her mother's guidance to unroll the writers of Rome and Greece',[112] and enjoin her to listen to the marital advice of Venus, Paulinus banished Venus, Cupid and Juno from the feast. They were replaced by *pax*, *pudor* and *pietas*.[113] There was no place for Claudian's 'rude crowd of Nereids' thronging around Venus, however tastefully described.[114] The true examples of marriage were Eve, Sarah, Rebecca and above all, the Virgin Mary; and while Claudian ends with the hope 'of a little Honorius born in the purple, to rest on his grandsire's [Stilicho's] lap',[115] Paulinus urges sexual abstinence on Julian and Titia, or if children did come then they should be dedicated to an ascetic life. The keynote was contained in the opening lines – 'Concordes animae casto sociantur amore Virgo puer Christi, Virgo puella dei'. Solemnity replaced joy, emotional intensity gave way to ascetic caution and the decorations and dancing in the city's streets gave way to celebrations more in keeping with a Christian occasion. Paulinus was following the teaching of Ambrose rather than Jerome. Marriage was not denigrated, but its object was the production only of Christians dedicated to God.

Paulinus' *Consolatio* (*Carmen* XXXI), written for Pneumatius and Fidelis who had lost their son, conformed to the same pattern. Paulinus cannot help reminding himself of his own loss years before, but the parents of the dead child are bidden to put away grief and to mourn instead the sin of man. The deceased is indeed praised, and the untimeliness of his death due to Invidia has a distinct pagan flavour, but Christian spirituality prevails. Paulinus depicts the resurrection in terms of Ezekiel's vision of the restoration of the dry bones (Ezekiel 37)[116] and of Christ's promises. At the Coming of Christ the parents would see their son again. While both poems show Paulinus drawing on Classical authors to add style and embellishment, his aim was to adapt their words exclusively to Christian ideas while rendering these acceptable to his educated readers.

The language of his other poems, such as the exhortations (*Protreptici*) addressed to Jovius (*Carmen* XXII) or the young Licentius, or the *Propemptikon* written on Nicetas of Remesiana's departure for Dacia in 400, contains the same mixture of Classical and Christian elements. In particular, Paulinus' poem to Jovius has the swing of one of Horace's letters and as one would expect in this context, the text is full of Classical allusions. All the same, Jovius is told to put away childish things. 'Non modo iudicium Paridis nec bella gigantum falsa canis. Fuerit puerili ludus.'[117] He should be writing of Creation not with the dreams of Epicurus as his source but of Moses and St John. In the *Propemptikon* also there are reminiscences of Horace, Propertius, Ovid, Tibullus and Statius which educated readers would recognise, but there is also the missionary motive of Nicetas' journey in Christ's service – to bring 'the faith that gleams before Christ to the remainder of humanity buried in error'.[118] Altogether, though in style, vocabulary and metre Paulinus imitates the classics, he was also borrowing from the new generation of Christian poets, such as Juvencus and Prudentius. Up to this moment, North Africa as in so many other aspects of western Christian civilisation had been the seed-bed of Christian poetry, and familiarity with its use had extended far down Christian society there. Tombs and churches were dedicated in verse by individual Christians and moral exhortations preserved for posterity in mosaics in verse. In making verse his normal vehicle of expression, even to the inscriptions on the walls of the basilica in honour of Felix, Paulinus pioneered the emergence of a Latin-Christian poetry outside Africa in what was to be the last creative age in the Western Empire.

In particular he influenced the development of a specifically Christian terminology through which the Scriptures could be naturalised into the former classical educational and literary traditions. In this he widened the foundations already laid down by the North African Christians.[119] He differentiated clearly between the use of words in a pagan and Christian context. The Christians were *fideles*. They worshipped in a *basilica, cella* or *aedes. Templum* is confined to a pagan temple. Curiously, *domus* for *domus Dei* common in North Africa in the sense of 'church' or 'chapel' does not appear to have been used. *Altaria* and *mensa* (the latter in common use in North Africa) are the terms for 'altar': the more traditional *ara* is neglected except for a Jewish altar. *Propheta* tends to displace *vates* in Paulinus' later works for 'prophet' and the Old Testament prophet's message is a *praedicatio*. The term *sacramentum*, beloved by Tertullian to describe the Christian's commitment to the exclusive service of Christ, was used by

Paulinus in the mediaeval sense for the sacraments of the Church, such as baptism and marriage or for the great occasions in the Church's year, such as Easter and Trinity. Pagans were still 'the nations' (*gentes*). *Paganus* used in North Africa for 'those outside the *militia Christi*' was not yet given its later popular meaning of 'pagan'.[120]

Paulinus' literary legacy may be traced through the North African poets of the Vandal period, Luxorius and Dracontius. North Africa, however, was destined to pass out of Latin Mediterranean civilisation, and it was to be many centuries before western European Christendom sought once more to harmonise Christianity with its classical heritage. Not until the last quarter of the eleventh century would something like a school of poets emerge who consciously drew their inspiration from the former greatness of Rome.[121] Paulinus gives no hint that he was aware that catastrophe overhung the western world in which he had grown up. South Italy is depicted in the same terms of peaceful prosperity as Gaul and Spain.[122] His conclusion that service to the Roman empire was incompatible with service to Christ had been influenced by a sense of futility resulting from his abundance of material wealth and power. His complaint was against the luxury and useless bustle of contemporary society. He was not in despair at its decline and fall. 'Let them enjoy their pleasures', he wrote to Severus while he was still at Barcelona in 395, 'their high offices and wealth, if indeed these are theirs. For they prefer to have those on earth where our life ends than in heaven where it abides.'[123] He shows that the contemporaries that he influenced such as Aper thought likewise.[124] His approach to life was purely individual. Like Augustine, his concern was with his inner self and how to save it from 'what is called the second death, nothing other than a life of punishment'.[125] He conceived this as requiring a complete abandonment of secular duties, and so far as possible the heritage of pagan Roman civilisation. There was no spark of the provincial patriotism that lights through the pages of Paulus Orosius. Like some antiquarian romantic, in his mind's eye he saw himself welcoming death at the hands, not of the barbarians but of persecuting authorities of a long past era.[126] In one letter to Severus he dwells on the wickedness of the Emperor Hadrian, believing that in building a temple of Jupiter over the spot where Helena found the True Cross he

aimed at destroying the Christian faith.[127] Radagaisus and Alaric
do not figure in his correspondence, though *Carmen XXI* written
in 400 rejoices in the defeat of the Goths thanks to the saints and
martyrs. When one compares his letters and poems with the
writings of Prudentius one appreciates the gulf that was opening
between the Christian in the west who believed that Rome purged
of aristocratic paganism might still be mistress of the world, and
those like Paulinus and Augustine who denied any such possibility.

For the historian who believes that human history is in part
directed by the wills of individual men and women, the collapse
of the Roman empire in the west resulted not only from military
disaster and economic and social tensions, but from the alienation
from public duty of a considerable number of the traditional
governing class. Alienation was due largely to theological attitudes, a fatal attempt to maintain the otherness of Christianity
in the changed situation following the Constantinian revolution.
What had once been a specifically North African interpretation
of Christianity, emphasising with fatalistic insistence the universal
penalty of Judgment except for those saved by Grace as the prime
result of the Fall, became the accepted doctrine of western
Christians, including the Roman aristocracy. It shared with more
material causes the undermining of the will to resist the Germanic
invaders in the west that resulted in the fall of the Roman empire.
Paulinus of Nola, Romano-Gallic aristocrat, Christian man of
letters, and seeker after perfection, fully represented the spirit
of his times.

Notes

* In this paper I have drawn on my article, 'Paulinus of Nola and the
last century of the Western empire', *JRS* 60 (1969), pp. 1–11. I have also
been encouraged by my colleague, Professor P. G. Walsh, and Dr
R. P. H. Green of St Andrews University to whose contributions on
Paulinus I am greatly indebted. I have used P. G. Walsh's translations
of Paulinus' *Letters*, published in *Ancient Christian Writers*, vols 35 and
36 (Westminster, Maryland, 1967).

1 E.g. by A. Momigliano in his essay in *Paganism and Christianity in the
Fourth Century* (Oxford, 1963), pp. 1–16.

2 The standard works on Paulinus remain Pierre Fabre's *Saint Paulin de
Nole et l'amitié chrétienne* (Bibliothèque des écoles françaises d'Athènes
et de Rome, fasc. 167, 1949) and *Essai sur la chronologie de l'œuvre de saint*

Paulin de Nole (Publication de la Faculté des Lettres de l'Université de Strasbourg, fasc. 109, Paris, 1948). See also Walsh, *op. cit.*; C. H. Coster, 'Paulinus of Nola', *Late Roman Studies* (Harvard, 1968), pp. 183–204, and R. P. H. Green's monograph, *The Poetry of Paulinus of Nola, a study of his Latinity* (Collection Latomus, vol. 120, Brussels, 1971). The text of Paulinus' *Epistulae* and *Carmina* are published by G. von Hartel in *CSEL* XXIX and XXX.

3 Ambrose, *Ep.* 58 ad Sabinum. For a full collection of *elogia* of Paulinus' decision to withdraw from the world, see Migne *PL*, LXI, col. 125ff.

4 Thus, Ausonius' description, *Ep.* 27, line 116 (ed. and Eng. tr. by H. G. Evelyn White). For Paulinus' estates and secular career, see A. H. M. Jones, J. R. Martindale and J. Morris, *PLRE* (Cambridge, 1971), pp. 681–2. That in addition, Paulinus had an estate near Narbonne, see Paulinus, *Ep.* 5.21.

5 Paulinus acknowledges his debt in *Carmen* X (ed. W. Hartel, *CSEL* XXX, Vienna, 1894), lines 93–6.

6 Jerome's view of a conformist provincial Christian society in north-east Italy is bitingly expressed in his *Ep.* 7.5. 'In mea patria rusticitatis vernacula deus venter est et de die vivitur. Sanctior est ille qui ditior est.'

7 Thus, *Carmen* IV, lines 8–12:

> Mens contenta suo nec turpi dedita lucro
> Vincat corporeas casto bene conscia lecto
> Inlecebras, turpesque iocos obscenaque dicta
> Oderit illa nocens et multum grata malignis
> Auribus effuso semper rea lingua veneno.

8 *Ibid.*, lines 15ff. Compare also *Carmen* XXIII.

9 *Carmen* V, lines 26–30.

10 Ausonius, *Ep.* 4, lines 9–10.

11 Ausonius, *Commemoratio Professorum Burdigalensium* (ed. H. G. Evelyn White). For Aquitaine in this period, see C. Jullian, *Histoire de la Gaule*, vol. VIII, pp. 130ff.

12 Ausonius, *Professores*, II, lines 9–12.

13 *Ibid.*, IV.

14 Sulpicius Severus, *Chronicon* II.48.3, For Ausonius' description of Delphidius and his family, *Professores* VI, 37–8.

15 Hilary, *Tractatus in Ps. 67.20* (PL IX col. 457).

16 For Lydney, see R. E. M. and M. V. Wheeler, *Lydney Park* (Reports of the Research Committee of the Society of Antiquaries of London, vol. 9, 1932), pp. 103–4.

17 For Augustine at Milan, see P. Courcelle. *Recherches sur les confessions de S. Augustin* (Paris, 1950), pp. 78–95 and *Les Confessions de S. Augustin dans la tradition littéraire* (Paris, 1963), ch. I, and P. R. L. Brown, *Augustine of Hippo* (London, 1967), pp. 79ff.

18 Paulinus, *Ep.* 38, 39 and 44 (to Aper), 40 (to Sanctus and Amandus), and 43 (to Desiderius). For Sulpicius Severus, see *Ep.* I and Victricius, *Ep.* 18. See P. G. Walsh's 'Paulinus of Nola and the conflict of ideologies in the fourth century', *Kyriakon (Festschrift Johannes Quasten)* P. Granfield and J. A. Jungmann (Münster, 1970), pp. 565–71.

19 An example of the fatalistic attitude of Christian bishops to these events
is provided by Maximus of Turin when he told the wretched city
councillors of Turin trying to prepare the defences of their city against
Radagaisus in 402 that they would be better employed preparing their
souls in readiness for the approaching Last Day (*Sermo*, 85.2, ed. A.
Mutzenbacher, p. 348).

20 *Carmen* XXI, lines 367ff.

21 *Ibid.*, lines 381ff.

22 Ambrose's description of Paulinus' 'conversion' (*Ep.* 58) suggests an
acquaintanceship but not a close one. To suggest a meeting during
Paulinus' stay in Italy seems reasonable. There is no evidence for a
later visit to Milan, about 387 (see N. K. Chadwick, *Poetry and Letters
in Early Christian Gaul* (London, 1955), p. 70).

23 He emphasises the latter in *Carmen* XXI, lines 397-8: 'te [Felix]
revocante soli quondam genitalis ad oram sollicitae matri sum
redditus'.

24 Melania was a Spaniard, like Therasia, and the connection with Paulinus
would seem more probably to come through her. Paulinus (*Ep.* 29.5) is
vague enough in claiming kinship: 'cuius (Melaniae) fides illi magis
quam noster sanguis propinquat'. Another clue is perhaps given in
Carmen XXI, lines 281ff, where Paulinus appears to associate the noble
family of Albina which was connected by marriage with Melania, and
Therasia. 'Prima chori Albina est cum pare Therasia; iungitur hoc
germana iugo,' Therasia it would seem had the closer connections with
the Christian Roman aristocracy than Paulinus.

25 Paulinus, *Carmen* I.

26 Ausonius, *Ep.* 23.

27 *Ibid.*

28 Paulinus, *Ep.* 18 to Victricius.

29 *Ibid.*, 18.7.

30 *Carmen* XXI. lines 416ff. Compare also, *Ep.* 5.4, with its reference to
the 'lying scandals' from which Paulinus was now finding rest.

31 *Carmen* XXI, lines 419-20.

32 For the early dating of these letters, see Fabre, *Essai sur la chronologie*,
pp. 66ff.

33 These poems contain no reference to Felix or to Paulinus' various
concerns when he was living at Nola. Paulinus was, however, adapting
the classical metre to the requirements of a devout Christianity. See
Fabre, *St Paulin de Nole*, p. 27, placing *Carmen* IV in the period 384-9.

34 As demonstrated in his defence of his life in Spain when he wrote his
reply to Ausonius, *Carmen* X, lines 199ff.

35 Paulinus, *Carmen* X, lines 1-5, = Ausonius, *Ep.* 31. Another factor that
undoubtedly affected Paulinus at this time was the death in infancy of
his son (*Carmen* XXXI, line 603: 'exoptata diu soboles').

36 Ausonius, *Ep.* 29, lines 54-61.

37 *Ep.* 27.

38 *Ep.* 28, line 31: 'Tanaquil tua nesciat istud'.

39 *Ep.* 27, line 60: 'Romana procul tibi nomina sunto'.

40 Paulinus, *Ep.* 9 and 10. Dating, see Fabre, *Essai sur la chronologie*, pp. 62ff.

41 *Ep.* 9.5.

42 *Carmen* XI = Ausonius, *Ep.* 30.

43 *Carmen* X, line 191.

44 *Ibid.*, line 192.

45 *Ibid.*, lines 202ff.

46 *Ibid.*, lines 330-1.

47 *Ibid.*, lines 285-6.

48 Thus Varro, *De re rustica* III.1.4, 'divina natura dedit agros, ars humana aedificavit urbes', and man had improved on the original divine handiwork.

49 Paulinus, *Carmen* X, lines 305ff.

50 Jerome to Paulinus, *Ep.* 58.6 (ed. I. Hilberg, *CSEL* liv, p. 535).

51 Paulinus, *Ep.* 1.17, and compare *Ep.* 2.2.

52 For the scenes at Thagaste, see Augustine *Ep.* 126 and 127.

53 This is suggested by Jerome's opinion (*Ep.* 58.8) of the work that 'cumque in primis partibus vincas alios, in paenultimis te ipsum superas'. There was clearly some evidence of inward strife whether Paulinus was willing to continue in the public service of even the most Christian emperor.

54 Jerome, *Ep.* 58.8: '[tu] qui talia habes rudimenta, qualis exercitatus miles eris'.

55 *Ibid.*, 58.10.

56 *Ibid.*, 58.11: 'Nihil in te mediocre contentus sum: totum summum, perfectum desidero', a very shrewd thrust touching Paulinus' vanity as a writer.

57 For the continued association in the minds of western Christians of public office with 'the world of the devil' and consequently debarring the holders from the priesthood, see Pope Innocent I, *Ep.* 2.2, to Victricius of Rouen and also *Ep.* 6.11 (*PL* XX, col. 500). Pope Siricius gave his view in *Ep.* 5.2: 'Item si quis post remissionem peccatorum cingulum militiae saecularis habuerit ad clerum admitti non decet'. Paulinus could, of course, claim that his period of office took place before his baptism. Compare, too, Lactantius, *Div. Inst.* VI.20.16.

58 Paulinus, *Carmen* XXI, lines 395-6:

> Ergo ubi bis terno dicionis fasce levatus
> Deposui nulla maculatam caede securim.

59 *Ep.* 17. Paulinus, however, seems to have known precisely what was happening in ecclesiastical Gaul, who was a newly appointed bishop and what were his views. See *Ep.* 48 (fragment).

60 *Ep.* 37.6.

61 Cited by Augustine in his long letter to Paulinus, *Ep.* 186.34.

62 For the essential spirit of Pelagianism in south Italy see Brown *op. cit.*, pp. 381ff.

63 Paulinus, *Carmen* XXI, lines 234-5.

64 Shown for instance by Paulinus in his letter to Alypius, *Ep.* 3. See Fabre, *St. Paulin de Nola*, pp. 138ff.

65 Augustine, *Ep.* 186.1 and 4.

66 His Letters 1, 9, 10, 35 and 36 were written before his departure to Spain, while Letter 34 is a sermon.

67 Severus had abandoned his career as a lawyer 'with a sudden urge to break the deadly bonds of flesh and blood' (Paulinus *Ep.* 5.5). The correspondence ends in 404 perhaps because of the growing insecurity of the countryside immediately preceding the great Germanic invasions of 405–6.

68 *Ep.* 32.5.

69 *Ibid.*, 32.8.

70 *Ibid.*, 32.10–23. On the basilicas see H. Belting, *Die Basilica der SS. Martiri im Cimitile* (Wiesbaden, 1961).

71 *Ep.* 39.

72 *Ep.* 38.10.

73 Paulinus the Deacon, *Vita Sancti Ambrosii* 36 (PL XIV, col. 42): 'In qua epistola [Ambrose] etiam admovuit ut suaderet viro Romanis pacem servare'.

74 Paulinus, *Ep.* 18.4.

75 *Ibid.*

76 *Carmen* XVII, lines 206–8, and compare lines 225–6:
> Mos ubi quondam fuerat ferarum
> Nunc ibi ritus viget angelorum.

77 P. R. L. Brown, 'The patrons of Pelagius', *JTS*, n.s. 21.1 (1970), pp. 56–72.

78 *Ibid.*, pp. 57–9.

79 *Ibid.*, p. 60.

80 Paulinus and Therasia to Romanianus, published among Augustine's correspondence as *Ep.* 32, at para. 2, 'verba caelestia Augustini'.

81 Paulinus, *Ep.* 8 to Alypius, line 83 (Hartel, p. 51).

82 Courcelle, *Les Confessions*, pp. 559–607.

83 Paulinus, *Ep.* 3.

84 *Ep.* 3.2, and compare Paulinus' letter to Alypius (=*Ep.* 24 in Augustine's correspondence). Alypius like nearly all westerners did not know Eusebius' work at first hand but attributed it to his namesake Eusebius 'of Constantinople' (i.e. of Nicomedia), as did Paulinus.

85 The incident which took place *circa* 399–400 is discussed by Courcelle, *Les Confessions*, p. 567.

86 On this important aspect of the *Confessions*, see L. F. Pizzolato, *Le Confessioni di sant' Agostino: da biografia a 'confessio'* (Milan, 1968).

87 See Brown, *op. cit.*, p. 159. These works would, however, seem to contribute only indirectly to the literary genre of the *Confessions*. The latter would appear to be the culmination of Augustine's ten-year crusade against the errors of Manichaeans and should perhaps be read in conjunction with *De Genesi contra Manichaeos*, both of which embody his own reprobation of his nine years with the sect.

88 Augustine, *Ep.* 186.40.

89 Paulinus, *Ep.* 3.4 to Alypius: 'Send me the whole account of your holy person.' Compare also the passage in another letter to Alypius, preserved in Augustine's correspondence as *Ep.* 24.4 (Goldbacher, p. 76).

90 Augustine to Paulinus, *Ep.* 27.5.
91 See Brown, *op. cit.*, p. 161-2.
92 Augustine, *Ep.* 27.5.
93 See Walsh, *Letters*, introduction, pp. 10ff.
94 Paulinus, *Ep.* 18.7.
95 Chadwick, *op. cit.*, p. 72.
96 *Ep.* 5.21. On the daily meal attended by Paulinus' household at Nola see *Ep.* 15.4 and 23.8, and the vegetarian diet observed, *Ep.* 19.4 and 23.5.
97 For Vigilantius see G. Bardy's article in *Dictionnaire de Théologie Catholique* XV, 2992, and Chadwick, *op. cit.* It may be reasonably assumed that the presbyter Vigilantius and Jerome's later opponent are the same person.
98 Paulinus, *Ep.* 23.7 and 9.
99 For Cardamas and his eccentricities, *Ep.* 14, 15 and 19.
100 The literary evidence is analysed by R. C. Goldschmidt, *Paulinus' churches at Nola* (Amsterdam, 1940), and the results of the excavations at Cimitile are analysed by H. Belting, *op. cit.*
101 *Carmen* XXVIII, lines 61ff. That peasants possessed no clear-cut property rights in Campania at this period is an interesting sidelight on prevailing social conditions in what has been generally thought to have been an impoverished province.
102 As described in *Ep.* 32.13ff.
103 *Carmen* XXVII, though no direct quotations from Statius are recognisable. Vergil *Aen.* V seems to be the most frequent source of Paulinus' inspiration here. See, however, Helm's article in Paulinus in Pauly-Wissowa *RE* 18.4, col. 2340, suggesting a reminiscence of Statius, *Silv.* I.3 and II.2.
104 For much of the information in this section I am indebted to R. P. H. Greene's book, especially ch. II. See also Helm, *op. cit.*, cols. 2336-44.
105 Augustine, *Psalmus contra partem Donati*, PL XLIII, cols 23-32.
106 Paulinus, *Carmen* XVI, lines 100 and 155-92.
107 *Carmen* XV, lines 309ff and 351ff.
108 *Carmen* XVI, lines 66ff, and compare lines 105ff for the exasperated ruminations of the pursuit party.
109 *Carmen* XIX, lines 378ff., and *Carmen* XX, lines 301ff.
110 *Carmen* XX, lines 388f.
111 *Ep.* 16.7.
112 Claudian, *Epithalamium*, lines 231-3.
113 Paulinus, *Carmen* XXV, lines 9-14. See also Helm, *op. cit.*, col. 2339, for Ovidian influence on this composition.
114 Claudian, *Epithalamium*, line 171.
115 *Ibid.*, lines 340-1.
116 Paulinus, *Carmen* XXXI, line 313.
117 *Carmen* XXII, lines 13-14.
118 *Carmen* XVII, lines 51-2.
119 For these, see A. A. T. Ehrhardt, 'Quaker-Latein', in *Existenz und Ordnung (Festschrift Erich Wolf)* (Frankfurt, 1962), pp. 167-71, and for

the Latin used in Christian communities as a jargon, see C. Mohrmann, *Augustinus Magister* (Paris, 1954), vol. I, pp. 111–16.

120 See, for these and other examples, Green, *op. cit.*, ch. IV.

121 See Colin Morris, *The Discovery of the Individual* (Church History Outlines 5, SPCK, 1972), pp. 51ff.

122 As showing Paulinus' description of the early spring breaking in on the countryside around Nola.

> Hinc vernat hiems, hinc undique nobis
> Spirat odoratos vegetabilis aura vapores;
> Hoc de corde venit benedicti spiritus agri
> > (*Carmen* XXVII, lines 164–6).

123 *Ep.* 1.7.

124 *Ep.* 38.

125 *Ep.* 40.11.

126 *Ep.* 1.8. 'I pray, brother, that we may be found worthy to be executed in the name of Christ.'

127 *Ep.* 31.3.

V

Claudian

Alan Cameron

In A.D. 395 Theodosius the Great[1] died, the last Roman emperor
to lead his troops into battle for two hundred years, and the last
to rule alone over an empire Augustus would have recognised
as his own. Another strong ruler might have arrested the process
of disintegration, but Theodosius left his realm to two feeble
sons: Arcadius, aged seventeen, and Honorius, aged ten, both
destined throughout their reigns to remain pawns in the hands
of unscrupulous ministers, incapable of exerting any influence on
the momentous events through which they lived.

A few months before his death, which took place in Italy
shortly after the suppression of the usurper Eugenius, Theodosius crowned his son Honorius emperor of the West. But in
order that he could himself return to the East (where trouble was
brewing), he appointed an informal regent for the child emperor,
the *magister militum* Stilicho.[2] In spite of a barbarian father, Stilicho had had the great good fortune to win for his wife Theodosius' (adoptive) daughter Serena. This marriage, together with his
appointment as generalissimo of all western forces, made Stilicho
the obvious choice, especially since his barbarian blood could be
expected to prevent him setting the child aside and usurping the
purple himself.

A regent for the ten-year-old Honorius was reasonable enough.
But the moment Theodosius was dead, Stilicho claimed that with
his dying breath the Emperor had appointed him regent of Arcadius as well. Arcadius' ministers at the eastern court in Constantinople, first Rufinus, then Eutropius and a succession of more
shadowy figures, were naturally reluctant to allow this barbarian
upstart to gain that ascendancy over the wretched Arcadius which
they themselves had hoped for, and vigorously opposed his every
attempt to return to Constantinople and establish his influence
there. Thereafter for the first time a sharp line of demarcation was

drawn between the two halves of the empire, and relations between the two courts rapidly deteriorated, never entirely to recover.

The story of the next fifteen years – a crucial period in western history – is largely the story of the intrigues of the two courts, intrigues that allowed Visigoths to devastate the Balkans with impunity, a band of renegade Ostrogoths to dictate terms to Arcadius, and finally, in 410, Alaric to sack Rome itself. Our knowledge of these events derives from writers who are biased, selective, and hopelessly unreliable. And if our knowledge of the *events* is sketchy, still less are we able to follow the motives behind them. 'It is impossible,' wrote H. St L. B. Moss,[3] 'to explain psychologically the actions of the chief Roman figures at this period: access has been forbidden to the courts of Ravenna and Constantinople, where . . . sat the two sons of Theodosius, . . . the centre of the multifarious intrigues of the palace.' Yet for the West at least this is not entirely true. If we can but learn how to read him, we have as a guide one who regularly attended Honorius and his entourage at Milan, entertaining them with a brilliant series of panegyrics, invectives, and epics over a period of four years. I refer, of course, to Claudian, a writer once as popular as any of the Silver Latin poets (Disraeli quoted him in the House of Commons as recently as 1852),[4] but now almost completely neglected, save for the occasional textual critic for whom subject matter is immaterial – and of course for the historian, for whom he is an indispensable and unique source.

Claudian was an Egyptian Greek, an adventurer who, like so many Egyptian poets of the age, left his native province to win fame and fortune with the aid of his sharp wits and ready pen. A contemporary, Eunapius of Sardis, writing of another Egyptian who was planning to earn his livelihood in Rome with his pen, observed that 'he seemed to be peculiarly suited to Rome, because he knew how to flatter and fawn on the great'.[5] If this was the minimum requirement, Claudian would certainly have passed muster. The Egyptians of the period seem to have specialised in the skills of which the works of Claudian are the only surviving example, for the sands of Egypt have turned up fragments of some half-dozen verse panegyrics of Roman generals of the fourth and fifth centuries. In fact, from the fourth to the sixth centuries we have a long procession of Egyptian poets, many of them (like Claudian) carried by their literary talents to high posts in the imperial administration.[6]

In January 395 Claudian recited in Rome what he later tells us was his first published poem in Latin, to celebrate the consulate of two members of the illustrious family of the Anicii. The poem is precisely what it purports to be. Although Theodosius was still alive at the time, holding court in nearby Milan, his recent victory over Eugenius is mentioned only to provide a context for further glorification of the Anicii. Nor as yet do we meet that widely misunderstood feature of Claudian's later poems, glorification of the Roman aristocracy as a whole. The consuls of the year and their famous forebears are the sole recipients of Claudian's eulogies.

It was a virtuoso performance, and it did not pass unnoticed. Later chroniclers record Claudian's début as one of *the* events of 395: 'hoc tempore Claudianus poeta innotuit' (at this time the poet Claudian rose to fame).[7] It was not unpredictable that twelve months later he would be at court delivering the customary panegyric on the third consulate of the Emperor Honorius.

In many respects this poem is much like its predecessor, a glittering example of what rhetoricians of the age called the basilikos logos. Yet at the same time it contains a good deal more than one might have expected to find in such a panegyric – and not merely because that colourless and insignificant emperor offered the panegyrist little direct scope. We find that Claudian has become the propagandist of Stilicho. Now since all Claudian's poems from now on to a greater or lesser extent praise Stilicho's virtues, military and civil, real and imaginary, expound his policies and answer his detractors, it is essential to make perfectly clear just what the relationship between Claudian and Stilicho was.

In the past scholars have tended to assume that Claudian's praises were dictated by a combination of simple servility and genuine conviction. It has been alleged that, like the Augustan poets, who at times prophesied victories over Britain, Parthia and even India (embarrassing, perhaps, to a *princeps* who had no such ambitions),[8] Claudian too sometimes overreached himself. In his poem on the consulship of Stilicho (400), for example, he devotes quite a bit of space to the regent's son Eucherius, stressing that he was the grandson of Theodosius and hinting at a royal marriage for him (there happened to be a spare princess at the time, Galla Placidia). It has been claimed that this must have embarrassed Stilicho, for we know from Orosius and Zosimus that Stilicho was believed to have intended to make Eucherius emperor of the East instead of the infant Theodosius II, and that Eucherius was allegedly a pagan who intended, when Emperor, to persecute Christians. Yet the very mention of Theodosius II dates these rumours to 408, when Arcadius died and Eucherius was twenty. Claudian wrote his poem when Eucherius was a child of eleven, long before such rumours came into being. In fact, there can be no serious doubt that here, as throughout his political poetry, Claudian was putting across Stilichonian policy of the hour. It was natural enough for Stilicho to prepare public opinion for the honours (however ill-judged – or in the event ill-fated) he was intending for his son.[9]

Let us now consider the panegyric on the third consulship of Honorius, the first poem in which Stilicho is mentioned. The scene is set in Milan. Theodosius, realising that he is dying, bids everyone leave the room, and carefully instructs Stilicho to look after his sons – emphasising particularly that Stilicho *alone* (that is to say, by implication none of the ambitious politicians of the eastern court) is to protect *both* sons (that is to say, not just Honorius). Claudian also stresses Stilicho's close personal relationship to that house of Theodosius. But, perhaps more significant than what Claudian says about the alleged regency itself is the way he introduces it. Historians who accept the double regency (most, that is) can scarcely have noticed Claudian's explicit statement that Theodosius and Stilicho were *alone* when this momentous decision was announced. Yet clearly it amounts to an admission that Stilicho's claim rested solely on his own report of Theodosius' last words (Claudian expressly states that Theodosius died the moment he had finished speaking). Is it really credible that Theodosius deliberately sent all possible witnesses (his son and successor Honorius included) from the room before making so startling and far-reaching an announcement? And the suspicious and increasing emphasis with which Claudian reiterates Stilicho's claim in poem after poem for the next five years strongly suggests that it was not universally accepted.

The credulous insist that Claudian cannot have hoped to get away with so monstrous a lie. But in our own day we have surely seen totalitarian régimes perpetrate successful (or tacitly tolerated) frauds of similar dimensions, and in any case 'lie' is too simple a term for Stilicho's claim. Everyone knew that Stilicho had been entrusted, at a time when Theodosius had no inkling that he himself was to die so soon, with an informal regency over Honorius. Nor need we doubt that, as he lay dying, Theodosius did in some sense entrust both sons to his daughter's husband. What he can hardly have either foreseen or approved is Stilicho's *interpretation* of such a request as an extension of his existing 'single' regency – hardly the truth, but not exactly a lie either. The claim as stated was the weaker in that there were no provisions in Roman constitutional law for the appointment of a regent to an emperor (whatever his age), and consequently no machinery for determining when the period of minority should end – especially since Arcadius, at seventeen, had already exceeded the age of minority in ordinary civil law. As for the 'eastern' regency, it remains only to add that (a) more sceptical than modern historians, Arcadius (who was most concerned) never accepted it, and (b) Stilicho himself never in fact behaved as though he had the legal right to act in Arcadius' name.

Thus Claudian's precise and circumstantial *yet false* account (especially the boldness with which he makes a virtue of necessity about the lack of witnesses) can only be satisfactorily explained on the hypothesis that he is consciously putting across an official Stilichonian version. But perhaps the best proof of Claudian's commitment to Stilicho is the consistency and coherence of the devices he employs to publicise and justify Stilicho's acts and aims throughout all his political poetry.[10] First and most obvious is his continual evocation of the alleged double regency. Next his repeated insistence on the essential unity of the two halves of the empire. The greater the hostility between the two courts, the better Claudian claims relations to be (he cannot admit that the unified empire was as much a myth as the regency through which Stilicho was supposed to be ruling it). When eventually forced to admit that Stilicho had enemies, he invariably represented them as demons of discord, whose sole object was to undermine this unity:

> geminam quid dividis aulam
> conarisque pios odiis committere fratres?
>
> (*Eutr.* I.281–2)

(Why do you divide the two courts, and seek to sow hatred between loving brothers?)

Whenever he can, Claudian stresses (even where it is demonstrably non-existent) the continuity of policy between Stilicho and Theodosius. The destruction of the African rebel Gildo is represented (quite falsely) as something Theodosius had been on the point of doing when he died. The marriage of Honorius to Stilicho's daughter Maria had been long since planned by Theodosius. Stilicho's (unpopular) enrolment of barbarians in his armies is carefully praised as a policy of Theodosius – truthfully, this time, but propaganda does not have to be false to be significant.

But perhaps the most instructive thing about Claudian's political poems is the way that at a different level his version can develop and change from year to year, sometimes even from week to week. As the political situation changed, so inevitably did Stilicho's policies – and, no less inevitably, Claudian's propaganda. Within the compass of this chapter his technique can best be illustrated in detail by a study of his treatment of just one incident, the war against Gildo (398),[11] a treacherous African chieftain appointed count of Africa by Theodosius in 386.

Now when war against Gildo broke out, Stilicho was in a particularly delicate situation. Soon after Theodosius' death, the prefect of the East, Rufinus, had been assassinated. Naturally enough Stilicho's name was heavily canvassed among possible suspects. But Eutropius, a cunning eunuch, succeeded to Rufinus as the power behind Arcadius' throne ('Rufini castratus prosilit heres', is Claudian's happy phrase), and opposed Stilicho's designs even more energetically than Rufinus – 'lording it over Arcadius as though he were an ox'.[12] When Stilicho failed to drive Alaric out of Greece in 397, Eutropius accused him of treachery and collusion with the enemy, and even went so far as to have him declared a public enemy in Arcadius' name. Then Eutropius intrigued with Gildo, and invited him to transfer his allegiance from Honorius to Arcadius – that is to say, to consider his province of Africa as belonging to the Eastern, instead of the Western, Empire. Both parties stood to gain by this. Gildo naturally preferred the nominal suzerainty of distant Constantinople to the tighter reign of nearby Rome, and Eutropius, by cutting off the corn supply on which Rome was completely dependent, hoped to destroy Stilicho's credit there, and impose his own terms on Honorius – terms which would naturally include the removal of Stilicho and, de facto, the extension of Eutropius' influence over Honorius. It was a clever plan, and could have succeeded. Stilicho was not without enemies in Milan, who were doubtless already urging Honorius to throw off the yoke of his overpowerful minister.

What was Stilicho to do? Declared a *hostis publicus* in the name of Arcadius, how could he lead an expedition in the name of Honorius against Gildo (who could legitimately claim to be a loyal subject of Arcadius), without causing an open breach between the two Emperors, and being obliged for ever to renounce his aim of uniting them both under his own influence? Yet swift action had to be taken if Stilicho was going to survive this crisis not merely with his authority intact, but his very life. By a remarkable stroke of fortune – perhaps Stilicho's only stroke of luck, except for acquiring Claudian – he was able to make use of the services of a disgruntled brother of Gildo named Mascezel. Mascezel had recently sought asylum in Milan to escape the clutches of Gildo, who had attempted to murder him and had in fact succeeded in murdering his two sons – a deed in comparison with which, so Claudian assures us, the crimes of the house of Atreus pale into insignificance. Mascezel went to Africa, and there was a battle of sorts, and treachery. The war was over more quickly than Stilicho could have dared hope. So quickly, indeed, that Eutropius had no time to consider whether or not he ought to support Gildo. So an open breach was prevented.

Stilicho had won. But he had not renounced his cherished design of establishing himself as protector of Arcadius, and was thus reluctant to antagonise further the still all-powerful Eutropius. So he entrusted to Claudian the difficult and delicate task of celebrating the victory over Gildo in such a way as to gloss over the intrigues of Eutropius and the highly embarrassing circumstance that Stilicho had been a declared public enemy throughout.

Not an easy task. In fact Claudian wrote two accounts. One in Book I of his epic *de bello Gildonico*, written in spring 398 immediately after the news of Gildo's defeat, the other a long section in Book I of his poem on Stilicho's consulship in January

400. There are major and significant differences of emphasis between the two versions, differences which should have made historians think twice about simply combining details from both into one composite picture before enquiring *why* Claudian chose to change his story two years after the event.

The opening words of the poem strike the keynote of Stilicho's policy: 'Concord has returned between the brothers' (*Concordia fratrum | plena redit*) – but without drawing attention to the fact that the concord had been broken in the first place in the name of one of the brothers, and restored without his aid and despite his hindrance. We are then told that the 'third tyrant' has fallen to Honorius, the only victory lacking to the arms of Theodosius. Now we must remember that Constantinople continued to recognise and support Gildo, so when Claudian bluntly dismisses him as a 'tyrant' (a word that at this period bears the specific meaning 'usurper'), and '*third* tyrant' at that, he is explicitly putting him on a par with Magnus Maximus and Eugenius, the two usurpers crushed by Theodosius in 388 and 394. By representing Gildo's defeat as the natural continuation and completion of Theodosius' suppression of ursurpers, Claudian is able to gloss over the delicacy of the situation and the dubious legality of Stilicho's action.

Next, a speech before Jupiter's throne on Olympus from the goddess Roma, a thin, emaciated figure, her helmet crooked and her spear rusty, vividly and forcefully recounting the hardships caused in Rome by Gildo's stoppage of the corn supply. Then Africa, similarly distraught, appears to add her complaints to those of Roma: by this device Claudian contrives to suggest that Gildo's actions did not represent the wishes of the people of Africa as a whole.

Jupiter reassures them, and sends two ghosts down to the world to set things straight: Theodosius, the lately deceased emperor, and his father Theodosius the elder, a general of Valentinian. Both descend picturesquely through the planetary spheres, Theodosius alighting in Constantinople to speak through a dream to Arcadius, his father in Milan to address Honorius. The selection and pairing of the four interlocutors was carefully thought out.

Twenty years earlier, the elder Theodosius had suppressed another African rebel, Gildo's brother Firmus. So the conqueror of Firmus was just the right person to tell his grandson Honorius that it was the destiny of the house of Theodosius (which of course included Arcadius too) to conquer the house of Gildo and Firmus. What Claudian carefully (and understandably) avoids drawing attention to is that on this occasion Gildo had fought for Theodosius against Firmus (whence his appointment as count of Africa). Similarly, the fact that Mascezel had fought for Firmus against the Romans is conveniently glossed over when his claims as an ally against Gildo are presented later in the poem! A more embarrassing detail which Claudian also 'forgets' is Gildo's marriage to a niece of Theodosius, linking him no less than Stilicho to the imperial house. None of them vital factors in the present situation – but better forgotten. By such devices of suppression and distortion Claudian presents a picture of Gildo's position and purpose which, if not directly mendacious, is misleading in every possible respect.

The speech of Theodosius the Emperor to Arcadius is no less a masterpiece of misrepresentation. Claudian could have attacked Eutropius directly, or at any rate reproached Arcadius for allowing himself to be talked into the affair by Eutropius. Instead, he pretends that all the initiative in the revolt had come from Gildo, who had undertaken to transfer Africa to Arcadius. Theodosius is merely made to chide Arcadius for being taken in by Gildo's specious promises (no mention of Eutropius). He warns that, since Gildo has been disloyal to both Theodosius himself and now Honorius, he will surely betray Arcadius too before long. The two brothers must pull together; united they will be irresistible.

The moment Theodosius has finished, Arcadius agrees. 'No kinsman is dearer to me than Stilicho. Let Gildo pay the penalty for his crimes, *redeat iam tutior Africa fratri*' (let Africa return, more secure now, to my brother).

Now there can be no question of Arcadius saying anything of the sort at the dramatic date of the poem, autumn 397. But by the time Claudian was writing, with Gildo defeated and Honorius' authority in Africa firmly re-established, he might well have wished that he had. Stilicho too was anxious that the whole unfortunate affair should be forgotten, and his propagandist skilfully prepared the way for reconciliation. If all blame for the revolt could be put on Gildo, then with Gildo gone no obstacle remained to the longed-for *concordia fratrum*. To admit that the eastern government had been responsible was to admit that, although the revolt was over, the *discordia* that had inspired it still existed. Had Eutropius been able to accept Stilicho's olive branch, then Claudian's listeners need never have known of the eastern involvement. One line in Theodosius' speech is particularly instructive in this respect:

> Sed tantum permitte cadat; nil poscimus ultra.
>
> (314)

(But grant that he fall; we ask no more.)

Now that the revolt is over, all Stilicho wants is for Arcadius to dissociate himself from it.

Mlle Demougeot was struck by the prominence accorded to Honorius in Claudian's account of the preparations for the expedition, and suggested that Honorius had already begun to resent Stilicho's domination, and manifested a certain independence on this occasion, which Claudian was obliged to represent.[13] Certainly Honorius appears nowhere else in Claudian's political poems in such an active role. The true explanation, however, is that Claudian is deliberately playing down Stilicho's role because of his compromised status as *hostis publicus* in the eyes of the eastern government. We find the same tactics in the *Epithalamium* recited only a matter of weeks earlier for the marriage between Honorius and Maria, a match which, in a desperate attempt to bolster up his position at court during the crisis, Stilicho had had to advance several years on his original plan (Honorius himself was still only 14, the bride even younger). Claudian, however, explains the suddenness of the marriage by a passion which the love-lorn Honorius, forgetful even of his hunting, could no longer contain. Stilicho is actually represented as trying to put off the happy day! There can be little doubt that this is why Stilicho is kept in the background in *Gild.*, praised only for his *consilium* (318) – significantly enough the very virtue singled out in the inscription to the statue erected to him in commemoration of the 'liberation' of Africa (contrast the martial qualities alleged on the inscription to the corresponding statue to Honorius).[14] What clearer proof could there be that Claudian was following (or formulating) official Stilichonian policy?

Gild. I takes the expedition no further than the storm which caused the imperial fleet to put in for Cagliari after leaving Pisa.

The sequel in which Claudian must originally have intended to describe the campaign itself was never published. Instead, by the end of the year we find Claudian launched on his two-part literary crucifixion of Eutropius, the cruellest (and most entertaining) invective that has come down to us from the ancient world. But he did in fact round off the story a year later in Book I of his panegyric on the consulship of Stilicho.

Much had changed between early summer 398 and January 400. The Gildonic crisis had been over for eighteen months, and Eutropius was now disgraced and dead. Things could be viewed in a different perspective now. Mascezel, who perforce was credited with the command of the expedition in *Gild.*, is not mentioned at all in *Stil.* Nor was there any need to pretend that the initiative came from Honorius; Stilicho was no longer *hostis publicus*, but consul. Hence if the victory is to be Stilicho's, not Mascezel's, it can be magnified instead of belittled. In *Gild.*, Gildo's troops are represented as cowardly, untrained and unarmed – the implication being that Mascezel's victory will be no great achievement, a mere formality, once Stilicho has advised Honorius to send the expedition. In *Stil.* we are treated to an impressive and fearsome list of Gildo's troops, concluding with a comparison of the swarthy Gildo himself to Memnon arriving at Troy, and to Porus leading his host of Indians against Alexander. Naturally, just as Memnon was laid low by Achilles and Porus by Alexander, so Gildo met his match in Stilicho. The reader is so carried away on the wings of Claudian's rhetoric that he almost forgets for the moment that Stilicho himself never left Italy! Very different was the picture in *Gild.* of Gildo staggering forth to battle half drunk at the head of his demoralised and debauched band of villains, decked out with garlands fresh from a carousal and wincing – a nice touch – at the raucous sound of the bugle. The victory, dismissed in *Gild.* as being won merely 'without a hitch' (*nullis victoria nodis / haesit*) and assigned to Honorius, is now extolled as greater than the defeats of Tigranes, Mithridates, Pyrrhus, Antiochus, Jugurtha, Perseus and Philip V; and all the glory is Stilicho's.

But the most significant difference of emphasis between the two poems is that the East is now blamed quite openly for the revolt. While Eutropius was still supreme, Claudian had suppressed his part in the affair in the hope of a *rapprochement*. But with Eutropius gone, all guilt could safely be fixed on him; he could be depicted as a second Rufinus, the only obstacle to the *concordia* which, with his removal, could blossom forth between the brothers once more. No need to pretend now that it was Gildo who made overtures to the East; he can reveal that

> coniuratus alebat
> insidiis Oriens; illinc edicta meabant
> corruptura duces
>
> (276f)

(The East nurtured war with treachery; thence came edicts to corrupt our generals.)

We learn of other dark intrigues, even of an attempted assassination (291f). Even here Claudian treads delicately; it has to be made perfectly clear that Arcadius himself has nothing to do with the wicked machinations of what is described as an 'iners atque impia turba / praetendens proprio nomen regale furori'.[15] At lines 295–6 Stilicho is praised

> responsa quod ardua semper
> Eois dederis, quae mox effecta probasti.
>
> (*Stil.* I.295–6)

(Because thou didst ever give haughty answer to the East – and later made that answer good.)

Now it may well be that Stilicho did give haughty replies to eastern ultimata about Gildo; but if so he was very careful not to publicise the fact at the time. Nothing was further from Claudian's mind when he wrote *Gild.* than to crow over the discomfiture of the East; on the contrary, the keynote of the poem was reconciliation with the East.

It could hardly be said that reconciliation was the theme of the two savage books *In Eutropium*. Yet even so, it is striking (and usually overlooked) that amid the seemingly indiscriminate abuse heaped on the luckless Eutropius, Claudian is careful never to suggest that he was a danger, much less a rival to Stilicho. Nothing but a brief and evasive allusion to his role in the Gildonic crisis:

Gildonis taceo magna cum laude receptam
perfidiam, et fretos Eoo robore Mauros
(*Eutr.* I.399–400)

(I say nothing of Gildo's treason, received with the highest
praise[*sc.* in the East], and Moors dependent on eastern power.)

One scholar has criticised the poem for 'proving very little'.[16] It
was never intended to 'prove' anything; rather to discredit the
eunuch in quite general terms. It was not till *after* his fall that
Claudian felt able to blame all Stilicho's recent embarrassing
dealings with the East on Eutropius.

It should now be a little clearer why we cannot hope to reach
the truth by *combining* details from different poems written at
different times; *contrasting* would be a more fruitful approach.
When Claudian says later what he did not say at the time, there will
usually be a good reason: too flagrantly false, too painfully true,
or just simply the requirements of the politics of the hour. We
will usually learn something about official attitudes at both times.

But Claudian is much more than a historical source of a particularly complex and illuminating nature. Steeped as he is
in the verse of Lucan, Statius and Juvenal, of whom he is the
only true pupil and heir in three centuries, he is also more than just
the 'last of the Roman poets', the title under which he is usually
squeezed onto the the last page of histories of Latin literature.
When a few scraps of Greek contemporary poetry of the late
Empire were dug up in Egypt early in the century, Wilamowitz
at once claimed them as the Greek originals of Claudian.[17] As
so often, the great man went too far. Claudian's poems are much
more than Latin versions of such pieces. Yet Wilamowitz none
the less saw a truth that has escaped subsequent researchers in
the field. Contemporary poetry of this sort is not found in
Latin before Claudian.

Most of Claudian's poems are panegyrics. Now in the West,
from Pliny onwards and above all in the fourth century, prose
was the rule for the formal panegyric (the corpus of the *Panegyrici
latini* has preserved eleven specimens written between 289 and
389). It is true, of course, that here as in the *Epithalamia* and
other occasional poems Claudian owes much to Statius,[18] yet

there was no continuous tradition that linked Claudian to Statius.

The other major genre represented in Claudian's œuvre (apart from the invective, which is a sort of inverted panegyric) is the epic (in fact *In Ruf.* II and *In Eutr.* II are both closer to epic than invective). Claudian may have been influenced here too by Statius (the lost *De bello Germanico*), but once more there was no living tradition of Latin historical epic in the intervening centuries (the 30-book *Antoniniad* ascribed to the elder Gordian is a fantasy of the *Historia Augusta*).[19]

It is to the lively fourth-century Greek tradition of both panegyric and historical epic (often not readily distinguishable)[20] that Claudian owes his immediate inspiration. He owes no less a debt to the Greek rhetoricians of the third and fourth centuries; it is unquestionably to the handbooks of Menander Rhetor rather than to the works of the Latin panegyrists that Claudian's panegyrics owe both their form and countless details of treatment.[21] And we have already seen that Claudian even used his poetry in the same way as his fellow-countrymen of the age. In fact everything about Claudian save only the language in which his surviving poems are written fits perfectly into place in the Greek literary scene of the fourth century. In Rome he is an isolated phenomenon.

Much the same is true of Claudian's remarkable contemporary Ammianus Marcellinus. Like Claudian a Greek, like Claudian, too, Ammianus revived an art unknown in Latin since the age of Juvenal. Though he is often known by the not unmerited title 'heir of Tacitus', once more there had been no continuing link between them. Ammianus too must have owed much more in the way of direct inspiration to the lively Greek tradition of large-scale historical writing (Dio, Herodian, Dexippus, Eunapius). Tacitus was his Latin model, just as Vergil and Lucan, Statius and Juvenal were Claudian's Latin models, but without the continuing Greek tradition, the Latin models alone could hardly have called forth powerful heirs in the Greek world.

But to acknowledge this Greek influence on Claudian is not to deny his debt to his Latin predecessors. This debt is indeed so overwhelming that for centuries no other was suspected. The task of the critic is to attempt a balanced assessment of the ways in which the two strands mingle, and the success with which the finished product, the style of Claudian, emerges.

In one respect Claudian's debt to the classical Latin poets was actually deeper than that of his contemporaries of western origin. The purity of his diction and prosody have often been held remarkable. So they are. But the reason is surely that the classical poets were quite literally his masters – those from whom he learned not just the secrets of their art but also the Latin language itself. In all probability he never spoke or read contemporary Latin before his arrival in Italy in 394.

Long lists of his 'borrowings' from the Latin poets have been compiled, though little serious attempt to examine the various ways in which Claudian used his predecessors was made before Ursula Keudel's 'Imitationskommentar' on the *de consulatu Stilichonis*.[22] Often of course he merely uses a phrase because it was the obvious and established 'poetic' way to say what he wanted to say. Latin poetic diction became so fossilised so early that it is hardly surprising that Claudian's diction is basically that of the Silver Age. There is however a smaller and more interesting category, where Claudian adapts a phrase or passage from Vergil or Statius or Juvenal in the expectation that the original will be called to the reader's mind. The intention will vary; sometimes to exploit the associations of the original, sometimes to impress by clever variation, sometimes by reversal, sometimes by parody. Two examples out of many must suffice.

Arcadius addresses the recently deceased Theodosius, who has appeared to him in a dream:

> *Unde* tuis optatus ades . . . quis tale removit
> praesidium terris? *ut te* mortalia pridem
> implorant longeque pium fortemque requirunt
>
> (*Gild.* 231f)

(Whence come you to your loved ones?. . . Who has robbed the world of such a champion? How long now has mankind prayed for your aid, missing your goodness and might.)

The verbal parallels are slight, but no one could fail to appreciate the evocation of Aeneas' words to Hector, recently dead and appearing to him in a dream:

> quae tantae tenuere morae? *quibus* Hector *ab oris*
> *expectate* venis? *ut te* post multa tuorum
> funera defessi aspicimus ...
>
> (*Aen.* II.282f)

(What delay has kept you so long? From which shores do you come, Hector, long expected? It is in weariness now, after the death of many of your kin, that we gaze upon you. ...)

Having once recognised the allusion the reader cannot but come to Claudian with the emotional associations of Hector's warning to Aeneas in his mind.

It was a 'tiny letter', Claudian claims, that brought about Eutropius' fall:

> concidit *exiguae* dementia [*sic.* Eutropii] vulnere *chartae*.[23]

(his folly collapsed at a blow from a mere scrap of paper.)

The letter in question can only be the (surviving) decree of Arcadius condemning Eutropius to exile. Seeck objected that this was a rather disrespectful way to refer to an imperial decree, normally styled 'sacred' in Claudian's day.[24] In my recent book I suggested in reply that Claudian meant 'merely that any letter was a small thing to have had such a result'.[25] I should have remembered how full the *In Eutropium* is of echoes and adaptations from Juvenal. Thus prepared, at a time when Juvenal was all the vogue in the fashionable circles of western society,[26] the contemporary reader would have thought of only one text when he came to an overpowerful favourite minister finally ruined by a letter from his emperor:

> '*verbosa et grandis epistula* venit
> a Capreis'   (Juvenal X.71-2)

(a long and wordy letter came from Capri.)

Claudian's letter is short simply because Tiberius' letter about Sejanus had been so notoriously long (cf. Dio, LVIII.8–9), a particularly neat 'imitation by reversal' – and (by comparison with Tiberius) an indirect compliment to Arcadius. This is a good illustration of the different levels at which allusive writing of this sort is meant to be appreciated.

Perhaps the most obvious and (to us) most distressing way in which Claudian recalls the poets of the Silver Age is in his taste for hyperbole and his continual straining for effect. There is nothing in Lucan and Statius he cannot match and more if he chooses. No compliment is too forced, no comparison too far-fetched for Stilicho or Honorius. The totally undistinguished teen-age consuls of 395 he thinks nothing of raising above the Decii and Metelli, the Scipiones and Camilli of old.

H. H. Huxley has interestingly traced through Latin epic the theme that death at the hand of a hero confers a sort of reflected glory. To the simple statement in *Aen*. X.829-30,

> hoc tamen infelix miseram solabere mortem:
> Aeneae magni dextra cadis

(In your wretchedness you have this consolation for your unlucky death: you fall to the sword of great Aeneas.)

Statius added the conceit that the man so slain should go down happy to the shades and boast of his glorious death (*Theb*. IX. 557f). Claudian must embellish even this. When Honorius goes hunting, [27]

> telis iacebunt sponte tuis ferae
> gaudensque sacris vulneribus leo
> admittet hastam morte superbior

(Beasts of their own accord will fall to your spears, and the lion, rejoicing in the sacred wounds you deal, will welcome your lance, still prouder in its death.)

The line of descent is clear.

Of course, it was not the Roman poets alone who delighted in hyperbole. A fantastic case a generation or so younger than Claudian from the Greek world is Nonnus, another Egyptian. The two poets have a lot in common. But Nonnus seems to have been influenced by Latin poets, certainly Ovid and in all probability Claudian too. [28] Whatever Claudian might have owed to his Greek predecessors and contemporaries, unquestionably the Latin tradition is the stronger influence here. And while there are many echoes of Vergil, and a brilliant pastiche of Lucretius in the opening section of the *In Rufinum*, it is above all on the poets of the Silver Age that he modelled his style. To Lucan in particular he owes his remorselessly polished hexameter line, improving further on such Lucanian affectations as the hephthemimeral caesura and the golden line. In the matter of elisions he goes far beyond any Latin predecessor: one in eighteen lines, as against one in six even in Lucan. No Latin-speaking writer ever penned a smoother line than Claudian.

One of the most remarkable features of Claudian's poetry, panegyrics, epics and invectives alike, is his extravagant use of personifications. Now on the available evidence, personifications are not a notable feature of Greek contemporary poetry – or even in Nonnus, for that matter. Here too the influence is all on the Latin side, above all Statius. Of course, personifications of every sort are common enough in earlier poets; there are many striking examples in Vergil and Ovid (the Megaera of *In Rufinum* owes much to the Allecto of the *Aeneid*). But there can be no doubt that Statius greatly expanded their role in the *Thebaid*, and that Claudian took up where Statius left off. It is in Statius that we first find personifications outshining the fast-fading Olympians, who themselves are sometimes little more than personifications. The Megaera and Tisiphone who put Pietas to flight in *Theb.* XI are less Furies proper than personifications of discord. It is the same in Claudian. The Mars who discusses with Bellona how best to chasten the eastern provinces in the *In Eutropium* is no longer the son of Jupiter. In the *concilium deorum* which opens *Gild.*, the long and fiery speeches of the distraught and elaborately described figures of Roma and Africa are rounded off with one perfunctory sentence from Jupiter, on whom not one word of description is wasted. Most of the other contemporary poems are similar. The Olympians proper play a very subordinate role. It is Justitia who persuades Theodorus to take the consulship for 399 in *Pan. Theod.*, and a badly overworked Roma who in poem after poem urges this or that course of action on Stilicho or Honorius.[29] In *Cons. Stil.* her sister provinces surround her, all pleading that Stilicho be given the year.

Scholars who have investigated Claudian's debt to Menander and his fellow professors have much exaggerated even the purely formal debt of his panegyrics to the Greek rhetorical tradition. The rhetorical pattern is there to be sure (though not followed quite so rigorously as unimaginatively compiled 'tables of sub-divisions' can imply), but the epic-dramatic framework Claudian gave to what Menander envisaged as primarily a speech gives an altogether different overall effect. Claudian's panegyrics are a new and hybrid form, children of the marriage between Greek rhetorical teaching and Silver Latin epic. Which element most impressed contemporaries is very easily demonstrated. Claudian's formula was an instant success, establishing itself overnight as the pattern for Latin panegyrics. Romas and Africas flit hither and thither throughout the depressing efforts of Merobaudes and Sidonius, spouting at inordinate and self-defeating length. But neither writer seems to have had any conception of the rhetorical pattern which underlay Claudian's dramatic form. The result is that they have lost the redeeming quality of shape and proportion that makes Claudian so readable.

If Claudian's panegyrics look back to the rhetoricians of the Empire, they also look forward to the allegory of the Middle Ages. One of the strangest and most beautiful scenes in Claudian is at the end of the second book of *Cons. Stil.*, where Sol visits the cave of Time:

> Far away, all unknown, beyond the range of mortal minds, scarce to be approached by the gods, is a cavern of immense age, hoary mother of the years, her vast breast at once the cradle and the tomb of time. A serpent surrounds this cave, engulfing everything with slow but all-devouring jaws; never cease the glint of his green scales. His mouth devours the back-bending tail as with silent movement he traces his own beginning. Before the entrance sits Nature, guardian of the threshold, of age immense yet ever lovely, around whom throng and flit spirits on every side. A venerable old man writes down immutable laws; he fixes the number of stars ...
>
> (*Stil.* II.424f)

Inside all the years are stacked in due order in varying metals. Not surprisingly it is from the gold pile that Phoebus picks one for Stilicho.

The other passage was much admired by eighteenth-century translators of Claudian,[30] and has inspired one modern critic to see him as the author of the *Pervigilium Veneris*.[31] Once more we are in a never-never land, where the frosts never whiten and the winds never beat: the garden of Venus, wherein flow two fountains, one sweet, the other bitter; where live the Amores, Licentia, Excubiae, Lacrimae, Audacia,

> incundique Metus et non secura Voluptas,

and 'wanton Youth with haughty neck shuts Age from the grove' (*Fesc.* 69f).

There is an important sense in which allegory of this sort is fairly superficial. There is little of the moral allegory that constitutes the essence of Prudentius' poetry, most obviously the stupefyingly predictable battles in the *Psychomachia*, between Luxuria and Sobrietas, Superbia and Mens Humilis, or (my personal favourite) Ira and Patientia (Patientia stands quietly waiting till Ira has lashed herself into such a fury that she takes her own life). The main purpose of both passages from Claudian quoted above is decoration – a purpose, let it be said straight away, that they fulfil superbly. But they do have an importance of their own none the less. As C. S. Lewis has so well put it:[32]

> the decline of the gods, from deity to hypostasis and from
> hypostasis to decoration, was not, for them nor for us, a
> history of sheer loss. For decoration may let romance in. The
> poet is free to invent, beyond the limits of the possible,
> regions of strangeness and beauty for their own sake. I do
> not mean, necessarily, that Claudian is a romantic. The
> question is not so much what these things meant to him as he
> wrote, but what they meant to later generations, and what
> they paved the way to. Under the pretext of allegory
> something else has slipped in, and something so important
> that the garden in the *Romance of the Rose* itself is only one of
> its temporary embodiments – something which, under many
> names, lurks at the back of most romantic poetry. I mean
> 'the other world' not of religion, but of imagination; the
> land of longing, the Earthly Paradise, the garden east of the
> sun and west of the moon. Just as the gods – and their
> homes – are fading into mere decoration, in the mythological
> poets of this age, we catch a glimpse of the new life and the
> new dwellings that poetry will find for them.

Failure to see that the old names and the old places in Claudian have undergone this subtle but decisive change, that the old bottles are filling up with new wine, has led to a vastly over-emphasised characterisation of Claudian as the 'last pagan poet of Rome'. 'Claudian writes' (I quote merely one out of a score of such verdicts), 'as if the old Roman state religion were in full bloom throughout the Empire'.[33] Yet what might at first sight appear to be the full panoply of Olympus (with many later additions, as we have seen) 'in full bloom' turns out on closer inspection to be little more than poetic decoration, an embellishment without which secular poetry of this sort would have been simply unthinkable, whether the poet was pagan, Christian or neither. The specifically pagan element in Claudian's poetry is very slight indeed, and such as there is can usually be paralleled in the work of secular Christian poets (notably Sidonius) anyway.[34]

It is a serious error to imagine that this 'pagan' imagery is a factor of real significance in either the making of Claudian's poetry or its appeal to contemporary audiences. But time and again Claudian has been claimed as a leading light in the 'pagan reaction' of the late fourth century, of which modern scholars have so much to say and the ancient sources so little. There is no evidence for any such connection, nor is it in the least probable. Claudian is not so much as mentioned in the extensive correspondence of that doyen of the pagan literary scene, Q. Aurelius Symmachus, nor is it at all likely that he frequented aristocratic society in Rome, pagan or Christian. For he spent almost all his western sojourn at court in largely Christian Milan. Furthermore, of all the many notables addressed in Claudian's poems, major and minor alike, not one is known to have been a pagan, whereas many are known to have been Christians. Honorius and Stilicho's wife Serena were notorious for their Christian piety. Serena, particularly odious to pagans for profaning the temple of the Great Mother in Rome, Claudian goes out of his way to praise for her devotion to prayer (*Laus Ser.* 223f); while for Honorius he wrote an Easter hymn (*carm.min.* XXII), where at *l.* 4 he writes,

> Impia tu *nostrae* domuisti crimina vitae,

(Thou hast conquered the sins of *our* life.)

and at *l.* 17.

ut *nos* surriperes leto.

(That thou savest *us* from death.)

It certainly looks as if Claudian either considered himself or wished to be considered a Christian. It need hardly be said that the authenticity of a poem that so sharply conflicts with *fable convenue* has been questioned, but on no adequate grounds.[35]

At *III Cons. Hon.* 93f Claudian describes (in lines which were quoted by both Augustine and Orosius) the miraculous storm which helped Theodosius to defeat the pagan usurper Eugenius in 394:

> O nimium dilecte deo, cui fundit ab antris
> Aeolus armatas hiemes, cui militat aether
> et coniurati veniunt ad classica venti.

(Beloved indeed thou art of god, for whom Aeolus frees armed tempests from his cave, for whom the very elements do battle, to whose bugles the winds flock in one band.)

A Swiss scholar has recently claimed that 'la pirouette la plus audacieuse de Claudien, c'est de rendre profane, mythologique, la victoire chrétienne de 394'.[36] This is quite misconceived. The superficial touch of pagan imagery can hardly conceal the fact that Claudian firmly follows the official Christian line: the hurricane which blinded Eugenius' men was sent by God – the Christian God, of course. Indeed Augustine and Orosius quote the passage precisely to show that Claudian, though a pagan (as they believed),[37] nevertheless did accept the Christian miracle.

As the acknowledged propagandist of Stilicho (distrusted by the aristocracy on political grounds), the confidant of Serena and court poet to a Christian court, Claudian cannot have appeared in a favourable light to the pagan party (if anything so coherent may be said to have existed). It is little short of absurd to claim him (as many have) as their spokesman. Refutation of this notion will bring us back full circle to Gildo and propaganda.

Stilicho did not declare war on Gildo in the name of Honorius; he got the senate of Rome to do the job for him. Claudian's eloquent account of the honour thus paid the senate by Stilicho has often been quoted as an example of his unbounded enthusiasm for the authority of the senate:

hoc quoque non parva fas est cum laude relinqui
quod non ante fretis exercitus adstitit ultor
ordine quam prisco censeret bella senatus.
neglectum Stilicho per tot iam saecula morem
rettulit, ut ducibus mandarent proelia patres

(Stil. I.325f)

(This too must not be passed over without full meed of
praise, that the avenging expedition did not embark until
the senate had, in accordance with antique usage, declared
war. Stilicho re-established this custom, neglected for so
many ages, that the Fathers should give generals charge to
fight.)

(Platnauer, Loeb)

According to Boissier, though this move of Stilicho's was 'a mere
formality, it overwhelmed Claudian with joy'.[38] Now in the first
place, it was not a 'mere formality'. Compromised as he was at
the time, Stilicho badly needed the shelter of an authority not
dependent on himself; and (hardly less important) declaration
of war, involving as it necessarily would complete stoppage of
the African corn quota, was bound to be very unpopular. More
significant still, however, is Claudian's failure to mention Stilicho's
gesture in *Gild.*, a poem wholly devoted to the preparations for
the war. If he had really been so overwhelmed by it, why wait
two years and then give it quite disproportionate space in a much
briefer and more schematic account? Indeed, in *Gild.* Claudian
makes Roma lament the passing of the good old days when Rome
could depend on the counsel of the senate to defend her (44f)! The
conclusion seems inescapable. In mid-398, when *Gild.* was recited
before court in Milan, Stilicho had no special wish to make capital
out of his consultation of the senate. Two years later, before an
audience which we happen to know comprised much of the
senatorial aristocracy (Symmachus included), he evidently did.
Such an inference is strongly supported by another fact which has
escaped general observation. All Claudian's most eloquent passages about Rome and its glorious past occur in the poems he
recited in Rome; no such passages are to be found in what he
performed in Milan.[39] It must be repeated, we shall never understand Claudian until we learn always to note where and when he

wrote each poem before reading it. There is no need to deny that he had *any* genuine admiration for Rome; but it would be equally naïve to take such passages as straightforward expressions of Claudian's own sentiments and opinions. Whatever else they may incidentally reveal, they were designed very specifically to win Stilicho senatorial support from senatorial audiences.

For reasons which no doubt have their origin in Romantic prejudice, *De Raptu Proserpinae* has long been Claudian's most popular poem. Those who feel impelled to try him at all will seldom be encouraged to probe further by a perusal of this pretty but irrelevant torso of a traditional mythological epic. It has been the purpose of the foregoing remarks to suggest that Claudian's contemporary poetry is more worth while – and not only because it is (in the modern sense) more 'relevant'. The invectives at least are certainly better poems by any literary standard that can be imagined (the similes and imagery of the *In Eutropium* are particularly striking and original). Claudian was no author of belles lettres living in a vacuum, an inferior disciple of Lucan and Statius. He is surely a much more important writer by any yardstick than Silius Italicus or Valerius Flaccus (Coleridge was quite right to commend Claudian and leave Silius unread). Propaganda and politics aside, with their finely balanced tension between tradition and innovation, between the world of fantasy and imagination and the very real world of the late fourth century, Claudian's panegyrics and invectives are a powerful and living symbol of the age.

Notes

1 The title is ancient, given only to distinguish him from his homonymous grandson.
2 For all details concerning the regency, see my paper 'Theodosius the Great and the regency of Stilicho', *HS*, 73 (1968), pp. 247–80.
3 *The Birth of the Middle Ages* (1935), p. 57.
4 For Claudian's popularity in the eighteenth and nineteenth centuries, see my *Claudian* (1970), ch. XIV.
5 *Vit. Soph.* X.7.12, p. 493.
6 I collected most of the evidence in *Historia*, 14 (1967), pp. 470–509; cf. too my *Claudian*, ch. I (a book to which, for fuller justification of the sometimes controversial statements in this brief sketch, I shall be referring more frequently than modesty might seem to dictate).
7 Quoted by P. Fargues, *Claudien* (1933), 12.

8 See H. D. Meyer, *Die Aussenpolitik des Augustus und die Augusteische Dichtung* (1961), with P. A. Brunt's challenging criticisms in *JRS*, 53 (1963), pp. 170–6.

9 See (e.g.), G. Boissier, *La Fin du paganisme* vol. II (1891), p. 291, with the fuller discussion in my *Claudian*, pp. 46f. The passage in Claudian (*Stil.* II.341f) is part of a description of a series of tableaux on Stilicho's consular robe. I would now withdraw my suggestion (pp. 48, 303) that these scenes really were embroidered on Stilicho's robe. The whole series, referring as they do to the hoped-for future, are more naturally to be taken as a purely imaginary ecphrasis on the model of the Vergilian shield of Aeneas, which likewise bore 'famamque et fata nepotum' (see now the excellent analysis in Ursula Keudel's commentary (see note 22), pp. 88f). This in no way affects the dynastic and propagandist significance of what Claudian says.

10 See, more fully, *Claudian*, ch. III.

11 Fully treated in *Claudian*, ch. V.

12 Zosimus, V.12.1.

13 E. Demougeot, *De l'unité à la division de l'empire romain* (1951), p. 180, n. 320.

14 *CIL* VI 31256; 1730.

15 *Stil.* II. 79–80 ('a feeble, vicious cabal cloaking its own madness behind the name of their emperor'). Did Claudian perhaps feel that he had gone a little too far in Book I?

16 F. J. E. Raby, *Secular Latin Poetry* I² (1957), p. 91.

17 *Berliner KlassikerTexte*, vol. 1 (1907), p. 107.

18 On the epithalamia of Statius and Claudian, see Z. Pavlovskis, *CP*, 60 (1965), pp. 166f.

19 *H. A. Gord.* 3.2: T. D. Barnes, *Tertullian* (1971), p. 191.

20 On the merging of the two genres, see *Claudian*, pp. 260f.

21 See particularly L. B. Struthers, *HS*, 30 (1919), pp. 49–87, and Fargues, *op. cit.*, ch. VI.

22 Ursula Keudel, *Poetische Vorläufer und Vorbilder in Claudians De Consulatu Stilichonis* (*Hypomnemata* 26) (1970).

23 *In Eutr.* II, *pr.* 19.

24 *Geschichte des Untergangs der antiken Welt* V (1913), p. 565.

25 *Claudian*, p. 144.

26 See the evidence collected in *Hermes*, 92 (1964), pp. 363f, particularly Ammianus, XXVIII.4.14.

27 'Glory in battle: variations on an epic theme', *PLPLS* (*Literary and Historical Section*) 8.3 (1957), pp. 155–65.

28 On the familiarity of late Greek poets with Latin poetry, see *Claudian*, 19–21; on Nonnus and Ovid see now J. Diggle's edition of Euripides, *Phaethon* (1970), pp. 180–200.

29 On the figure of Roma, much misunderstood, see *Claudian*, pp. 273–6.

30 *Claudian*, p. 439.

31 Gladys Martin, *CJ*, 30 (1935), pp. 531–43.

32 *The Allegory of Love* (1936), pp. 75–6.

33 H. L. Levy, *TAPA*, 89 (1958), p. 345.

34 *Claudian*, pp. 193f.
35 *Claudian*, p. 214; on Shelley's strange misinterpretation of Claudian, based on this one poem alone, *ibid.*, pp. 450–1.
36 F. Paschoud, *Roma Aeterna* (1967), p. 146.
37 Augustine, *Civ. Dei* V.26 *ad fin.*; Orosius, *Adv. Pag.* VII.35.21. Scholars have tended to assume that what can only have been the *opinion* of these writers is self-evidently decisive in the matter of Claudian's religious allegiance. Yet a 'paganus pervicacissimus' (Orosius' phrase) would have been something of an embarrassment for Honorius and Stilicho at a Christian court, and it is surely likely that Claudian would have had the tact (whatever his true convictions) to profess a nominal Christianity (which is certainly what the use of the first person in his Easter hymn suggests). No one now takes very seriously Orosius' claim that Stilicho's son Eucherius was a pagan, and it is probable that similar allegations about Claudian derive from the same anti-Stilichonian propaganda which we know to have been spread by the faction that encompassed his fall, backed up by the well-known fact that Egyptian poets of the period usually were pagans (*Claudian*, p. 192, quoting the parallel of Cyrus of Panopolis, a favourite at the court of Theodosius II; founder of a famous church of the Virgin and friend of St Daniel the Stylite, he could still be ruined by an accusation of paganism – and then condemned to a bishopric!)
38 Boissier, *op. cit.*, vol. II (1891), p. 290, and cf. (e.g.) Paschoud, *op. cit.*, p. 146.
39 *Claudian*: ch. IX.

VI

Prudentius

Valerie Edden

The second half of the fourth century was a watershed in the history of the Latin West. The Empire, though long past the Golden Age of the Caesars, was still the dominant world power, but it was now Christianity rather than any pagan religion or philosophy which won men's allegiance and fired their imaginations. It was the end of one world and the beginning of another, but for a short while the old era retained much of its civilising power whilst the new faith gave men a sense of purpose and a new vitality. If the fourth century had an unusually large share of great men (a fact to which this volume bears witness), it is surely because the greatest minds were able to move freely within the two different worlds, putting to the service of the new religion much that still seemed good in the culture of the Roman West. But of course there was conflict between the two worlds, the one with its centuries-old heritage of Graeco-Roman civilisation, the other still firmly rooted in Hebraic thought; the strength of many of these fourth-century giants lay in their ability to reconcile their conflict.

One of these giants, straddled between two worlds, was Aurelius Prudentius Clemens, the first great Christian Latin poet, who like so many original minds, made the fullest use of the traditions in which he was nurtured. By the time of his birth in 348, in Saragossa in Spain,[1] Christianity was no longer the belief of a small persecuted minority but the official religion of the Empire, since it had been espoused by the Emperor Constantine and his sons who had tried, not entirely successfully, to establish their own brand of Caesaro-papism. But it was in the schools of the Empire that Prudentius learnt grammar and rhetoric in the Roman style and, though the precise date of his death is unknown, it is almost certain that he died before the fall of Rome in 410. It is no wonder that the two men to whom he was most indebted, if we are to believe his poems, are a Roman poet and one of the Fathers of the Latin Church: Vergil and Tertullian. Indeed he may well have taken his attitude to pagan learning from Tertullian, whose condemnation of the pagan classics went alongside a realisation that without them there would be no Christian learning. 'Quomodo repudiamus saecularia studia, sine quibus divina non possunt?' (How can we reject secular learning, without which there would be no divine learning?) [2] Prudentius certainly made no attempt to abandon pagan learning; his poems are heavily indebted to Vergil, [3] but significantly he never mentions him by name.

He gives us brief details of his life in the *Preface* to his poems, where he tells us that after his school-days (he seems to have been an unwilling pupil, who 'flevit sub ferulis'), he attended a school of rhetoric in preparation for a career as an advocate. It is difficult to know how seriously to take his confession of youthful depravity, since the theme has almost the status of a *topos* amongst Christian apologists. He was twice governor of a province and was finally given some high position in the service of the Emperor. In the *Peristephanon* he refers to a visit to Rome, where he visited the tombs of the martyrs. In 405, at the age of fifty-seven, he presented the world with his poems, repudiating his past worldly folly and dedicating the remainder of his days to the fight against heresy and the praise of the apostles and martyrs; the categories listed correspond to his poems: (1) *Apotheosis*, 'The Divinity of Christ'; (2) *Hamartigenia*, 'The Origin of Evil'; (3) *Psychomachia*, 'The Battle for the Soul'; (4) *Cathemerinon*, 'The Daily Round'; (5) *Peristephanon*, 'Crowns of Martyrdom'; (6) *Contra Symmachum*, a reply to an address of Symmachus; (7) *Dittochaeon*, 'Twofold nourishment'. Despite the Greek titles, there is no evidence that he had more than an elementary knowledge of Greek.

That these poems fulfilled a particular need, or rather several needs, is evidenced from their popularity, which seems to have been immediate and was certainly immense in the Middle Ages. They were to be found in almost every library which contained more than patristic writers. [4] They continued to be popular until long after the Renaissance, and even the great classical scholar Richard Bentley spoke of Prudentius as 'Christianorum Maro et Flaccus'. [5]

One of the problems which faced the early Church was the

need for specifically Christian literature. The first converts were Jews who continued in their use of the Jewish scriptures and liturgy. After the writing of the Gospels, the energies of the earliest Christians were directed into homiletic and exegetical works and into producing a Christian liturgy and translations of the Bible into Latin. On the other hand, most early Christians were educated in the schools of late pagan antiquity and their education was based on classical, pagan texts. The content of a Christian education was a vexed question for many centuries. Whilst the pursuit of eloquence was not incompatible with Christian holiness, the study of pagan texts was difficult to justify in an education aimed at fitting the soul for the eternal city. The portrayal of the pagan gods and their involvement in the affairs of men and the glorification of the delights of the world all must have been distasteful to the Christian intent on eradicating all traces of a pagan culture and religion which had long since ceased to exert any widespread moral influence. And if they were unsuitable study for the mature Christian how much more unsuitable for the nurture of the Christian boy or youth. In theory it seemed desirable to limit the reading of the young Christian to the scriptures, but in the western world this was never the practice.

The earliest Christian literature, as Raby has pointed out,[6] drew not on the literary language of classical literature but on the vulgar tongue and the Latin of everyday usage, and thus in style (though not in matter) they often fell short of the pagan authors with which educated men were acquainted. In particular, the rough and simple language of the New Testament in Greek and in the early Latin translations in which it was widely known in the West were a source of distaste and bewilderment to many lettered men. Jerome speaks of the 'simplicitas et quasi vilitas verborum'[7] of the scriptures. The pagan classics retained an aesthetic appeal which the earliest Christian literature could not displace.

Under Julian the problem of Christian education became more acute since, in a vain attempt to restore the old religion, Julian forbade Christians to teach literature; this edict had consequences far beyond anything he could have anticipated: not only did it result in the resignation of some of the most famous professors but in a renewed vigour in the production of Christian writings.

It was Prudentius' achievement to write Christian poems which did not deeply offend the lover of Vergil, by using all the eloquence and rhetoric he had learnt from his study of the pagan classics. Bentley's phrase (quoted earlier) is in a sense literally true, for Prudentius' poems were written and read precisely as Christian substitutes for Vergil and Horace, though one must add that neither these poems nor those of any other Christian poet ever really ousted the classical authors they were designed to replace, and Christian and pagan were read side by side for centuries.

Prudentius' originality becomes clear in a comparison with his predecessors. He was not, of course, the first to write Christian Latin verse. The psalms had long been supplemented by Christian hymns for liturgical use and the hymns of Ambrose and Hilary (for example) were in wide circulation. Commodian (whose date and provenance have both been disputed) wrote didactic verses for the instruction of new converts; the main purpose of his *Instructiones* was to attack the false beliefs of the heathens and the Jews and the errors into which converts might fall; the *Carmen Apologeticon* which relates sections of the *Bible* in hexameters, seems to have its origin in the belief that verse is more readily memorable than prose. But neither poem could ever have been intended to satisfy the converted classical scholar; indeed they seem to have been designed for a comparatively unlettered audience. On the other hand, there were attempts to replace the pagan classics with Christian poems. Juvencus, a fellow-countryman of Prudentius, who lived a little earlier in the fourth century, retells the Gospel story in his *Evangeliorum Libri IV* as an epic much indebted to Vergil. Severus Sanctus Endelechius wrote a Christian bucolic *De Mortibus Boum*. Prudentius' achievement was two-fold: he extends the matter of Christian poetry from Biblical narrative and liturgy to cover the whole range of the Christian life and secondly, as Curtius points out,[8] he writes independently of the system of antique genres. *Cathemerinon*, though heroic, combines devotion with didacticism in verses extolling the cult of martyrs which are certainly not epic. *Psychomachia*, despite its debt to the *Aeneid*, is not an epic but an extended allegory.

Psychomachia indeed best represents the blend of old and new, Roman and Christian, in Prudentius' works. The origins of the allegory of the virtues and vices are complex. The idea of conflict within the soul of man was familiar from both Christian and Roman thought, and allegory provided preachers and teachers with a simple way of expressing complicated inner psychology by externalising and thus identifying the opposing factors. St Paul extends the allegory to include the weapons and armour available to the Christian:[9]

> For we wrestle not against flesh and blood, but against principalities, against powers, against the rulers of the darkness of this world, against spiritual wickedness in high places.
>
> Wherefore take unto you the whole armour of God, that ye may be able to withstand in the evil day, and having done all, to stand.
>
> Stand therefore, having your loins girt about with truth, and having on the breastplate of righteousness; And your feet shod with the preparation of the gospel of peace;
>
> Above all, taking the shield of faith, wherewith ye shall be able to quench all the fiery darts of the wicked. And take the helmet of salvation, and the sword of the Spirit which is the word of God.

The particular source of *Psychomachia* may be found in Tertullian, who when condemning fighting and wrestling, suggests that the Christian who has a taste for such things satisfy it instead in contemplating the fight for virtue:[10]

> Vis et pugilatus et luctatus. Presto sunt, non parva et multa. Aspice impudicitiam deiectam a castitate, perfidiam caesam a fidem, saevitiam a misericordia incontusam, petulantiam a modestia adumbratam.

> (Do you want fighting and wrestling? Here they are at hand, and in plenty. See here, immodesty cast down by chastity, faithlessness slain by faith, cruelty crushed by pity and impudence thrown into the shade by modesty.)

But classical moralists such as Seneca also wrote of the inner conflict, and *Psychomachia* is certainly as much indebted to Rome as to patristic writings. Prudentius represents his virtues and vices as female figures; some of the virtues derive directly from Roman deities, such as Fides, Pudicitia and Concordia, which had become little more than personified virtues as early as Vergil; others derive from a tradition of personified abstractions which had been popularised particularly by Statius and Claudian. Prudentius typically marries Roman to Hebraic tradition by identifying these personified abstractions with Biblical characters who had long been considered types of particular virtues in Jewish (and hence Christian) scriptural exegesis. Thus David's defeat of Goliath is cited as representing the triumph of Mens Humilis over Superbia; Judas and Achar are given as examples of Avaritia; Jonathon breaking his fast by eating the honeycomb as an example of Luxuria; Judith is cited as a type of Pudicitia (she is an unexpected example of this virtue) and the triumph of the virtue is confirmed (more predictably) by the Virgin birth. The Preface indicates the subject of the poem by telling the story of Abraham slaying the barbarian kings as an allegory of the victory of virtue over vice. But into this one central allegory he weaves allegories of several other events in the patriarch's life.[11]

The battle proceeds as a series of seven combats in which each virtue in turn defeats its appropriate vice[12] in battle scenes drawn largely from *Aeneid* X. The military exploits of these Amazonian virgins in shining armour have struck some critics as aesthetically weak or morally undesirable. C. S. Lewis was offended at the impropriety of Humility triumphing over her foes and of Mercy striking her enemies.[13] Nowadays no doubt our sympathies tend to be with Christian pacificism, but that ought not to blind us to the psychological realism of many of Prudentius' details: the ruthlessness of Pride; Anger destroying itself whilst Patience looks on; Avarice cleverly disguising herself as Thrift; the way in which Pride condemns the uselessness of spiritual virtues such as Fasting, Purity and Simplicity.

The virtues and vices are presented with vivid physical detail, as though following some longstanding tradition of iconography, but no such tradition has yet been identified and we must attribute these miniatures to Prudentius' imagination; they were the inspiration of many later artists.[14] Thus Luxuria has perfumed hair, shifting eyes and a languid voice; Superbia has her hair piled high on her head, a cambric cloak on her shoulders and a gossamer streamer billowing behind her, she rides a spirited horse which is covered with a lion's skin; Ira has bloodshot eyes and foams at the mouth. Only Discordia with her 'scissa palla' has clear origins (in Vergil's Discordia,[15] though in *Psychomachia* she presents Heresy rather than discord). Unlike the presentation of

individual characters, the scenes after the battles (with each vic-
torious virtue standing in triumph over the body of the van-
quished vice) are presented in an established iconology of battles
dating from early Roman times.

As its title indicates, *Psychomachia* deals at one level with the
fate of a single Christian soul, like a fourth-century version of
The Holy War, describing 'ancipites nebuloso in pectore sensus
sudare alternis conflictibus' (emotions pulling in opposite directions [which] sweat in continuous clashes within the dark recesses
of the breast).[16] But the poem moves out beyond this level of
meaning, for the time-scale is both the eternal one of the Redemption and also the particular one of the history of the Christian
Church, moving from the temptation in Eden to the present
day, from the creation to the New Jerusalem, yet it makes the
reader constantly aware that the battle is ever-present as well as
everlasting by references to contemporary affairs.

For like another Christian poet many centuries later, Prudentius
realised that allegory provided a good opportunity for social
satire. Just as the allegoric and symbolic characters in *Piers Plow-
man* became involved in many of the injustices and evils of the
late fourteenth century so Prudentius' vices are characteristically
late Roman. In the train of Avaritia we find soldiers killing fellow-
soldiers to steal their armour; sons plundering their fathers'
corpses; there are even Christian priests who succumb to the
temptation of greed. Luxuria, a traditionally Eastern quality, is in
Psychomachia a western vice and may apply specifically to Rome,[17]
since the licence and decadence described matches the pictures
of Rome given by contemporary writers such as Jerome and
Ammianus Marcellinus.

Whatever its reputation among modern critics, *Psychomachia*
was the most prized of Prudentius' poems in the Middle Ages and
became one of the most widely read of all poems. The reasons for
its popularity are not hard to seek. It is pious and didactic without
ever becoming dry, presenting Christian morality simply and
graphically. It is exciting and full of action, packed with battles
and combats. And of course it is a triumphant work, reminding
the Christian reader that since Christ's triumph over sin on the
cross, the battle is already won, however hard the present struggle
against the powers of darkness within the individual soul and
in the world about him.

More to modern tastes are the lyric pieces in the *Cathemerinon*.[18]
Each piece is too long ever to have been intended for liturgical
use in its entirety and here again Prudentius seems to have introduced a new type of poem – a meditation including prayer, praise
and exposition. The first six poems celebrate the hours of the
day; the remaining six cover events in the Christian life. Prudentius shows himself master of a variety of classical metres.
Trochaic tetrameters and elevated diction are used with great
solemnity in the 'Hymn for Every Hour', in which the poet
invokes the Muse to assist him in proclaiming the glories of the
Christian hero, Christ. The following lines describe the eclipse
of the sun when Christ died and descended into hell.[19]

> Sed deus dum luce fulua mortis antra inluminat,
> dum stupentibus tenebris candidum praestat diem,
> tristia squalentis aetrae palluerunt sidera.
> Sol refugit et luguri sordidus ferrugine
> igneum reliquit axem seque maerens abdidit;
> fertur horruisse mundus noctis aeternae chaos.

(But while God poured out his golden light into Hades and
made day shine bright on the bewildered shades, the dim stars
in the darkening sky grew pale. The sun, clad in dismal
mourning-clothes, shrank from the earth, leaving its fiery
region in the sky, and in its grief hid itself away. They say the
world quaked in fear of the chaos of eternal night.)

In strong contrast are the muted, halting lines of the hymn for
the burial of the dead:[20]

> Non, si cariosa uetustas
> dissoluerit ossa fauillis
> fueritque cinisculus arens
> minimi mensura pugilli,
>
> nec, si uaga flamina et aurae
> uacuum per inane uolantes
> tulerint cum puluere neruos,
> hominem periisse licebit

(Not if the passage of time reduce his decaying bones to dust,
and the few, dry ashes are just a small handful in measure;
not if far-ranging gusts and the breezes which blow through

the empty air bear away his sinews with the dust, not even
then will a man be allowed to perish.)

or the graceful, fluent metre of the Epiphany hymn:[21]

> Hic ille rex est gentium
> populique rex Iudaici
> promissus Abrahae patri
> eiusque in aeuum semini.
>
> Aequanda nam stellis sua
> cognouit olim germina
> primus sator credentium,
> nati inmolator unici.
>
> Iam flos subit Dauiticus
> radice Iessea editus
> sceptrique per uirgam uirens
> rerum cacumen occupat.

(He is the king of the Gentiles, he is the king of the Jews,
promised to our father Abraham and to his seed for ever.
For the father of all the faithful, who offered his only son
in sacrifice, knew that one day his seed would equal the stars
in number. And now arises the flower of David, sprung
from the root of Jesse, flourishing through the rod of
dominion, he takes possession of the lofty place.)

The central theme of the *Cathemerinon* (if it can be said to have
one at all) is the consecration of the daily round, to which God
alone gives meaning and purpose, 'te sine dulce nihil, domine'
(without you, Lord, nothing is sweet).[22] Prudentius (like many
a later devotional poet) had learnt to see God in even the simplest
activities. When he eats, his mind turns to the supersubstantial
bread provided by God, 'hic pastus animae est saporque uerus'
(He is the true sustenance and savour of the soul),[23] and to the
sacrament in which Christ feeds man on his flesh and blood.[24]
Once established, the theme of sustenance recurs throughout
the series of poems: in the poems on fasting and when a mention
of Moses and manna from heaven (or of the marriage feast at
Canaa) prompts the reflection that we too are fed on God's
mystic feast.

The first group of six poems begins with daybreak and ends

at nightfall; light and darkness are woven in and out throughout the *Cathemerinon*, giving it an apparent coherence. Light is of course traditionally associated with Good, darkness with Evil; the coming of Christ had from the earliest times been represented as 'Light shining in darkness'.[25] Spiritual knowledge is acquired through 'illumination'.[26]

The very fabric of the first poem is composed of such symbolism: the cockcrow shatters the dark and heralds the light just as Christ stirs up the soul to abandon the powers of darkness. This daybreak calls to mind also Christ's warning of doomsday, lest men are slumbering in their sins at that fateful hour, forgetful of the true light, 'lucis oblitum suae'. Inevitably it recalls also Peter's denial before the cock crowed thrice (that is in the night literally and in the night of the human race), and again it recalls the tradition that Christ rose from the dead at cockcrow. The final prayer incorporates both literal and figurative meanings:[27]

> Tu, Christe, somnum dissice,
> tu rumpe noctis uincula,
> tu solue peccatum uetus
> nouumque lumen ingere.

(O Christ, rouse us from sleep, break the bonds of night, cleanse us from our old habit of sin and illuminate us with thy new light.)

The second poem takes its theme from the first: the coming of daylight brings to mind the coming of the true light (Christ) on the last day, when darkness will be banished once for all and all things revealed; the poem concludes with a prayer for that illumination which will cure man's blindness. The hymn for the lighting of the lamp (V) takes up the theme again in a prayer that God who created the heavenly bodies which give light to the earth and who taught man to make fire and artificial light should give to men also the light of Christ, 'nostris igniculis unde genus venit' (the source of our little flames). It concludes by describing a festival with a myriad lamps burning to the glory of God (possibly a vigil for Easter Eve):[28]

> O res digna, deus, quam tibi roscidae
> noctis principio grex tuus offerat,

lucem qua tribuis nil pretiosus,
lucem qua reliqua praemia cernimus!

Tu lux uera oculis, lux quoque sensibus.

(It is meet and right, O God, that at the beginning of the
dewy night your flock should offer you light, the most
valuable of all your gifts through which we are able to see
all your other bounty. You are the true light of our eyes,
the true light of our minds.)

With the coming of the night, the poet considers sleep and that
illumination which comes to men in dreams when 'splendor
intererrat, qui dat futura nosse' (a shining light appears which
reveals what the future will be). [29]

Throughout the *Cathemerinon*, Christ is seen as the true light;
he is the author of light, 'lucisator' [30] 'Lux Bethlem'. [31] His nativity
is indicated by the returning sun. [32] At the Epiphany a shining
star marks the advent of a ruler to whom even Light must bow
(XII).

The *Cathemerinon* has been criticised for being digressive and
disorganised, a criticism partly due no doubt among older critics
to a desire for 'organic unity'. Clearly neither the collection as a
whole nor the individual poems are unified according to neo-
classical rules, but they have rather more coherence than has
often been acknowledged. I have already mentioned one factor
which makes for coherence – the recurrence of ideas and images
linked with light and sustenance. Sometimes the real theme is
implied rather than stated. 'Before sleep' is principally concerned
not simply with sleep but with dreams and the Biblical examples
all serve this theme, for it tells of Joseph interpreting the dreams
of Pharaoh's butler and baker and then of Pharaoh himself, and
of John's dream on Patmos. Each of the poems uses Biblical
examples.

The poem on the lighting of the lamp links the main theme (of
light from God) with the theme of the previous poem (sustenance
from God) by the career of Moses, to whom God was revealed
in a flame of light (in the burning bush), under whose leadership
God guided the chosen people with a fiery pillar (drowning their
enemies in the Red Sea), and fed them with quails and manna and
water which he enabled Moses to purify. By interpreting these

Old Testament stories allegorically the poet brings his readers back to the present hour by reminding them that God feeds all men also with his mystic feast and guides them with his true light (Christ) to the Promised Land (Heaven).

The poems in the *Cathemerinon* insist repeatedly on the sanctity of the human body, alongside the need to control the lusts of the flesh. Mortification of the flesh (through fasting) nurtures the soul,[33] but Christ, by his incarnation, has freed the body from the passions which can tyrannise it.[34] The body is the home and temple of the soul.[35] This emphasis is revealed more explicitly in *Apotheosis*, one of two theological treatises which will be passed over briefly in this essay, for though they are fluently and vigorously written their interest is primarily theological rather than literary, and unlike his other poems, they make little attempt to present Christian material in a classical fashion, except possibly in the choice of hexameters as a metre suitable for discursive subjects. That is not to suggest that either is intended primarily as a contribution to contemporary religious controversy; the issues under discussion were no longer burning ones and Prudentius' aim seems instead to provide a poetic affirmation of orthodox belief.

The aim of the *Apotheosis* is praise of Christ, as the central paean of praise indicates;[36] it affirms the twofold nature of Christ as God and man, and refutes in turn the various heresies which misrepresent his true nature, including a long section attacking the Jews for their failure to recognise his divinity. Through the incarnation, mortal flesh is hallowed, and the resurrection of the body assured.

If *Apotheosis* exalts human nature in its potentiality, *Hamartigenia* stresses the depths to which human nature has fallen, analysing the origin of evil. It is one of several treatises from the period which attack the heresy of Marcion, who believed that there were two Gods, one of the New Testament and one of the Old. No particular source for *Hamartigenia* is now accepted with any certainty. Prudentius presents Marcion's two Gods as authors of good and evil respectively, confusing his teaching with Manicheism. Prudentius acknowledges the pervasive presence of sin and depravity and asks the perennial question, if God is good, how does such evil arise? He dismisses the idea that there can be dual powers of good and evil and the belief that sin springs from the flesh (as we would expect from the *Apotheosis*) and concludes that sin is not an external force but an ever-present possibility within the soul of man because of his capacity for free choice. It is not a new argument of course; Prudentius' aim seems to be not originality but to present his material in a striking and memorable fashion. The treatise is marked by vivid comparisons: the inner source of sin is compared to a viper which hatches young which soon destroy it; man's free choice is compared to birds, some of which succumb to the temptation of deceptive grains and find themselves snared by bird-lime, whilst others, such as the doves, escape the traps because they are not so greedy.

The two treatises assert orthodox belief against the threats of heresy, but Prudentius was at least as much concerned with the threat to Christian truth from those who sought to compromise it by diluting it with long-held pagan beliefs. If Prudentius clung to pagan literature with only a few scruples, he felt only repulsion for pagan religion and culture.

From the earliest times the synoptic gospels had been expounded by men whose interpretations were substantially affected by their classical education, most notably of course by St Paul, the Romanised Jew, and by the Hellenised Jews of Alexandria in the second century. Whether or not Christian doctrine was enriched by this addition of Graeco-Roman philosophy is a moot point but there can be no doubt that it made Christ's teaching more easily acceptable by the Gentile world. But by the fourth century times had changed: Christianity was no longer in any danger of being dismissed as a mere sect of Judaism, but since it had become the official religion of the Empire, most men styled themselves as Christians and there were now well-grounded fears that a religion was spreading which blended a belief in the Christian God with pagan superstition and Roman moral values. There is evidence of a definite pagan revival at this time[37] and Prudentius' attitude is not difficult to understand when we reflect on the weak impression made by Christianity on some of his contemporaries. Though no one now doubts Boethius' authorship of orthodox theological treatises, his *Consolation of Philosophy* shows not a trace of Christian belief and Ausonius is plainly puzzled at the effects of the new religion (which he too ostensibly professed) on his young friend, Paulinus of Nola.

In 382 the Emperor Gratian, under pressure from St Ambrose, had the statue of Victory removed once more from the

Senate-house to the dismay of many pagan members of the Senate. The following year Gratian died and was succeeded by Valentinian II; in 384 the pagan party, with Symmachus as their spokesman, pleaded for restoration of the statue. Symmachus' arguments are masterly and must have seemed very persuasive.[38] He does not attack Christianity but pleads for tolerance and the maintenance of time-honoured traditions. He argues that Victory is to be regarded not as a goddess but as a mere name and that respect for the customs of antiquity is not incompatible with Christianity, particularly since Victory has brought nothing but good to Rome. But, predictably, these arguments were seen as an attempt to compromise Christian truth and Symmachus and the pagan party were firmly defeated by Ambrose, who wrote a formal reply to Symmachus' speech.

Twenty years later when Prudentius wrote his own reply to the speech, *Contra Orationem Symmachi*, the issue was still a live one. The altar of Victory had become the symbol of paganism and, as I have said before, the relationship of Christianity to pagan culture was still the burning issue of the era. But it is not only the issues involved which interested Prudentius: the praise he confers on his opponent's oratory is one pointer to the fact that he is concerned also to prove that the pagans do not have a monopoly of rhetorical skill. For Symmachus himself he shows only respect.

The points he makes are ones which recur in his works – the importance of Rome as the imperial city of Christendom, the depravity of the pagan gods, and the low moral standards encouraged by the old religion. The first book gives the spiritual history of Rome with an analysis of the old religion and the history of the conversion to Christianity. Symmachus had argued that Victory was responsible for Roman military success, Prudentius retorts by citing the triumphs of Constantine under his new Christian standard.[39] But the point he makes most strongly is the depravity of the Roman gods; he repeatedly stresses their sexual immorality and points out that even the city of Rome itself was founded as the result of rape. He shows distaste for pagan religious rites and customs, with their bloodshed, animal sacrifices and auguries and scorns the great multitude of minor deities and the pagan habit of deifying natural phenomena. (The Christian insistence on the unity of God must have been one of its more attractive doctrines, if also a difficult one, judging by the way in which heresies continually threatened it.)

The second book follows Ambrose's speech fairly closely, answering Symmachus' points in turn, arguing that Rome has not always been true to her past, and has had many new gods; that there could be no impelling moral law without a belief in the unity of God and in immortality. He continually stresses the importance of Rome, transmuting triumph in the glorious victories of Rome into a Christian belief that Rome is the city chosen by God for the centre of his earthly kingdom, a kingdom of peace.

The same attitude to paganism can be seen in his poem on the martyrdom of Romanus, [40] where he places in Romanus' mouth an attack on the depravity of Roman morals, deploring the sexual exploits of the pagan deities and the superstitions and religious rites which were rife. [41]

> Venerem precaris, conprecare et simiam.
> Placet sacratus aspis Aesculapii,
> crocodillus ibis et canis cur displicent?
> Adpone porris religiosas arulas,
> uenerare acerbum caepe, mordax allium.
>
> Fuliginosi ture placantur lares
> et respuuntur consecrata holuscula?
> Aut unde maior esse maiestas focis
> quam nata in hortis sarculatis creditur?
> si numen ollis, numen et porris inest.

(You pray to Venus, then pray earnestly to an ape as well. The sacred viper of Aesculapius [the god of healing] is considered acceptable, why shouldn't a crocodile or an ibis or a dog be acceptable as well? Make your pious little altars to leeks, revere the harsh onion or the pungent garlic! Are your grimy household gods [grimy because near the hearth] pleased with incense, while they reject consecrated vegetables? Why do people believe that the majesty of the hearth is greater than that in cultivated gardens? If there is a divine presence in a hearth then there is a divine presence in a leek!)

As we have seen, the decadence of Roman life is graphically presented by Luxuria in *Psychomachia*.

But however much Prudentius deplored the decadence of contemporary Rome, he felt also a great deal of pride in being a Roman. This is not merely imitation of a classical common-place; he transforms pride in the achievements of Imperial Rome into pride in Rome as the Imperial city of Christ's new spiritual kingdom. He puts into the mouth of the dying Lawrence a prayer that Rome might be the supreme Christian city of a Christian Kingdom. [42] The establishment of peace in the Empire is said to have paved the way for the earthly life of Christ; [43] in *Apotheosis*, the Imperial leaders are presented deserting their old pagan temples and divinities to follow Christ. [44] The waters of the Tiber are sacred still, only now because they flow between the tombs of Saints Peter and Paul. [45]

But pride in Rome is matched with pride in his native Spain, as his predominantly Spanish *Peristephanon* shows. The martyrs in honour of whom these hymns are written are largely Spanish. The fourth poem combines its praise of heroes with the traditional Laudes Urbi in an encomium of Saragossa, city of eighteen martyrs: [46]

> Sola in occursum numerosiores
> martyrum turbas domino parasti,
> sola praediues pietate multa
>   luce frueris.
>
> Vix parens orbis populosa Poeni,
> ipsa uix Roma in solio locata
> te, decus nostrum, superare in isto
>   munere digna est.

(You only have furnished great crowds of martyrs hastening to their Lord, you alone will enjoy great light because of your wealth of piety. Even Carthage, prolific mother of the Punic world, even Rome, set on her throne of dominion, are scarcely able to surpass you in tribute, who are our glory.)

Emetrius and Chelidonius are an honour to Spain. [47]

Whilst the poems in the *Cathemerinon* are suitable for any Christian anywhere, those in the *Peristephanon* are particularised in both time and place. Some were apparently written for congregational singing, despite their length. [48] Some refer to specific occasions and places, such as VIII, written for the baptistery at Calagurris, scene of the martyrdom of Emetrius and Chelidonius; IX, written for the passion of St Cassian, was inspired by the poet's visit to his tomb en route for Rome; XI and XII are to celebrate martyrs whose tombs Prudentius visited at Rome.

The cult of the martyrs was strong in the late fourth century. Martyrdom was no longer a real threat in the Empire, yet the fierce persecution under Diocletian was still in living memory; men looked back with admiration to an era when faith seemed strong and the Church seemed triumphant against almost impossible odds. It is a pointer to the popularity of the cult that, whereas Prudentius' other poems are largely dependent upon learned sources, *Peristephanon* relies largely on oral tradition (hence a number of confusions, such as the confusion of two distinct Cyprians in XIII). The first poem praises two martyrs, Emetrius and Chelidonius, but, as a prelude to the whole series, includes also an encomium of martyrdom. Martyrs are Christ's witnesses and though they make the ultimate sacrifice for their faith, the price of mortal flesh is cheap when measured against the reward of eternal salvation. Scorn of any hurt done to the body is characteristic of the *Peristephanon*; the Hymn in honour of St Vincent describes the torture-place as the wrestling place of glory ('palaestra gloriae'). [49] Martyrs are soldiers of Christ, bearing his standard, a metaphor which enables Prudentius to bring into use all the heroic style and sentiments of the classical epic.

Each poem follows a similar pattern: a protestation of faith, a torture and a series of miracles. The confessions of faith are often achieved in remarkably unpropitious circumstances: Romanus delivers a long diatribe against paganism when his tongue has been torn out (X); Quirinus addresses the crowd lying prostrate floating on a river, after he has been cast from a bridge by his torturers. All remain staunchly defiant, confident that they are in the right and that their due rewards will soon be forthcoming. When St Lawrence is asked to pay the Churches' gold over to Caesar, he responds by handing over a company of poor and infirm old men, whom he claims to be the real wealth of the Church; afterwards on the griddle, in the same spirit, he makes his famous, grotesque joke. [50] The child Eulalia proudly and defiantly presents herself before the civil authorities and upbraids them for their burnt offerings and other pagan practices, and when invited to save herself by touching a speck of pagan incense, retorts by spitting in her persecutors' faces and kicking over the sacrificial meal (II); Vincent's torturers cry out with annoyance, [51]

> Gaudet renidet prouocat
> tortore tortus acrior!

(He rejoices! He is smiling. The tortured cries out with more spirit than the torturer.)

Each martyr's passion is distinctive and the tortures are embraced eagerly as an opportunity to glorify God. Cassian is stabbed with the writing-styles of his young pupils; St Lawrence is roasted alive; St Vincent is tortured on the rack and then thrown to lie on broken pottery; Quirinus is drowned. If the reader is expected to respond with awe and admiration to these deaths, then the ensuing miracles bring a further response: reassurance about the omnipotence of God and his concern for his faithful believers. Snow instantly covers Eulalia's corpse and her spirit is seen to depart from her body in the form of a dove (III). Miraculous light breaks into the dungeon where Vincent lies and the broken pieces of pottery are covered with flowers (V). Fructuosus, Augurius and Eulogius stand unscathed in a fiery furnace, like Shadrach, Meshach and Abednego (VI). Quirinus is miraculously saved from death on so many occasions that he has to ask God to let him die (VIII). This assurance of God's power is extended into contemporary time, by references to the miracles still worked by the remains of the martyrs, and the faithful reader of the fourth century is reminded of his union with the Church triumphant and the constant prayers of the Saints, as the closing lines of the martyrdom of Cassian make clear. Prudentius relates his own feelings of gratitude on visiting Cassian's tomb: [52]

> Tunc arcana mei percenseo cuncta laboris,
> tunc quod petebam quod timebam murmuro,
> et post terga domum dubia sub sorte relictam
> et spem futuri forte nutantem boni.
> Audior, urbem adeo, dextris successibus utor,
> domum reuertor, Cassianum praedico.

(Then I reckon up all my secret distresses and mumble my
desires and fears and consider the home which I have left
behind me for an unknown destiny and my perhaps
wavering hope of future blessings. I am heard, I approach
the city of Rome and am lucky to enjoy there a happy
outcome of events, and so I return home, acclaiming
Cassian.)

Within this framework of hagiography are passages on other
topics. The martyrdom of Romanus contains a long passage
attacking paganism (already mentioned) in some ways similar to
the *Contra Orationem Symmachi* (X). The martyrdom of Agnes
contains a long passage of contempt of the world (reminding
modern readers unmistakably of the end of Chaucer's *Troilus
and Criseyde*):[53]

> Miratur orbem sub pedibus situm,
> spectat tenebras ardua subditas
> ridetque solis quod rota circuit,
> quod mundus omnis uoluit et inplicat,
> rerum quod atro turbine uiuitur,
> quod uana saeclimobilitas rapit:
> reges tyrannos imperia et gradus
> pompasque honorum stulta tumentium.

(She wonders at the world placed beneath her feet, from on
high she surveys the darkness beneath her and smiles at the
sun's revolving orb, the whole world twisting and turning,
men living in a dark whirlpool of affairs, the mutability of
the passing centuries snatching away vain glories: kings,
tyrants, the dominion, rank and pomp of those puffed up
with the stupidity of honours.)

Apart from the Epilogue to the whole collection of poems,
which dedicates both poems and poet to the service of God, the
last work of Prudentius for our consideration is the *Tituli Historum*
(commonly called the *Dittochaeon*, a title for which there is doubtful authority), forty-eight quatrains[54] apparently designed to
accompany a series of paintings in a church. Since the precise
subject and treatment of each quatrain is predetermined and great
brevity is required, there is little scope for elaboration or impro-

visation, thus *Dittochaeon* tells us little about Prudentius, except
to confirm what the other poems reveal – that he habitually
interprets Old Testament stories as types of New Testament ones
or allegorically. The scenes described in the *Dittochaeon* tell the
story of the Fall and Redemption. There are New Testament
scenes from Christ's life and early Apostolic times and incidents
from the Old Testament which prefigure later events. For example,
the twelve springs in the grove of Elim and the twelve stepping-
stones in the Jordan prefigure the twelve Apostles; the story of
Samson and the foxes is used as a comparison with the contemporary situation in which the fox of heresy scatters sin around;
David's royal insignia are appropriate for Christ, the supreme
King. Some stories are allegorised: Abel is the soul and Cain
the flesh; the five loaves and fishes are 'aeternae . . . opulantia
mensae' (the riches of the eternal table).[55] As a whole the New
Testament passages do not appear to have been chosen to match
the Old, number for number, though there are one or two cor-
respondences. Eve, who corrupted Adam (I) is paralleled by
Mary, the instrument in God's plan for redemption (XXV);[56]
Abraham's angelic visitors (IV) are paralleled by the angels an-
nouncing Christ's birth to the shepherds (XXVIII).

Such typology and allegorisation is found throughout Prudentius' work. The murdered, innocent Abel is a type of Christ;[57]
Moses escaped Pharaoh's decree that first-born male children
should be slain just as Christ survived the massacre of the Inno-
cents;[58] the cleansing power of the Jordan prefigures the sacrament of Baptism;[59] Abraham's sacrifice of Isaac shows how a
man must offer to God the thing he holds most dear.[60]

Prudentius' use of scriptural material places him in a long line
of Hebraic poets and prophets; his aim, to encourage piety and
devotion and to keep the faith free from both heresy and paganism
is uncompromisingly, at times militantly, Christian. But he is
nonetheless a Roman, with a Roman grounding in grammar and
rhetoric and a heritage of classical culture. Sometimes the two
traditions pulled him in different directions; at others he was able
to blend the two into a new whole. Roman religion and superstitions he could only condemn; Roman mythology he cites only
to condemn or compare unfavourably with Christian stories; yet
the Christian God becomes, like Jove, 'Tonans' (the Thunderer),
and he does not scorn to make use of pagan literature for his own

purposes. His adaptation of classical styles and genres for Christian poetry has already been discussed; but he is able also to adapt specific passages for his use, describing Christ the Good Shepherd in a bucolic setting with Vergilian vocabulary,[61] and the natural world greeting the new-born Christ in language drawn from the fourth Eclogue.[62] Many men find that trying to resolve the conflict between old and new ways of thought is a crippling experience; it is Prudentius' achievement that where many men could find only irreconcilable opposites, he could select and blend and, without ever compromising his faith, create an entirely new type of Christian literature.

Notes

There are three good editions of Prudentius by: J. Bergman (*CSEL* LXI, (Vienna–Leipzig, 1926); M. Lavarenne (Collection des Universités de France, Paris, 1943–51, with a French translation); M. P. Cunningham (*CC* 126, Turnholt, 1966). The text quoted in this essay is that of Cunningham. There are several English translations; the most easily accessible is the prose translation in the Loeb Classical Library, translated by H. J. Thomson (2 vols, London and Cambridge, Mass., 1949–53). Recently there has also been an increasing number of scholarly studies of Prudentius; Cunningham's edition contains a full bibliography.

The following general essays are recommended:
T. R. Glover, *Life and Letters in the Fourth Century* (Cambridge, 1901), ch. XI.
F. J. E. Raby, *A History of Christian-Latin Poetry* (2nd edition, Oxford, 1953), ch. II.
Bernard M. Peebles, *The Poet Prudentius*, Boston College Candlemas Lectures on Christian Literature 2 (New York, 1951).

1 His place of birth has been disputed, see Bergman, *op. cit.*, pp. ix–x.
2 *De Idololatria* X.4.
3 See Albertus Mahoney, *Vergil in the works of Prudentius* (Washington, 1934).
4 For example, Gustavus Becker. *Catalogi Bibliothecarum Antiqui* (Bonn, 1885) lists eighty-three volumes noted in the catalogues of twenty-five named libraries and two unnamed libraries. There is an unpublished dissertation on the influence of Prudentius in the Middle Ages: E. B. Vest, 'Prudentius in the Middle Ages' (diss., Harvard, 1932).
5 On Horace II.2.15.
6 F. J. E. Raby, *op. cit.*, p. 10.
7 *Epistola* LIII Ad Paulinam. 10.
8 E. R. Curtius, *European Literature and the Latin Middle Ages* (trans. W. R. Trask, London, 1953), p. 459.
9 Ephesians VI: 12–17.

10 *De Spectaculis* XXIX.

11 See Morton W. Bloomfield, *The Seven Deadly Sins* (Michigan, 1952), p. 63. This allegory is derived from Philo Judaeus.

12 Prudentius of course writes before the seven deadly sins and their corresponding virtues have become strictly codified and his particular list of seven vices (Veterum Cultura Deorum, Sodomita Libido, Ira, Superbia, Luxuria, Avaritia and Discordia) is unique. See Bloomfield, *op. cit.*, pp. 64–5.

13 C. S. Lewis, *The Allegory of Love* (Oxford, 1936), p. 69.

14 See Emile Mâle, *L'art religieux du XIIIᵉ siècle en France* (Paris, 1910), Book III; Helen Woodruff, *The Illustrated Manuscripts of Prudentius* (Cambridge, Mass., 1930); Adolf Katzenellenbogen, *Allegories of the Virtues and Vices in Mediaeval Art, from Early Christian Times to the Thirteenth Century* (London, 1939); Louis Reau, *Iconographie de l'art chrétien* (Paris, 1955–9), vol. I, pp. 175–91, which includes a useful bibliography.

15 *Aeneid* VIII.702.

16 Lines 893–4.

17 As T. R. Glover suggests, *op. cit.*, p. 264.

18 Their popularity is confirmed by the inclusion of small sections in modern hymnbooks. John Mason Neale's translation of 'Corde Natus ex parentis' (from IX) is particularly well-known.

19 *Cath.* IX.76–81. The emphasis on God's light dispelling darkness recurs throughout the *Cathemerinon*, see below.

20 *Cath.* X.141–8. The literal prose translations fail to convey that very mastery which the quotations are chosen to illustrate. For a more poetic and more successful translation of this passage see *Mediaeval Latin Lyrics*, trans. Helen Waddell (London, 1929, reprinted in the Penguin Classics, 1962), p. 55.

21 *Cath.* XII.41–52.

22 *Cath.* III.11.

23 *Cath.*IV.33.

24 *Cath.*IX.61–3.

25 St John I:4–9.

26 Illumination is now only a fossilised metaphor, but originally (in St Augustine, for example) illumination is the way in which the soul grasps the divine light.

27 *Cath.* I.97–100.

28 *Cath.* V.149–53.

29 *Cath.* VI.43–4.

30 *Cath.* III.1.

31 *Cath.* VII.1.

32 *Cath.* XI.1–2. If Prudentius is here suggesting a parallel between Christ and the returning sun, he is, I think, the first Christian poet to do so.

33 *Cath.* VII.6–25.

34 *Cath.* VII.

35 *Cath.* IV.16–18; X.129–30.

36 *Apoth.* 386–96.

37 See Herbert Bloch, 'The pagan revival in the West at the end of the fourth

century' in *The Conflict between Paganism and Christianity in the Fourth Century*, ed. A. Momigliano (Oxford, 1963), pp. 193–218; Kurt Latte, *Römische Religiongeschichte* (Munich, 1960), pp. 360–72.

38 For Symmachus' speech see: 'Relatio de ara Victoria'. *MGHAA*, ed. O. Seeck. 6, I, 280.

39 Constantine's standard bore the *Chi-Rho* monogram.

40 *Per.* X.

41 *Per.* X.256–65.

42 *Per.* II.413–84.

43 *Contra Symm.* II.620–2.

44 *Apoth.* 435–48.

45 *Per.* XII.29–30.

46 *Per.* IV.57–64.

47 *Per.* I.4–6.

48 M. P. Cunningham, 'The nature and purpose of the *Peristephanon* of Prudentius', *SE* 14 (1963), pp. 40–5.

49 *Per.* V.213.

50 The joke itself does not originate with Prudentius but is found in several authors, notably Ambrose. See E. R. Curtius, *op. cit.*, p. 426. This section of *Excursus* IV contains an interesting discussion of Prudentius' place in the history of hagiography.

51 *Per.* V.131–2.

52 *Per.* IX.101–6.

53 *Per.* XIV.94–101.

54 Two sixteenth-century editions carry an additional quatrain, 'Sepulchrum Christi'. This is not thought to be by Prudentius.

55 This sort of scriptural exegesis is of course commonplace at this time. For those unfamiliar with this tradition J. Danielou, *From Shadows to Reality*, trans. W. Hibberd (London, 1960), provides a general introduction.

56 The poet does not make the usual play on Eva/Ave.

57 *Hamart. Praef.* 20–6.

58 *Cath.* XII.141–4.

59 *Cath.* II.63–4.

60 *Psycho. Praef.* 1–8.

61 *Cath.* VIII.41–8. Christ is commonly presented as a shepherd in early Christian paintings, often using motifs of classical art, which suggest, if unintentionally, the life of bucolic repose, but Prudentius seems to be the first to fuse the classical pastor with the Good Shepherd in a poem.

62 *Cath.* XI.65–76. The fourth eclogue was commonly interpreted as an unwitting prophecy of Christ.

Subject Index

Name Index